Building the **Dynasty**

Building the
Dynasty

Manchester United
1946–1958

Iain McCartney

First published by Pitch Publishing, 2015

Pitch Publishing
A2 Yeoman Gate
Yeoman Way
Durrington
BN13 3QZ
www.pitchpublishing.co.uk

A CIP catalogue record is available for this book
from the British Library.

ISBN 978 178531-046-1

Typesetting and origination by Pitch Publishing

Printed by TJ International, Cornwall, UK

Contents

Acknowledgements 9

Introduction 11

Chapter One
The Appointment and Those Tentative First Steps 13

Chapter Two
Back To Normality: Season 1946-47 52

Chapter Three
Heading For Wembley: Season 1947-48 74

Chapter Four
The Good, The Bad and The Title: Seasons 1948-49 – 1951-52 . . 101

Chapter Five
Sow and Ye Shall Reap: Seasons 1952-53 – 1955-56 148

Chapter Six
Jousting With Giants: Season 1956-57 197

Chapter Seven
The Dream Becomes a Nightmare: Season 1957-58 261

Sources 320

**This book is respectfully dedicated to all those
who lost their lives as a result of the
Munich Air Disaster, February 6th 1958**

Manchester United Players

Roger Byrne

David Pegg   Geoff Bent   Tommy Taylor

Eddie Colman   Liam (Billy) Whelan   Mark Jones

Duncan Edwards

Manchester United Officials

Walter Crickmer (secretary)

Tom Curry (trainer)

Bert Whalley (coach)

Journalists

Alf Clarke (*Manchester Evening Chronicle*)

Tom Jackson (*Manchester Evening News*)

Don Davies (*Manchester Guardian*)

George Follows (*Daily Herald*)

Archie Ledbrooke (*Daily Mirror*)

Henry Rose (*Daily Express*)

Frank Swift (*News of the World*)

Eric Thompson (*Daily Mail*)

Crew

Captain K. G. Rayment (co-pilot)

Mr W. T. Cable (steward)

Others

Mr B. P. Miklos (travel agent)

Mr W. Satinoff (supporter)

And to those who survived...

Manchester United Players

Johnny Berry   Jackie Blanchflower   Bobby Charlton

Bill Foulkes   Harry Gregg   Kenny Morgans

Albert Scanlon   Dennis Viollet   Ray Wood

Manchester United Officials

Matt Busby (manager)

Journalists

Frank Taylor (*News Chronicle*)

Press

E. Ellyard (*Daily Mail* telegraphist)

P. Howard (*Daily Mail* photographer)

Crew

J. Thain (captain)

M. Bellis (stewardess)

R. Cheverton (stewardess)

G. W. Rodgers (radio officer)

Others

Mrs V. Lukic

Miss V. Lukic

Mrs B. P. Miklos

Mr N. Tomasevic

Acknowledgements

(In no particular order) – Mark Wylie, Jim Murphy, Steven Sullivan, Mike Carey, Jane Dyer, Stan Dunn, Roy Cavanagh, Joy Worth, Ray Adler, David Meek, Tim Ashmore, Tom Clare, Ray Evans and Tony Park.

I would also like to offer a special thanks to my editor Derek Hammond.

Dedicated to the Memory
of
Jimmy Murphy, Bert Whalley
and
Joe Armstrong

Without whom the post-war history of
Manchester United
would have been so different

Introduction

IN the modern game, Sir Alex Ferguson's managerial achievements may be unique; but, at Old Trafford, it was as if he had found Matt Busby's recipe book, had blown away the cobwebs and was merely following it word for word from those bygone days of a wildly different era in football.

Initially, Ferguson endured a strenuous and almost demoralising few years in the manager's chair which had, in previous years, proved far from comfortable – before he went on to handsomely repay the faith shown in him by the board of directors. He assembled a squad like some leader of old and marched them to undiluted success, conquering England, Europe and the world to the acclaim and disdain of millions. Back in the 40s and 50s, however, Busby's task had been much greater than that of his Scottish counterpart, as the man from Bellshill had to start from scratch on all fronts, without the benefit of a superclub's resources behind him.

Looking back beyond these twin Scottish-Mancunian success stories, a starkly contrasting picture existed in the long-forgotten decades when the fledgling Manchester United, and its previous incarnation of Newton Heath, struggled with bankruptcy, dark days in the Second Division and the threat of dropping even further down the Leagues. Yes, there were First Division championships in 1908 and 1911, with an FA Cup success in 1909, but for long periods United were living in the shadows of others.

In 1937, Manchester United fell under the guidance of club secretary Walter Crickmer, so with the resumption of League football on the horizon following the Second World War, a new manager was a real priority.

One name that arose as a potential candidate was that of Matt Busby, who was no stranger to Manchester or indeed United, due to his association with neighbours City and his current employers, Liverpool. Busby himself had been contemplating his future as war raged in Europe and North Africa, holding ambitions to get involved in the coaching/managerial side of the game, so when the United approach was made, he decided to grasp the opportunity.

The appointment itself represented a gamble by United, trusting their future in an individual untried at managerial level, with no coaching qualifications or experience other than that gathered in the army and gleaned from his time at Maine Road and Anfield. But the man from Bellshill relished the challenge and, in a relatively short period of time, transformed Manchester United into the club it had always craved to be – with a team that was the envy of British football.

Building the Dynasty takes you back to those war-torn days and the appointment of the man who was to set about building one of the greatest football clubs in the world. It narrates the club's struggle to return to its bomb-ravaged Old Trafford home whilst guesting at the Maine Road accommodation of neighbours City, and its attempts at recapturing the silverware that had for so long eluded them. It rekindles Busby's vision of producing his own home-grown talent, building on the existing MUJACs (Manchester United Junior Athletic Club) set-up, and evaluates the huge, all-too-frequently forgotten part played by his assistant Jimmy Murphy in nurturing those talented youngsters from the junior sides through to the first team. The book profiles countless players of yesteryear who are still remembered with reverence some seven decades later, and brings to life those pioneering days of European football – Busby's fight against the footballing authorities, the games, the ups and downs, and the stories of countless fans and club insiders who made a contribution.

It was at this time of icons and legends that Manchester United stretched out its tentacles and reached so many people, dragging them into the womb of what is no normal football club. But there was, of course, a cruel twist to the tale, as Busby's dream and the expected dominance of his home-produced team in the late 1950s failed to materialise due to events on foreign shores.

Building the Dynasty is more than just another football club history. This is the story of how Matt Busby lay the foundations of the modern-day Manchester United.

Iain McCartney

Chapter One

The Appointment and Those Tentative First Steps

I T was an innocuous, cold December morning in a Surrey army camp. Being miles from home, the mind would always float back to loved ones and the familiar, yearned-for environment, no matter how drab and discouraging it may have been in reality. Communication from those sitting by the fireside patiently awaiting the return of their beloved conscripts was at times infrequent, so every letter was treated with the excitement of an invitation to a royal garden party.

The buzz created by the arrival of the mail on this particular morning was little different than that of any other day, but for Matt Busby, one envelope carried an unfamiliar scrawl, the Manchester postmark intriguing him even more. The tasks at hand were now momentarily forgotten as this particular letter became the focus of his attention. Sitting down, he opened the single page and read:

"Dear Matt. No doubt you will be surprised to get this letter from your old pal Louis.

Well Matt I have been trying for the past month to find you and not having your reg. address I could not trust a letter going to Liverpool, as what I have to say is so important.

I don't know if you have considered about what you are going to do when the war is over, but I have a great job for you if you are willing to take it on. Will you get in touch

with me at the above address and when I know there will
be no danger of interception.

Now Matt, I hope this is plain to you. You see, I have
not forgotten my old friend either in my prayers or in your
future welfare. I hope your good wife and family are well
and please God you will be soon home to join their happy
circle.

Wishing you a very Happy Xmas and a lucky New Year.
With all God's Blessings in you and yours.
Your old pal Louis Rocca."

It was a morning and a letter, dated December 15th 1944, that not
only changed the life of its recipient but also the history of a football
club. One that had tasted both the highs and lows of the English
game. A club that was a slumbering giant, as success in recent years
had passed it by, mother fortune off-loading her wares on others.
The 1930s had been spent primarily in the Second Division of
the Football League, with only a final-day success at Millwall in
May 1934 salvaging pride and preventing an ignominious drop
into the third tier of the English game, along with the yet more
daunting prospect of financial ruin. It was a club that had been
run by secretary Walter Crickmer since November 1936, and one
in need of much more than a manager.

The letter, although entirely unexpected from this particular
source was, in content alone, something that the Scottish
international wing-half had been waiting and hoping for. Busby,
considering his playing days more or less over, had aimed to secure a
coaching/managerial position back in his native Scotland, but much
to his disappointment no offers of employment were immediately
forthcoming. Still, he lived in hope that, once clubs began to get
back to some sort of normality following the hostilities of the
Second World War, then something would materialise.

Little did he know that the wheels to such an appointment had
actually been set in motion three years previously at Penny Cottage,
near Cranborne in Dorset, during a late night/early morning chat
between the Manchester United chairman James Gibson and
his friend Captain Bill Williams, sports officer for the Southern

Command, who had at his disposal some of the best players in the English game. Over a few drinks, the conversation got round to Gibson enquiring of his friend if he knew anyone who might be suitable to take on the role of manager with his club once the war was over. One or two names were bandied about, but Williams put forward a strong case for a certain Matthew Busby – and slowly, as the glasses were refilled, a plan was put in place. Through his connections, Williams said he would arrange for Busby to play a couple of games as a 'guest' player with Bournemouth so that Gibson could run the rule over him on the pitch, whilst obtaining an insight into the Scottish international's character.

Gibson was duly impressed and what he saw was enough to convince him that here was someone who could have a profound effect on those around him as he was clearly a born leader. Little could be done however, with Busby still in the army and also, more to the point, still on Liverpool's books; but Williams agreed to keep an eye on the situation and inform Gibson if the need for hasty action on his behalf materialised.

It was not, however, until early 1945 that Williams contacted his friend to inform him that if he was still interested in Busby, then he should make his move sooner, rather than later. Busby was about to be demobbed and other clubs were beginning to show interest – so it was thanks to Louis Rocca that the ball started to roll.

With much more important goings-on throughout the country than sport in general, transfers and the day-to-day affairs of football clubs were only newsprint fodder for the 'local' papers. Even then, it was easy for stories to slip under the radar un-noticed, with the Busby-Manchester United story being a prime example. The news was soon to break, but not on the cobbled streets of Manchester.

Whilst Busby was north of the border on February 14th, in conversation with 'Waverley' of the *Daily Record*, he hinted strongly that his future lay in his homeland, and it was hoped that only a matter of time would see his appointment with a Scottish League club. In the same paper the following day, it was suggested that Hibernian were keen to give him the opportunity he craved for, but their chairman gave a flat denial when asked. Busby was also tight-lipped, keeping the rumour mill alive. He had good reason to be circumspect, as despite harbouring hopes of a return north, he had cast them aside and kept secret the fact that he had already been approached by a club and accepted their offer of employment.

But it was during those days in Scotland whilst on leave and visiting family, that his 'secret' was eventually to become common knowledge, as he was approached by 'Rex' of the *Sunday Mail* for nothing more than a friendly chat whilst attending the Queen's Park v Clyde Scottish Southern League fixture at Hampden Park on February 17th. But during the course of the conversation all was revealed.

Busby had returned north 'hoping for some peace and quiet', but was persistently asked about his future employment plans and although he had hoped to keep United's offer secret for a few more days, the *Sunday Mail* reporter was given the scoop, breaking the news in the following day's paper:

> "About two weeks ago he (**Busby**) received a grand offer of the managership of Manchester United. As it happened, he had a verbal understanding with his own club, Liverpool, concerning the job of player/coach. Nothing binding of course, but Matt thought it only right he should formally ask for his release from his promise.
>
> "On his way home on leave, he dropped off at Liverpool and explained the situation. Unknown to him, the Liverpool club held a board meeting to discuss the matter and decided to agree to his release. The press had tagged onto this story and presumed his journey to Scotland was linked with a job north of the border."

The offer may well have been made 'about two weeks ago', but it was only a matter of days since it had been discussed at Manchester United board level, with chairman J. W. Gibson reporting at the meeting on February 15th that he had been impressed with Busby during their recent conversation. He urged his fellow directors to sanction the appointment of the former Manchester City player as manager on a five-year contract, starting one month after Busby's demobilisation.

The appointment was 'officially' announced on February 19th, the day after the news had been broken north of the border, the United board more than likely forced into making the announcement earlier than they had intended. The new Manchester United manager had been granted a five-year contract and a reported salary of £750 per annum.

Busby himself was obviously delighted in securing such a position, but was also disappointed that no job opportunities had arisen in Scotland, saying: "I had been waiting for three years to see if a Scottish club would offer me a post." Strangely, he was to change his tune on this matter in later years, saying; "I could have returned to Scotland to take over Ayr United, but having lived for so long in Lancashire, I was not particularly keen to leave – even for the homeland." He had grown to realise what he had at his disposal, but his nationalistic drawstrings were to remain in place for a few more years yet.

Matt Busby had originally left Scotland in February 1928, but had everything gone to plan, it would not have been on a train journey south to Manchester, but on a steamer across the Atlantic to America to forge a new life in a land many of his fellow countrymen already called 'home'.

Opportunities to better oneself amongst the coal mines of Central Scotland, and indeed many other over-populated areas of Britain, were few and far between. For the Busby family, poverty was never far away, mainly due to his father having been killed during the First World War, leaving Matt as the main breadwinner. Many relatives had also lost their lives during the hostilities of 1914-1918, leading their families into forsaking their homes and friends for a new life across the Atlantic Ocean, and this move was also contemplated by Matt's mother in 1927. Although there were initial plans for her son to make a life for himself away from the coalface as a schoolteacher, the paperwork for a visa was duly filled in and the pipe dream that was America came a step closer to reality.

Due to a six-month waiting list, however, the Busbys never did say goodbye to those heather hills of home, as a visitor appeared on their doorstep with the offer of a trial with Manchester City. Matt's performances with local Lanarkshire junior side Denny Hibernian (having previously turned out for the quaintly named Alpine Villa and Orbiston Celtic, where Arsenal legend Alec James was a team-mate) had not gone unnoticed. Although caught in two minds, the offer was accepted and following a trial with City's second string against Burnley, a professional contract was offered – £5 per week during the season and £4 in the summer. Those plans for America were quickly dismissed.

But life at Maine Road was certainly no bed of roses, and Busby's dreams of becoming a professional footballer were suddenly looking far from certain. Failing to make much impression in the City reserves side at inside-forward in the latter half of the 1927-28 season, he was switched to the unfamiliar outside-right spot and from there to every other position along the front line. Such moves did little to instil confidence, and neither did City's signing of other forwards.

The close season offered time for thought and, had it stretched out any longer, there was every possibility that the City staff would have been one player less when the 1928-29 season kicked off; but the disillusioned young Scot decided to have one final attempt at making the much wanted breakthrough. It was to prove the correct decision, as he suddenly found himself propelled into first-team action against Middlesbrough in November 1929, but despite City's 2-0 victory, it was Central League football once again the following Saturday. This disappointment rekindled those lingering doubts of making the grade at Maine Road, whilst also doing little to abate the homesickness that had recently materialised. Only the intervention of his room-mate Phil McCloy prevented the purchase of a single rail ticket from Manchester to Glasgow.

There was, however, another intervention, although unknown to the unhappy young Scot, and one that could have changed his career and perhaps Manchester United's wartime search for a manager. Harold Hardman, United's chairman, had watched one or two of his neighbours' reserve-team fixtures and noted something in Busby's performances that prompted an approach as regards his availability. "£150 and he is yours" came City's reply, but the United chairman had to admit that his club were unable to find "150 pennies", so no deal materialised.

During his conversation with City's manager Peter Hodge, Hardman had revealed that if he had signed Busby then he would have switched him from an inside-forward to a half-back role. This information was not only promptly noted but acted upon by City, and this sudden change was to see the player finally make the breakthrough that he had thought was never going to materialise, going on to enjoy FA Cup success in 1934, whilst also winning Scottish international honours. Such were his performances that Liverpool were more than happy to pay £8,000 to take him to Merseyside in March 1936, where he took on the role of captain, but any hopes of further honours within the game were thwarted with the outbreak of the Second World War.

Having met the Manchester United directors, thirty-four year-old Busby soon became Manchester United's seventh manager[1]. But had Busby not been so desperate to secure employment in a coaching/managerial capacity, to enable him to continue his career within the game, then he may have contemplated taking over the reins at United for a shade longer and indeed with a little more thought, as it was far removed from the ideal appointment.

The man from Orbiston, despite his inexperience, could be considered as no random choice, selected by closing the eyes and sticking a pin into a list of possible candidates. He was a sought-after commodity. Reading would have been more than keen to employ him, having offered him the post of assistant manager, while his former club Liverpool had, as mentioned, shown more than a passing interest. But it was just a couple of miles across Manchester from his old Maine Road stomping ground that Busby decided to cut his managerial teeth.

During the war, Busby – more correctly, 'Company Sergeant Major Instructor Busby' – had served in the Territorial Army where he had honed his coaching credentials in North Africa as player-coach of an army team that could boast individual talent such as Frank Swift, Joe Mercer and Tommy Lawton. The 'player'

---

1 Or thirteen if you really want to delve into the record books, throwing secretaries A.H. Albut, James West, T.J. Wallworth, J.J. Bentley and Walter Crickmer into the mix, along with jack-of-all-trades Louis Rocca. All these men held the reins as manager, in all but name, for periods of varying length.

part was important, as Busby could still 'strut his stuff' over the course of ninety minutes, competing with the best – and despite being a Liverpool player, he was called upon to guest for the likes of Reading, Middlesbrough and Hibernian during those wartime seasons. Indeed, he had represented Scotland as recently as 3rd February 1945, the last of his seven wartime caps, all strangely enough against the Auld Enemy. His playing CV, however, only shows one 'official' Scotland cap, won back in 1933 against Wales at Cardiff, along with representative matches with the British Army and the United Services.

Taking up his new form of employment, surveying the relatively unfamiliar surroundings at United, Busby's eyes would have been opened to the size of the task ahead, and his thoughts and ideas may well have taken something of a bump against his preconceptions. Yes, he had a team. A handful of individuals, one or two little more than run-of-the-mill players and only one, Johnny Carey, who could boast of any sort of international pedigree. That, plus his own enthusiasm and ambition was about it, as Manchester United were now also homeless. Not evicted for the non-payment of monies owed, but forced to leave the confines of the Manchester Ship Canal due to the heavy bombardment of the surrounding Old Trafford area by the Luftwaffe.

Air raids on the evening of December 22nd 1940 had left some three hundred Mancunians dead. Such was the damage to United's ground, the Christmas Day fixture against Stockport County in the North Regional League was hastily switched to Stockport's Edgeley Park, along with the next home match against Blackburn Rovers, scheduled for December 28th. Strangely, moving both fixtures had little effect on the actual attendances with the 5-5 draw against Blackburn watched by 1,500 at a time when home gates would range from 700 to 3,000.

Old Trafford was consequently tidied up and normality resumed, but the 7-3 victory over Bury in the North Regional League (which saw both Rowley and Carey claim hat-tricks) on March 8th 1941 was to be the last United competitive fixture played at the ground until August 1949. On the evening of Tuesday March 11th, the 556th day of the war, the German air force once again flew over Manchester, with a sustained attack causing more damage and devastation than before. Although Trafford Park was the prime target, the Old Trafford stadium was once again caught in the line of fire, leaving it far removed from the pictures cast up in the new manager's mind's eye from his previous visits as an opposition player.

> "At times the concentration of gunfire was heavier than had been heard previously in the district," reported the *Guardian*. "The planes came over in procession and for a long period of attack, which ended before midnight, there was not a minute during which the drone of the engines could not be heard.
>
> "The earlier planes dropped some flares and incendiary bombs, while later planes dropped some high explosive bombs, but the barrage from the ground defences appeared to prevent the raiders from making a heavy concentrated attack."

During the war, there were heavy reporting restrictions with exact areas and buildings that had suffered bomb damage going unnamed, but the article did go on to state that "slight outbreaks of fire were reported from a football ground." With the following day's issue mentioning: "At the football ground, incendiaries fell on the main stand and the dressing rooms were damaged by heavy explosive." That 'football ground' was Old Trafford.

On this occasion, there was no possibility of a patch-up job. Manchester United Football Club were now homeless and while arrangements were being made with the Stretford Corporation to dismantle what was left of the stand to salvage the steel, and to demolish other unsafe parts of the ground, claims for war damage to property were put forward to the authorities. This was all very well in the long term, but what was to happen in the meantime, with half a season's fixtures still to fulfil and an overdraft of £15,000 at the bank?

Assistance came from neighbours City, who offered their unfortunate rivals a helping hand, suggesting that they used their

Maine Road ground for 'home' fixtures until the time came when Old Trafford was playable again. It was a lifeline United needed and grasped thankfully, as they were determined to continue with their commitments as best they could. Following clearance from the Football League, Maine Road became 'home' for both the Blue and the Red factions of Manchester, while Old Trafford lay dormant several miles away, eventually used only for the Central League fixtures of both clubs.

When season 1939-40 had kicked off, with only a hint of the impending danger in the air, Manchester United had a cast of twenty-nine professionals, the *Manchester Evening Chronicle* hinting that they "must be the envy of nearly every club in the country" as they had "three – possibly four – first-class centre-forwards in Smith, Hanlon, Hullett and perhaps Asquith, the new man from Barnsley." That current list of professionals was soon, however, to be decimated, as was that of other clubs, with all professional contracts cancelled. Advancing age and the hostilities were soon to claim both lives and football careers.

If having no ground was the greatest minus point in Busby's notebook, the more positive points included the progressive steps that the club had already made in laying the foundations of a prestigious junior system – the MUJACs.

The 1930s had seen Manchester United struggle, in more ways than one, the new decade kicking off with a 2-0 home defeat to Swindon Town, then members of the Third Division South, in the third round of the FA Cup. The campaign drew to a close with United in 17th place, a drop of five from the previous season, with a further drop of five places twelve months later leaving the club propping up the table and sending them into the Second Division. Conceding twenty-six goals in the opening five fixtures then did little to instil confidence.

The future looked as grim as the skyline around the Trafford Park Industrial Estate, due mainly to the financial clout of J.H. Davies having evaporated upon his untimely death in October 1927. The remaining directors had neither the wealth nor the business acumen to keep the club going for any foreseeable length of time.

A journalist close to the club, Stacey Lintott, had been part of a lunching circle that included a Mr James Gibson, a "successful businessman with a weakness for taking over failing companies and restoring them to solvency." An approach was made and Gibson, who knew little or nothing about football, let alone United, agreed to step into the breach and to shoulder the ever-growing debt; but this arrangement carried conditions. Gibson wanted to start at Old Trafford with a completely clean sheet which included the resignation of the current board, although at the suggestion of Lintott, secretary Walter Crickmer was retained.

Following the influx of the much-needed cash, a manager was the next priority on the list as Crickmer had been juggling his role with secretarial duties – and, once again, Gibson passed the job of finding a capable individual over to Lintott. The journalist had no hesitation in earmarking Frank Buckley for the position, a friend who had cut his teeth as a manager with Norwich City and Blackpool before moving to Wolves, where he was beginning to attract attention. Coupled with that, he was himself a Mancunian and had played three games for United in season 1905-06.

Buckley was favourable to returning to Manchester and a meeting was arranged, but nothing more was to come of the get-together, mainly due to the fact that the prospective manager and the new chairman had something of a personality clash, the latter wanting to retain supreme control of the club, the former not wanting to be little more than a superior office boy. Although he had never guided a team to a notable triumph, Buckley had certainly made his mark as a manager of note with a wealth of ideas, and would have brought undoubted success to Manchester United. But it was not to be.

Mid-table in 1931-32 was followed by a jump into sixth place in the Second Division, with the hope of further improvement, but season 1933-34 turned into a near catastrophe, with only a 2-0 victory at Millwall on the final day of the season saving the club from relegation into Division Three and an unknown fate.

The future, however, soon looked brighter as, within two seasons, United were back in the top flight, having won the Second Division championship in 1935-36. But it proved to be a false dawn, as they were to spend only one season back amongst the elite, finishing second bottom, arguably due to the fact that manager Scott Duncan left the club in the November. Thankfully, only one season was spent in the lower division, as they were again promoted, as runners-up, at the end of 1937-38.

In their determination not to simply maintain their place in the First Division, but also to build the club into a formidable force, much discussion was held at boardroom level and it was decided that while there would always be some activity in the transfer market, if and when required, the club would attempt to nurture their own footballing talent.

Agreement was reached that an approach would be made to schoolmasters and other individuals interested in schoolboy and junior football in the Manchester, Stretford and Salford area, with a committee of fifteen elected. Trials would be held and the most promising youngsters invited to come and train at the club, under the watchful eyes of Tom Curry, Jim McClelland and other members of the coaching staff. A further proposal held that the team or teams, depending on the number of suitable players, would be entered into one of the local Manchester leagues, under the name of MUJACs – the Manchester United Junior Athletic Club.

In the Altrincham, Hale and Bowdon *Guardian* from mid-August 1957 to March 1958, Harry Renshaw penned a history of Manchester United and in the weekly segment of December 27th wrote:

> "At school a boy's progress was closely watched by the teachers, who are and always have been the real foundation of soccer.
>
> "But once they had to make their way in the world the boys were left to their own devices for most part, for the youth organisations with their lack of funds could never be expected to cater for the thousands of youngsters who become available each year. In consequence many thousands of promising boys dropped out of the game through lack of encouragement and it was this tragic gap that United set out to fill within the limits of their means when they formed

the Manchester United Junior Athletic Club, commonly called the 'MUJACs'.

"By running these junior teams they were able to take youngsters straight from school, and by playing them in leagues of their particular age group gradually bring them to maturity without any harmful effects that inevitably fell to the boy who, because of superior skill was forced with open age teams and then suffer the consequences."

During the summer of 1938 the trials were concluded and season 1938-39 saw two teams, one made up of players aged around sixteen thrown into an open league set-up, with the younger lads enjoying a more leisurely introduction into competitive football with friendly fixtures.

Initially, the foray into an open league was difficult, but the experience gained was priceless, as local leagues were made up of a variety of players on different levels of fitness and skill.

United's set-up was certainly not unique, as other Football League clubs had also embraced a youth programme and towards the end of that inaugural MUJACs season, their fixture list was expanded to take in fixtures against two neighbouring Lancashire clubs, Everton and Preston North End, who had also become involved in bringing local youngsters into the fold.

The first such outing was against a previously undefeated Everton side at Old Trafford, the home side clearly geared up for the confrontation and stunning the visitors with a 3-0 victory. In the 'return' at Goodison Park, Everton were certainly not going to underestimate their opponents for a second time and, in a pulsating encounter, eventually ran out 5-3 winners. The fixtures against Preston North End produced identical outcomes – victory at home, but a defeat away, the latter mainly due to an emphatic display from a youngster by the name of Tom Finney.

A look at the team sheet for the match against Everton reveals only two names of note in the United side – Harry Haslam, who failed to make the grade with United, but who made a name for himself as manager of Luton Town, guiding them to the old First Division in 1974, while the other name of note was J. Aston, lining up as an inside-forward, one individual at least who was to progress through the ranks.

So, with that initial season out of the way, the men in charge sat down and discussed how things had gone, deciding that the scheme had indeed been a success that could be built upon. But no sooner were the MUJACs up and running when war was declared and suddenly the recently established committee of fifteen found itself reduced to four, with three of those remaining being unable to devote as much time to club business. On the playing side, many of the older boys joined the services, so in order to continue, the age of the players dropped to around fifteen.

In order to keep this area of the club alive, Mr John Bill was asked by United secretary Walter Crickmer if he would take on the role of secretary/manager of the MUJACs, to which he readily agreed and in November 1939 the first fixture of the new season was finally played.

Between that opening game and the first week of the New Year, a total of ten fixtures had been fulfilled, all against teams of an older age group, with one such outing, against Moss Rovers on Boxing Day, bringing considerably more than a dramatic 9-0 defeat.

With an average age of 17, the Moss Rovers side were one of the youngest teams the MUJACs had come up against, but they were still almost 18 months older and were predominantly individuals who had made up the Manchester Schoolboy side for the past two years. Not only that, they were commonly acknowledged as being 'unofficially' affiliated to Manchester City, adding an additional touch of spice to the fixture. John Bill, however, was reluctant to set his youngsters up for what would undoubtedly be a bruising defeat. In the end, he decided that there was more to lose by not playing, and in any case, whatever the outcome, it would simply be part of the learning curve for the youngsters. Although defeated, the manner in which the MUJACs played did not go unnoticed and, at the end of the game, they were invited to join the South Manchester and Wythenshawe Football League for the remainder of that season.

Due to the war creating a shortage of teams, the South Manchester and Wythenshawe League had only run their league programme up until the end of 1939, with Moss Rovers clear winners, but it was proposed to run a cup competition during the second part of the season. Being members of this well-established league also ensured closer contact with other clubs, opening more doors – and so the MUJACs had their first taste of competitive football.

Early forays brought instant success, with four wins out of four, scoring twenty-nine goals and conceding only two, but on Saturday March 2nd 1940 the fixtures conjured up a return against Moss Rovers. John Bill still expected to endure a defeat, but did insist that his team had "improved" and that "if we can reduce the deficit to 5-0 or so I shall be very pleased".

In the early exchanges, the United youngsters held their own with right-half Tony Waddington[2] stamping his authority on the game. Their opponents struggled to gain any sort of momentum as the half wore on and were somewhat stunned to find themselves a goal behind at half time. The Rovers did, however, manage to find a smattering of their usual form during the second forty-five minutes, finally managing to break down the MUJAC defence, but this solitary goal mattered little, as John Bill's youngsters scored two more, to earn a notable victory in those early days of the fledgling club.

The Second World War continued to have a telling effect on the MUJACs progress as a club and also for their players, as many could find themselves in their regular employment on a Saturday afternoon instead of pulling on their football kit. Much to John Bill's relief, however, he usually managed to field eleven players except on one occasion, in April 1940, he found himself without five first team regulars, all calling off at the last minute. Recruiting two reserve players, he was still three players short, but instead of calling the game off, decided to play with only eight men.

---

2   Tony Waddington was to move to Crewe after the war, where he enjoyed a seven-year career before moving into coaching with Stoke City. After a spell as assistant manager, he stepped into the hot seat in 1960, lifting the beleaguered Potters from a relegation-threatened side to Second Division champions and Football League Cup winners, while also bringing European football to the Potteries.

Playing something akin to a 2-1-4 formation, with Joe Walton doing the work of two men and on this occasion outshining Waddington, United surprisingly took the lead mid-way through the second half through leading scorer Hall, and held on to it to secure a surprise victory.

Throughout the Second World War, it was difficult to maintain the momentum of those early days, but nevertheless, the club never faltered in its decision and through consistent endeavour, success was achieved in various competitions with the United 'Colts', as they were to become known. Well, can you imagine standing there shouting "Come on ye' Manchester United Junior Athletic Club"?

Although there were league and cup triumphs, few of those youngsters who represented the club at this level during those war years were to make the step up to the Football League with United, but the seeds had been sown and through time would be cultivated with the club to reap the benefits.

The Football League had been forced into a premature hibernation after only three fixtures of the 1939-40 season, with United having beaten Grimsby Town 4-0 at home on the opening day, going on to draw 1-1 at Chelsea and losing 2-0 at Charlton before war became more than simply a passing threat. With football understandably taking a back seat, it was a few weeks before competitive fixtures were considered by the powers that be. In the months and years that followed, football was played on a regional basis in order to keep travel to an absolute minimum, with United playing in the War Regional League Western Division, then the North Regional League and Football League North, as well as numerous cup competitions and friendlies.

Although games were competitive, results were relatively unimportant, with actual team selection often unknown until minutes before kick-off. 'Guest' players were the norm due to actual signed professionals being engaged in the hostilities on a foreign field, while players from other clubs, unable to make their way 'home' for certain fixtures, would line-up for a club, or clubs, near wherever they happened to be stationed with the various armed forces.

Such circumstances led to United fielding what is arguably their best forward line of all time against Everton on June 1st 1940 – the only time they have ever played a League fixture in that month – with the front five reading: Stanley Matthews, Alex Herd (father of David), Tom Burdett (the odd man out), Peter Doherty and Raich Carter. Even with such illustrious individuals in the line-up they could do little to prevent a 3-0 defeat.

Almost all of the United players were, by now, in the forces, including Johnny Carey who could have opted to return to his native Ireland, a neutral country, but he decided his duty was to follow the route of his team-mates and join the army, spending most of his active service in Italy. Charlie Mitten was in the RAF, with Stan Pearson, Allenby Chilton and Johnny Morris in the army. The latter found himself stationed at Stromness in the Orkney Isles, while Smith, Warner and Bryant all worked in munitions.

Crowds in those wartime days would vary considerably from week to week with travelling support at a minimum, if any at all. A couple of thousand would be considered about average for a Maine Road 'home' fixture, although the ninety minutes against City would see 10,000 click through the turnstiles. Attendances for many of those wartime fixtures can be found as simply rounded up to the nearest hundred or thousand, but even giving or taking a few, something of a record was set on November 30th 1940, when the crowd for Liverpool's visit to Maine Road was given as a mere 700. The lowest attendance ever to watch a United home fixture?

The forced move from Old Trafford to Stockport in December 1940 saw little change in numbers. As previously mentioned, the attendance for the fixture on the 28th against Blackburn Rovers was given as 1,500. For those who made the short journey from Manchester, or the locals who decided they had eaten and drank enough, they were treated to a real goal feast, with United putting nine past their opponents without reply. For those who were not present, the result was somewhat misleading, showing a considerable turnaround from three weeks previously when the two teams shared ten goals.

With kick-off approaching, Blackburn had still been four players short, and a blackboard with a chalked-up message requesting players was carried around the ground. In true pantomime fashion, if the boots fitted, you got a game.[3]

Guest players, unknown men off the street and seasoned professionals littered those early wartime games, producing an excellent ninety-minute distraction from the events on foreign fields and the night-time bombings. The entertainment may not have been of the highest quality, but it often conjured up goals by the barrow load.

Season 1940-41 for example, not only produced the 9-0 and the 5-5 scorelines against Blackburn, as Bury were beaten 7-3 on March 8th, Manchester City 7-1 on April 14th and Chester 6-4 five days later. Such results were certainly not simply oddities throughout a particular season, as 1941-42 kicked off with a 13-1 victory over New Brighton, Jack Rowley claiming seven (two more items of note that would never feature in the record books), bettering his four against City and three against Bury the previous season. Ironically, Brighton held United to a 3-3 draw on their own ground the following Saturday. Stockport County, however, were not so fortunate in the next two fixtures, as United hammered them 5-1 away and 7-1 at Maine Road, that man Rowley scoring four in both fixtures. Chester fared little better, losing 7-0 at home and 8-1 in Manchester, while Tranmere leaked six at Maine Road, Rowley scoring five, with Wrexham returning to north Wales on the back of a 10-3 defeat, Rowley on this occasion overshadowed by Johnny Carey who scored four to the United sharpshooter's three.

Such results saw United lift the North Regional League title. Well, sort of, as it was played in two sections with the first up to December 25th and the second to May 23rd. To confuse matters even more, some games in the second phase were also War Cup qualifiers and Lancashire Cup fixtures.

---

3 Strangely, a similar story unfolded at Norwich, where Brighton arrived with only five players and soldiers on leave made up the numbers – again to no avail, as the home side went on to win 18-0. Further trivia can be gathered from the Christmas Day fixtures when some clubs actually played both morning and afternoon, with England international Tommy Lawton having the distinction of playing for two clubs in one day, turning out for Everton against Liverpool in the morning and Tranmere Rovers against Crewe in the afternoon.

In the first section, United finished fourth, three points behind Blackpool, but in the final placings were top following the application of a further set of complicated rules, as only teams who had completed eighteen or more games qualified for the championship. Their results over twenty-three games were taken into consideration and the average points adjusted accordingly. Complicated or what? In any case, United came out on top with an average of 33.89!

Despite this 'success of sorts', wartime football was relatively unproductive from a financial point of view for club and players alike. In the seasons leading up to the war, United were not exactly one of the wealthiest clubs around and had spent considerable time contemplating what the future held in store. Even before season 1941-42 had got underway, the problems were beginning to pile up.

At a board meeting on August 21st, it was reported that "arrangements had been made with the Stretford Corporation to salvage the damaged steel from the site (Old Trafford) and carry out demolishing operations as required." Only a couple of months earlier that all-important arrangement had been made with neighbours City regarding the use of their Maine Road ground while Old Trafford was out of action. A debt of £74,000 was already hanging over the club, but the generosity of their neighbours in offering their ground as a temporary home was something of a lifeline and more than gratefully appreciated. The terms of the rental, as per a letter from City secretary Wilf Wild to his United counterpart dated 4th June 1941, was laid out as £10 up to £100 taken at the gate, less tax, £15 for between £150 and £200 taken at the gate, increasing in multiples of £5 for every £50 over and above.

Ground rental, day-to-day running costs and of course wages all added up, but the latter was certainly nothing extravagant for the individuals who combined playing with their time in the forces or in a regular job of national importance. Most were simply paid appearance money, with 30/- (£1.50) the going rate, while match officials on the other hand could expect 10/6d (approx. 53p) per game plus expenses, with a locally based linesman pocketing 5/- (25p) per match.

The goals continued to flow during the following two seasons with United scoring five on three consecutive November afternoons in 1942 against City and Tranmere Rovers (twice). In the second half of the campaign, Blackpool, Everton and Bury also conceded five to the United goal machine, with Crewe being hammered 7-0 in a League Cup qualifier and then 6-0 in a Lancashire Cup tie. This was just as well, as minimum admission prices were raised at the start of the former, from 1/- (5p) to 1/3d (around 6p). During 1943-44, Stockport, Tranmere and Halifax all conceded half a dozen, although the Tranmere match was abandoned after 85 minutes with United winning 6-3, while Burnley were beaten 9-0 at Maine Road. There were, however, times during both seasons when the defence did not enjoy the best of afternoons, losing for example 6-1 at Everton and 5-4 at Chester in the opening months of season 1943-44.

Strangely, those free-scoring days seemed to dry up during 1944-45, the action unfortunately seeming to swing to the opposite end of the pitch, as goals were leaked on a more than frequent basis. Stockport were to score four on consecutive Saturdays with the season only four games old, the defence going on to concede a further eight over the course of the next three games. Liverpool were also to score eight in the two fixtures between the clubs in early November, while City managed two less in the following two games. Thankfully in one of those, United scored three to ensure victory! There were, however, goals for the support to celebrate with Tranmere Rovers and Stoke City leaking six and four respectively on consecutive Saturdays in October and April.

It was not until the second half of the season that some sort of consistency was reached, timed to perfection to coincide with the start of the League Cup North competition. Fifteen thousand turned up at Turf Moor, Burnley for the first round first leg tie, where the home side were beaten by the odd goal in five, much to the surprise of many, leaving much to play for in the second leg.

United 'outclassed' Burnley in that second leg, but in the second round first leg tie against Stoke City, their victory was once again considered a surprise – despite the 6-1 scoreline – although the 45,616 spectators in the season's biggest crowd to date might have thought differently. A weakened Stoke side in the return leg put up little resistance, but managed to keep the score down to a more respectable 4-1.

The odd goal in three gave United the advantage over Doncaster Rovers in the first leg of the quarter-finals. A performance extolling "energy, elegance and resourcefulness, wondrous to behold" gave them a 3-1 victory in the Maine Road return, nudging them into the semi-finals where Chesterfield stood in their way of a passage into the final.

Such were numerous United performances of late, they were fortunate to come out of the first ninety minutes against Chesterfield at Maine Road with a 1-1 draw. Had it not been for a resounding defensive display in the second leg and a 57th minute goal from Port Vale 'guest' McDowall, they would not have scraped through to the final. All that Chesterfield had to show for their efforts were gate receipts of £3,187.

In the final, a solitary goal from Lofthouse, five minutes into the second half, was enough to give Bolton a first leg advantage, while the Maine Road return, found the *Guardian* correspondent as intrigued by the 'pre-match entertainment' as much as the ninety minutes of football itself:

> "The entertainment began fully an hour before kick-off, the most arresting item being a display of energy by a one-legged man in red singlet and white shorts who insisted in hopping round the field as a mark of confidence that United could 'do it on one leg', so to speak. And when Wrigglesworth scored in the twenty-third minute and cancelled for a while the vital goal lost at Bolton the previous week, it seemed as though the whimsical supporter's gesture was justified."

Bolton equalised two minutes before the interval, but sixteen minutes into the second half, Bryant restored United's lead and the game remained on a knife edge until the final minute. Again, it was the United defence who excelled, keeping the visitors at bay. But with only seconds remaining, the game slipped from United's grasp when Barrass headed home Butler's corner. So near to forcing half an hour of extra time and the possibility of silverware, but such things would have to wait. The team had at least shown spirit for the fight, despite some unflattering results – and with Matt Busby's arrival impending, the future was beginning to take on something of a red glow. But all of the results, the successes, the failures, were ultimately of little consequence, as it was the appointment of Matt Busby that captured the imagination and interest of the supporters, not the eleven individuals on the pitch.

In the first half of that 1944-45 campaign, conceding goals – eighteen in the opening half dozen fixtures – and the overall inconsistency of the performances were only a minor concern compared to the ongoing problem of the Old Trafford ground. There was some relief to be had in a letter from the War Commission in mid-November, informing the club that "Old Trafford was not considered a total loss", but it would be months before any repair work could be carried out.

Local MP Ellis Smith, himself a keen United supporter and a man to whom the club should be more than a little grateful, became involved in their attempts at obtaining grants towards the rebuilding of the stadium. His efforts were finally rewarded in August 1945, when the War Damage Commission granted the club the sum of £4,800 to clear the debris around the ground, with local youngsters earning themselves some extra pocket money by painstakingly walking up and down the pitch picking up broken glass.

It is difficult to imagine the actual extent of the damage caused during those air strikes, but a visit to the ground by the *Manchester Evening Chronicle*'s United correspondent Alf Clarke prompted the following article in April 1946, under the heading 'They Are Putting the "Home" In Order':

> "Demolition work has now been completed. A difficult job has been done. The entire centre of the grandstand and the stone wall behind have been pulled own. All that remains is an open space, with many protruding struts from the girder foundations.
>
> In a few days' time workmen will begin to rebuild the wall and others will start on the task of erecting players' dressing rooms.

On the opposite side of the ground, the covered accommodation structure was also badly blitzed. But the workmen will find it easy dealing with this compared with the task of demolishing the main stand.

I understand that when United restart 'at home' next season the entire space of the old grandstand will not be used at all. This means that there will be standing accommodation only all-round the ground, with a blank space in the former grandstand area.

This cannot be used even for standing spectators for two reasons. First, there are no crash barriers and secondly, because there are no concrete steps. Spectators, however, will be able to stand in the paddock in front of the former stands.

It will mean that the ground capacity for the time being will be reduced, but I anticipate there will be room for 60,000 spectators.

How long it will take to rebuild the stand I don't know. The work has to be done in stages as Ministry of Labour permits are secured.

Meanwhile, what about the playing pitch? That is still as good as ever. In fact it will be in better condition when September comes round again.

Three hundred tons of special soil has been used on the ground and there will be new turf down the centre of the field from goal to goal. The seed will be sown in a few days' time down this stretch of soil.

It is a pity that we shall not have the Old Trafford that we knew for next season, because you can take it from me that though they shall be without seating accommodation, they will have the best team in the country. A sweeping statement, but I make it after careful consideration, and I believe my optimism is justified."

A further sum of £1,430 was granted in November 1946 for the demolition of what was left of the stand. Then, some time later, another cheque, this time for £17,478, popped through the

Cornbrook Stores letterbox, this being the figure granted towards the stand's rebuilding. Those payments were made in instalments, with the final sum of just over £710 for the demolition work not being paid until February 1947.

But Alf Clarke's belief that United would make a swift return to Old Trafford was to prove far off the mark. Much further than he could ever have anticipated.

The 1-1 League Cup North semi-final first leg draw with Chesterfield at Maine Road raised little cause for celebration, other perhaps than the gate receipts of over £3,700, as the visitors enhanced their reputation and retained their record of having drawn all their away leg cup-ties and were clearly the better of the two sides. But there was to be widespread rejoicing, with street parties the length and breadth of the country three days later, when victory in Europe was finally declared. Fighting still raged in the Far East, but it was to be only a matter of another seven days before Japan finally surrendered.

So, with the war now over, although there was still an enormous amount of work to be done at home and abroad, people could begin to return to as normal a life as was possible in the circumstances. On the football front, the administrators could begin to plan for a much fuller and more organised fixture list. Players began the slow, painstaking job of demobilisation, which would enable teams to field more settled elevens and end the reliance on 'guests' – or indeed members of the paying public – to enhance their starting line-ups.

Season 1945-46 had kicked off with the poorest start of all the wartime seasons, with only one victory in the opening eleven games, the players contributing little for their newly upgraded wage of £4 per game, whilst continuing to discuss striking for more. Gone were those entertaining, goalfest afternoons. "Crowd Groaned; No Real Thrill or Skill", "United's Attack Missed Openings Galore" and "Missed Chances" were just three of the headlines that accompanied reports from the opening half dozen fixtures. The incoming manager was going to have a far from easy baptism.

Thankfully there was a team of dedicated men behind the MUJACs project, as Matt Busby could not be expected to concentrate on first-team matters as well as overseeing the running of the junior sides, although he was to take more than a passing interest in the latter organisation. Similarly, as a novice manager, he quickly decided on the verity of the old adage 'two hands are better than one' and looked to appoint a trusty assistant.

Searching for help and guidance in his new and unfamiliar role, Busby needed to look no further than club secretary Walter Crickmer, who had held the position of temporary manager since chief scout Jimmy Porter had departed to become Bury manager in March 1944. Crickmer's opinion was always appreciated and, in reality, Busby was lucky to have such a strong and knowledgeable figure alongside him. Meanwhile, Crickmer himself was lucky to be alive, as he had been out and about in his position as a special constable stationed at the Old Trafford County Police headquarters on that March night when Old Trafford suffered at the hands of the German Luftwaffe and was buried under the rubble of a bomb-hit building, escaping with relatively minor injuries.

But Crickmer had enough on his plate without becoming involved again with the playing side of things, so Busby looked further afield for for a reliable assistant. He did have Tom Curry, the former Newcastle United wing-half, alongside him as trainer. Curry had played over 200 games for the Tyneside club and after hanging up his boots with Stockport County in 1930 had joined Carlisle United as trainer, moving to Manchester United under Scott Duncan four years later. He was a more than reliable aide, but Busby was looking for someone with a stronger coaching pedigree, someone who he could turn to and bounce ideas off. An afternoon at an army camp in Bari was to produce just that man.

A gruff Welsh voice had made Busby stop and take notice as it delivered a team talk to a group of soldiers under his guidance as a sergeant in charge of sports recreation. It was delivered with a passion the Scot had never witnessed before. It was as if this individual was leading his men into battle, not a nondescript football match. "I heard this man talking to a crowd of footballers in Italy. His audience was entranced," related Busby, "it was as if he was delivering a sermon. It was clear that he had some special quality for getting his message across." So impressed was the Scot that he introduced himself and informed Jimmy Murphy that whenever he managed to obtain suitable employment with a football club back in Britain, he would get back in touch with the offer of a job.

Born in Pentre, in 1910, in the heart of the Rhondda Valley, Jimmy Murphy played for Wales at schoolboy level, but he later dismissed himself and fellow players as "a non-entity, but in my year we beat England 3-2 at Cardiff and then drew 2-2 with Scotland at Hampden Park. Those results fired my imagination and brought me to the attention of English League clubs. He continued:

> "I went to West Bromwich Albion at the age of 16 for a month as an inside-forward, becoming a full time professional and worked my way through the A team to the reserves. After two years I appeared to be getting nowhere until suddenly 'Dame Fortune' appeared.
>
> "I had run out of goals as an inside-forward and one day with the reserves when we had lost a player through injury I dropped back to wing-half. I was promoted to the first team on the strength of that appearance.
>
> "Curiously enough, the transformation in my career was an exact parallel with Matt Busby."

Murphy made just over 200 appearances for West Bromwich Albion, as a tough-tackling wing-half, winning a runners-up medal in the 1935 FA Cup Final; but

> "It was the war that really ended my playing career though not before I had won sixteen caps for Wales and lost perhaps another eight because my club wouldn't release me," he continued. "I was a Desert Rat with the Royal Artillery and went through the North African campaign before becoming involved with football again.
>
> "At Bari Transit Camp in Italy, I took over from Stan Cullis as the sergeant in charge of sport. It was there that I met Matt Busby who had come out with a British Army team packed with stars like Joe Mercer, Frank Swift, Arthur Rowe and Cliff Britton."

Upon his demob towards the end of April 1946, Jimmy Murphy left the family home in the Midlands, heading for Manchester to take up the coaching job offered by Busby. It was a relationship that was to become not so much a 'good cop – bad cop', more a Batman and Robin or, for the preceding generation, the Lone Ranger and Tonto. The former Welsh internationalist was to become a hard taskmaster, a coach who demanded a lot, but who would give as much in return if he sensed a player had the ability and the determination to do well. There was no timescale on Murphy's contract of employment, making his days long, but there was never any form of complaint. Instead, Murphy was to thrive on those daily routines, assisting Busby with first-team training in the morning, then on Tuesdays and Thursdays also taking the club's junior players, part-timers and amateurs for their sessions at the Cliff. His dedication was unsurpassed. Looking back he recalled:

> "The ground was little more than a rubbish tip. The club just didn't have the money. The training area was just outside the ground on rough ground, covered with stones that was not even surfaced properly.
>
> "The so-called gymnasium was in a wooden hut, and Ted Dalton, our physiotherapist, had to work in a cramped room that only had one machine, and that was just an infrared lamp.
>
> "But we found those early days exciting enough. I brought a couple of players who were in the RAF at Bari – Billy McGlen and centre-forward Ronnie Burke."

So it was to the Cornbrook Cold Stores on Hadfield Street that Matt Busby made his way in October 1945 to take up the position of Manchester United, not nearby Old Trafford which stood desolate, a mess of fallen masonry, broken glass and tangled metal, as the premises owned by chairman J. W. Gibson were now the club's temporary headquarters.

United had been League champions, of a sort, in 1941, and Lancashire Cup winners that same year, beating Burnley 1-0 thanks to a Johnny Carey goal – then repeating the feat in 1943 following a 6-4 aggregate win over Liverpool. They had been League North Cup runners-up in 1945, scoring goals for fun at times, whilst leaking them like novices, all accomplished with an assortment of players. Coupled with a ground that resembled a building site, this was basically the Manchester United that Matt Busby inherited.

Having accepted the position of manager back in February, Busby had some eight months to gather his thoughts and to plot his path, but there had been little or no time to assess his playing staff in detail, with his first opportunity to see them in action coming at Barnsley on September 29th 1945. His presence did little to inspire his charges, with the game finishing 1-1. Two of the following three fixtures failed to produce a goal, never mind a victory, giving the new manager much to consider before he got behind his desk for the first time on October 22nd.

> "It is my intentions to develop young players," he told the *Manchester Evening News*, "I think I can do it all right and I am certain from what I have already seen of the team that we shall have a side second to none when normal football resumes next season."

It took him little time to become involved in some wheeling and dealing, securing an old RAF hut so that the players would have somewhere to change when training resumed at Old Trafford. The Cliff at Lower Broughton had been secured in the summer of 1938, but this was the regular haunt of the MUJACs and had been at the disposal of the RAF until 1944.

So, seven days after making himself comfortable in the manager's chair Matt Busby put pencil to paper and began to scribble down his first United line-up for the visit of Bolton Wanderers to Maine Road on Saturday October 27th 1945. He opted to make one personnel and three positional changes to the eleven who had drawn 1-1 with the same opponent at Burnden Park seven days previously; but it was a far cry from the team that had faced Charlton Athletic at the Valley on September 2nd 1939, the last 'official' Saturday of League football prior to the outbreak of hostilities. The pre-war team – Breedon, Redwood, Griffiths, Warner, Chilton, Whalley,

Bryant, Wassall, Asquith, Pearson and Wrigglesworth – had been totally transformed over the intervening weeks, months and years.

Breedon was now on his way to Burnley; Redwood had died of tuberculosis, contracted whilst in the army; Griffiths, like Wassall, had seen his career cut short due to the war, the former joining Hyde United as a player-coach and the latter making only a brief appearance with Stockport County; Bryant was soon to be a Bradford City player, while Asquith, a £7,000 signing from Barnsley, had only made one appearance for United prior to the war and that was to be his solitary entry in the record books, as he had re-joined his former club during 1945-46. Warner, Chilton, Whalley, Pearson and Wrigglesworth were of course still with the club, comprising the half-back line that was the backbone of Busby's first selection.

For that first game in charge, a Football League North fixture against Bolton, he was not exactly spoilt for choice as some of his squad was still unavailable, but decided on the following side: Crompton, Walton, Roach, Warner, Whalley, Cockburn, Worrall, Carey, Smith, Rowley and Wrigglesworth. Goals from Carey and Worrall gave United a 2-1 win, only their second victory of the season. Those newspaper headlines of a few weeks earlier suddenly changed to – "Magnificent First Home Success", observers reporting that it was by far the best game seen at the ground all season, with plaudits given to Carey, making only his third appearance of the season, along with Cockburn and Whalley. The majority of the 27,272 crowd went home happy, looking forward to continued success under the new manager.

Johnny Carey's return to the fore was to be fleeting, as he was soon to return overseas, with team-mates Johnny Morris, Stan Pearson, Charlie Mitten, Johnny Anderson and John Aston also on postings abroad. Johnny Hanlon, who had scored a dozen goals in twenty-seven appearances during 1938-39, had started the opening three fixtures of the season, but having been interred as a prisoner of war, had found those outings too demanding and had asked not to be considered again until he felt something like his old self. Vose, a stalwart defender in those immediate pre-war years, made a fleeting return in February, his first start in a red shirt since 1942, but the ninety minutes against Blackpool were to be his last with the club.

And continued success there certainly was, as seven days later, again at Maine Road, Preston North End were sent back up the A6 debating their 6-1 defeat, with Johnny Carey once again the star man. Although there were to be blips – a run of three consecutive defeats in late December – results certainly improved and although having to be content with fourth place in the first section of League results (seven behind winners Blackpool) and sixth in the second (this time seven behind Liverpool), Matt Busby did crown his first season in charge with a trophy, lifting the Lancs Cup with a 1-0 victory over Burnley.

Attendances were, overall, an improvement on previous years, although like that previous campaign, those towards the end of the season were considerably higher, with over 112,500 at Maine Road on consecutive Saturdays for the 'home' and away fixtures against City. Few matchgoers today will have experienced being part of a human mass upon a packed cinder-strewn terrace, with randomly erected crush barriers all that prevented you from tumbling forward into uncertain oblivion. Only a month prior to those City fixtures, an estimated 85,000 had managed to gain entry into Burnden Park in Bolton for their FA Cup tie against Stoke City. Some seven minutes after kick-off "a barrier collapsed and threw hundreds of people to the ground. Many were trampled underfoot in the wild rush to escape." Further eyewitness accounts stated that spectators had broken into the ground at the railway end, forcing movement in the crowd behind that goal which had kick-started the incident which saw thirty-three killed and around four hundred injured.

Those events at Bolton cast a dark cloud over the game, just as it was preparing to return to some sort of normality.

Like the 4-1 defeat by Manchester City, the 4-2 reversal at Sunderland and losing three without reply at Goodison Park against Everton, Busby took any setback in his stride, looking at the bigger picture and of course the future.

"With so many good players not yet available because of Service requirements, it will not be easy to start building up," admitted the United manager, "but I hope I may form some concrete plans for team strengthening later on in the season. United have a first class side, if only I could get them together in one place." He continued, "It is my intention to develop young players. I think I can do it all right and I am certain from what I have already seen of the team that we should have a side second to none when normal football resumes next season."

This was certainly no bullish statement, made in order to rally the support, as the MUJACs idea was slowly beginning to show fruition, as was the local scouting system. This had been inadvertently kick-started with the £250 (or £200, depending on the source) signing of seventeen-year-old Johnny Carey from St James's Gate in Dublin in 1936, nudging the United directors into the realisation that there would be other nuggets out there and finding them would save on transfers and compensation. Carey's signing, however, was certainly not planned, nor were a number of others, their names not even registered on United's radar, or in the notebooks of any of their scouts.

In the case of Carey, man-of-all-trades Louis Rocca had ventured across the Irish Sea to watch a centre-forward, Benny Gaughran, playing with Bohemians – a venture which turned out to be a complete waste of time, as the player in question had already signed for Celtic for a fee of £400. United's man in Ireland, Billy Behan, once on United's books and able to claim one solitary first-team appearance to his credit, had seen Carey play, and rather than have Rocca return to Manchester without seeing a ball kicked, persuaded him to spend another night in Dublin to take in the game involving St James's Gate the following day. Perhaps encouraged more by the Irish hospitality, Rocca stayed, watched St James's Gate against Cork Athletic, liked what he saw in Carey, who was playing as an inside-forward, and at the final whistle made an immediate approach to the St James's Gate secretary. A committee meeting was called there and then and a transfer fee agreed, Carey's father was asked for his permission for United to take his son over the water and following yet more Irish hospitality shown towards Rocca, all was agreed.

Along with a somewhat under-the-weather Rocca, the new signing made his way to Manchester, where the pair were greeted by newspaper headlines stating "United Sign Star" – only for the paragraphs below to reveal it was a player by the name of Thompson who had arrived at Old Trafford from Blackburn Rovers. Through the passages of time, however, it was to be the unknown Irishman who was to make the greater impact, the man from Blackburn disappearing into obscurity.

Jack Rowley was one exception to the rule, signed from Bournemouth for £3,000, although initially, he was another who had been spotted as a mere fifteen-year-old, playing with Cradley Heath in the Birmingham League. Following those initial reports, Ted Connor, a former United player and now a scout with the club, was sent to watch him. Due to his age, United decided to cast their eyes over him on another one or two occasions, only to find that when they made the move to sign him, he had joined Wolves. His name was filed away and re-emerged as a Bournemouth player, where he was once again beginning to attract much attention. As it happened, United chairman James Gibson was then spending considerable time on the south coast, often taking in games involving Bournemouth, and he reported back that here indeed was a player worth signing. Contact was made with the south coast club and a fee agreed.

Stan Pearson had been brought to Louis Rocca's attention by Jimmy Matthews, the Adelphi Lads' Club secretary, telling his friend that the player in question was showing tremendous promise. With that being seen as recommendation enough, Mr Ablett, manager of the United 'A' team, was sent to the Pearson household to obtain the youngster's signature on amateur forms. Following a handful of 'A' team appearances, the teenager was invited to join the United ground staff, going on to make his first-team debut as an eighteen-year-old against Chesterfield in November 1937, after a mere two Central League appearances, playing his part in a notable 7-1 win.

Before the war, United trainer and former player Jimmy Porter had happened to overhear a casual conversation between a group of supporters on a Manchester to Bury train journey. They were discussing a player who was turning in good displays with Radcliffe St Johns – a happy coincidence which resulted in the signing of Johnny Morris. A mental note was made by Porter, Radcliffe was visited by a United scout and Morris was duly signed. A star of the United 'A' team prior to the war, he was soon to shine in India playing alongside the legendary Tommy Walker of Hearts before returning to England and United.

Joe Walton had been signed from the revered local junior side Goslings, where goalkeeper Jack Crompton had also enjoyed a few outings (the latter also having seen service with his local side Newton Heath Loco, who had supplied goalkeeper Jack Hall to United). Although Walton had started his playing career as an inside-forward, he had first stepped between the posts in an emergency when the regular keeper failed to turn up. His performance that afternoon was to prevent him from ever returning to his outfield position. Joining United initially as an amateur, Crompton was to take over from Jack Breedon.

But it wasn't only in England that United had 'eyes', as reports relating to Charlie Mitten, who was at military school in Scotland, began to seep through. Spotted by United's Scottish-based scouts as the fourteen-year-old star of Queen Victoria Military College, where his father was an instructor, the club had to act quickly. Talk on the grapevine indicated that there were also a number of Scottish clubs making covetous glances in the youngster's direction. Within a week, he was on the United groundstaff.

Towards the end of season 1945-46 John Aston had broken into the first-team scene with a handful of appearances in the inside-right and centre-forward positions. One of the original MUJACs, Aston graduated through the ranks, before serving as a commando during the war, but like some of his former team-mates his signing was simply by pure chance – or at least one version of the story relates it as such.

According to Louis Rocca – whose countless tales have, on occasion, been seen to be little more than exaggerated myths – Aston's cousin, also named John Aston, a schoolboy international and captain of the Lancashire county side, had been signed by the club, but had failed to make a telling breakthrough. Prior to his departure, he asked if the club had seen his cousin who was a much better player than himself. Not wanting to leave any stone unturned, United subsequently dispatched Billy Malone, one of numerous local scouts, to watch the player in action for his club Clayton Methodists. With a favourable report being returned, John Aston mk2 was duly signed. The player himself was to relate a slightly different tale, saying that upon learning of the newly formed MUJACs, his father had, without his knowledge, written to the club regarding his son's ability and a trial was subsequently offered, with a contract duly signed following favourable showings.

Allenby Chilton had been invited to Merseyside for a month's trial with Liverpool, having been spotted playing for north-east side Seaham Colliery. Following his four weeks at Anfield he had the opportunity to sign on a permanent basis, but decided to return to the north-east before committing himself.

Back home, he was subsequently visited by Louis Rocca who, along with his trusted band of scouts who seemed to be everywhere, and asked if he would like to join United; but the visitor was told amateur forms had been signed with Liverpool at the start of his trial. Unperturbed, Rocca then asked if he would sign for United if his release could be obtained from Liverpool. With a professional contract in the offing, Chilton readily agreed, a deal was cast, and a fortnight later Chilton was a Manchester United player. He was also an individual that Matt Busby was more than familiar with, the pair having locked horns in opposition during the War League Cup South semi-final between Charlton and Reading at White Hart Lane when both were guest players – Chilton for Chelsea and Busby with Reading – the Biscuitmen coming out on top, winning 3-2 after extra time.

Harry Worrall was signed from Winsford United around the same time as Stan Pearson; Billy Wrigglesworth, like Rowley, arrived from Wolves, while Bert Whalley, who was to bring fellow Ashton-under-Lyne resident Henry Cockburn to Old Trafford, made the step up from Cheshire League level and Stalybridge Celtic. Jack Warner moved from Welsh junior football, with John Roach stepping up from the amateur ranks.

The diminutive Henry Cockburn was another who had graced the Gosling set-up, originally having played with the Avro's works team in Failsworth. A missed bus with his fellow team-mates to play against Goslings saw him offered a lift by the opponents' manager and an inspired performance shortly afterwards saw him offered a permanent place with the noted Manchester side. Those performances continued to improve and an invitation to a trial with Blackpool was duly received, but due to illness, he was unable to accept the offer, the Seasiders' loss proving to be Manchester United's gain.

Most of those individuals were to play an important part in Matt Busby's vision of the future, but for one player, the war robbed him of his best years and had it not been for the hostilities then the Old Trafford record books might well have taken an entirely different look.

John 'Jack' Smith was Yorkshire born, starting his professional career with Huddersfield Town, scoring 24 goals in 45 League appearances, but it was with Newcastle United that he came to the fore following a £2,500 transfer, scoring 69 times in 104 outings. Noting his scoring ability, United paid £6,500 for his services in February 1938, and he went on to score a modest eight goals in his 17 league games before the season's end. He began season 1938-39 with six goals in the opening 15 games, but was to spend the majority of that campaign in the Central League side. He returned to the first-team set-up during the war years, scoring a remarkable 163 goals in 206 games, including thirteen hat-tricks and five in the 9-0 victory over Blackburn Rovers in December 1940. Although only thirty when the war ended and despite his goalscoring prowess, he was sold to Blackburn Rovers in March 1946, his record confined to the miscellaneous sections of the record books rather than the main pages of Manchester United's history.

The club's overall performances, like their attendances, had improved as season 1945-46 progressed. Both Preston North End and Leeds United were hit for six as autumn rolled into winter, while February and March saw Liverpool concede seven over the course of two Saturday afternoons and Blackburn Rovers nine in their two outings against United a matter of weeks later. Jack Rowley was enjoying a run in the side, scoring regularly, while Hanlon, having re-established himself in the first team, had re-discovered his form in front of goal, scoring six in four games. But one of the major differences to the United line-up was the inclusion of a thirty-two-year-old, a player only five years younger than his manager, who had not only played alongside Busby a mere twelve months previously, but who many considered as being past his best.

Jimmy Delaney was born little more than a mile from where Matt Busby had spent his early days and like many others took the only real career path open to him upon leaving school, working down the mines. Football for Delaney and countless others was a godsend, a couple of hours or so away from the daily grind, and whilst playing with Stoneyburn Juniors he attracted the attention of Celtic and was soon to begin a lifelong love affair with the Glasgow club.

Success for Celtic and 'old brittle bones' Delaney ran on a parallel, his deft touches and the ability to move inside defenders for attempts at goal soon endearing him to the Parkhead faithful. On the domestic front, over the course of 178 appearances, in which he scored seventy-nine goals, he won League championship medals in 1936 and 1938, along with a Scottish Cup winners' medal in 1937 (a match in which he made the winning goal with only ten minutes remaining). He could also boast that he played in front of over 300,000 spectators on successive Saturdays at Hampden Park with Celtic and Scotland, winning nine caps with the latter.

A badly broken arm, sustained when stamped upon by an Arbroath defender in 1939, required a bone graft, after a surgeon had wanted to amputate, and this injury was to keep him on the sidelines for some two and a half years. It also led to a minor dispute with Celtic, who were wary about playing an individual who was now considered injury prone, resulting in problems obtaining insurance cover. For the same reason, the SFA were also cautious of selecting him for the Scotland side: on one occasion, with an international side due to be named, a crowd gathered outside the SFA offices in April 1944, shouting "We want Delaney".

Perhaps concerned for their future wellbeing, the Scottish selectors chose Delaney to face England ten days later. But after turning in a superb performance at Hampden, he returned home later that evening to find his infant son close to death. The hero of a few hours earlier could do little, as his son passed away.

Due to the ongoing problems relating to his fitness, Delaney soon became unsettled at Celtic and when his request for a £2 per week rise in wages in May 1945 was turned down, with his name placed on the transfer list, he knew that his career in the green and white hoops was coming to an end. The supporters, however, made their feelings known about what they thought was poor treatment of one of their favourites.

Many clubs were put off by both the player being suspect to injury and the insurance cover which would be involved in signing him, but neither bothered Busby and he surprised many by paying out £4,000 to take him south.

A fortnight after starring for Scotland at centre-forward against Belgium at Hampden Park, scoring twice, Jimmy Delaney made his United debut on February 9th 1946 against Liverpool. He was soon to prove that his career was far from over.

With Delaney supplying the ammunition, United were not long in reaping the rewards. Not only did they put five past Liverpool at Anfield, they scored six against Blackburn at Maine Road, five against Blackpool at Bloomfield Road and four against Bradford Park Avenue, Sheffield Wednesday and Newcastle United, all at Maine Road, as City's turnstiles clicked merrily away with only Bury and Blackburn Rovers in early March attracting less than 34,000.

Back in those distant, trouble-torn days, Manchester United were far from a glamorous club and certainly not considered one of the game's leading lights, but they were to find themselves in demand in March 1946 when they were asked to travel to Germany to take on a BAOR eleven in Hamburg. Having received new shirts from soldiers in India, they were more than happy to do their piece for the troops abroad; however it proved to be a fixture fraught with problems from start to finish, and served to make the United directors more than a little apprehensive about accepting similar invitations in the future.

The original plans were for the United party to fly from Manchester's Ringway Airport on the Monday prior to the game, but those were cancelled at the last minute, due to the plane they were to travel on not having had its planned overhaul. The departure was therefore scheduled for the following day.

As fate would have it, their Tuesday flight also encountered problems and the party were forced to land at Celle, about seventy miles from Hamburg, due to poor flying conditions. Two 'motor lorries' were then arranged to take them to their intended destination, but they broke down, forcing the United players and directors to spend the night at an RAF station at Celle.

Wednesday morning saw alternative transport arrangements made, an RAF three-ton lorry, and it was a rather tired and fed-up United team that arrived in Hamburg a mere two hours prior to the intended kick-off time. On their arrival, they were then informed that they would have to make their return journey to England by rail and sea, as no planes were available as had been originally agreed.

It is little wonder then that Matt Busby's team failed to get the better of their Rhine Army opponents in a rather uninspired match, played before a crowd of around 25,000 servicemen inside the stadium and a considerable number of interested Germans who claimed various vantage points outside overlooking the ground as they were prohibited from being present inside.

As the events on the field progressed, high ranking army officers tried unsuccessfully to charter a special plane to take the United players and officials back to England. As it was, they had to travel to Badenhausen by road and then catch a train for Calais, using a special duty train, normally reserved for brigadiers and colonels.

Matt Busby told Tom Jackson of the *Manchester Evening News*, "I spoke to a major-general after the game and told him that plans for our flight back to England had broken down. He was very concerned and said he would get in touch with Rhine Army Headquarters and try and arrange a Stirling Bomber to take us back. However, he was not able to do this and we must return by the longer route. League clubs have fixtures to fulfil at home and it is very unfair and very unsatisfactory that we shall get back only a few hours before we are due at Bradford on Saturday."

The United manager did add, however, that the army arrangements for the visit were very good, but an unfortunate series of events had marred the trip.

Due to the change in arrangements, there was every possibility that the United party would not manage to reach Bradford in time for their Saturday afternoon fixture. When the club informed the Football League, secretary Fred Howarth stated:

"The responsibility so far as we are concerned rests with Manchester United. If the match is postponed, then United will have to pay compensation to Bradford. Clubs will probably think twice about going to play matches on the continent if they meet difficulties like this."

Luck was finally on United's side, as they arrived at London's Victoria Station on Friday afternoon, after a long land and sea trip. The party was then rushed across the city in special transport to Euston, where they caught the 1.00pm train to Manchester, arriving back at the familiar London Road Station around 6pm, with thoughts of their own comfortable beds more to the fore than ninety minutes against Bradford a few hours later.

As could be expected, the trek across Europe did have an effect on the players and Bradford Park Avenue took full advantage of this and inflicted the first defeat in eight games on Busby's weary side, but only by the odd goal in three. But the show was soon back on the road with a trip to the seaside, blowing away the cobwebs with Blackpool beaten 5-1, and revenge taken out on Bradford to the tune of 4-0 the following Saturday.

So season 1945-46 ended on a high, with only four defeats since the turn of the year, Matt Busby having proved his worth in those early months in charge, leaving the support eager in anticipation of what the future had in store.

Chapter Two
Back To Normality

ALTHOUGH the war had come to an end, there was much to be done at home and abroad before everyday life could get back to any form of normality, with many of those in the forces still overseas employed in the mopping-up exercise. In Manchester, Matt Busby continued to gradually ease himself into his new managerial role, and must have been relieved to see season 1945-46 draw to a close: now he could take stock of his playing staff and Manchester United Football Club as a whole, could assess what was required in order to make progressive steps and what his priorities were to ensure a positive future.

Old Trafford was, for the time being at least, far from ideal as a training facility, so the Manchester University Firs Ground was leased for £50 to enable Busby to get pre-season training underway. The open spaces were ideal for putting his players through their paces and, as it offered proper changing facilities, it was an ideal replacement until Old Trafford was tidied up to an acceptable state.

Busby, now with Jimmy Murphy alongside him, was to kick off season 1946-47 with a squad of twenty-seven professionals, not adequate by any means if injuries befell the first eleven, with the goalkeeping position perhaps the biggest worry. Jack Crompton had little opposition for his jersey, but a distinct loss of form or an injury would give his manager cause for concern. Signings had been made in that department during the close season in order to provide cover, with Robert Brown joining the ranks from West Hartlepool along with Cliff Collinson, a local amateur from

Urmston. However, the former was still in the RAF while the latter, despite his undoubted promise, was far from ready to face up to the rigours of First Division football.

Content the United manager might have been with his playing staff, other than the goalkeeping situation, but he was under no illusions that he would have to make alterations as time went on, as age caught up with individuals, or when the management duo decided that a player might adapt better to a new position. In his very first programme notes for the opening fixture of the 1946-47 season he was to write:

> "I do feel our boys will provide many happy afternoons for us all. When I came here, I set out to have a team play methodical and progressive football. Without method a team gets nowhere. Without making progress after creating an opening or position, the opportunity is lost and the team is back where it started. This will always be my policy, so I leave it to the players to supply the answer, and I hope you will have something to shout about."

Johnny Carey, Henry Cockburn, John Aston, Johnny Anderson and Allenby Chilton all fell into the latter category of players. Chilton simply side-stepped from half-back to a more central position, moving backwards from more forward-lying roles. But the age issue did give Busby some concern as Jack Warner was now almost thirty-five, only two years younger than his manager, and Bert Whalley was thirty-seven, the same age as Billy Wrigglesworth, the latter two both having featured in the final game of the 1945-46 season.

'Old timers' Whalley and Wrigglesworth, however, were missing from the United line-up for the curtain raiser of season 1946-47 against Grimsby Town at Old Trafford, the Football League having retained the same fixture list as that of 1939-40. Also absent was Eddie Buckle who, it could be argued, was Matt Busby's first signing for the club rather than Jimmy Delaney, having joined United as an amateur in October 1945, and signing professional a month later. Buckle had also featured, and scored, in that final encounter of 1945-46 against Stoke City and perhaps could feel aggrieved at not having more appearances under his belt considering that he had scored four goals in his six first team outings during 1945-46, including one on his debut against Leeds United.

But Busby and Murphy had debated that first post-war starting eleven long and hard, deciding that it was to be Crompton, Carey, McGlen, Warner, Chilton, Cockburn, Delaney, Pearson, Hanlon, Rowley and Mitten who took to the Maine Road pitch on August 31st to face Grimsby Town. Billy McGlen, signed as an amateur from Blyth Spartans in January 1946, was making his debut, while for Johnny Hanlon it was a fixture that he could only have dreamed of, having been interred as a prisoner of war in Stalag IVB in Germany for three years after having been captured by the Italians in Crete. On the closure of the hostilities, he returned to Britain, regained his physical fitness and was rewarded with a return to the United starting eleven on the opening day of 1945-46, going on to make twenty-eight appearances, scoring thirteen goals.

United had hoped to kick off season 1946-47 back in the familiar surroundings of Old Trafford, instead of the shared, rented accommodation at Maine Road, but the club accounts for season 1945-46 mention that "owing to the persistent acute shortage of building materials it had not been possible to reinstate the club premises and they would continue to use Manchester City's ground". Some 30,000 did squeeze into the ground in early August to watch a Reds v. Blues practice match, which ended in a 3-3 draw. The more serious business of League football was, however, still played a few miles away across the city, although the tangled mess that was Old Trafford was never far from everyone's thoughts. As chairman James W. Gibson wrote in that first *United Review* for 1946-47:

> "A lump rises in my throat when I think of our premises at Old Trafford damaged beyond repair by fire and blast in March 1941 and still looking a sorry spectacle owing to government policy of issuing only limited licences for building materials whilst the housing problem is so manifest."

Also writing in the match programme for the visit of Grimsby Town was Matt Busby, his first opportunity to greet the United support since taking over the reins. In his notes, entitled 'Matt Busby Watches the Field', he wrote:

"You and I look forward to the opening of the 1946-47 season and what it has in store for us. How often have I felt the tingle run through me, known to all the players on the first match of a new season, wondering in what form it would find me and how kindly the ball would run. I am finding all the same reactions as a manager.

"A great number of people have asked me about our prospects for the coming season. To this I have replied that our boys are in good heart and excellent physical condition, and will hold their own. Others have remarked that the team should do very well if they start off as they finished last season. Yes, I would be a very happy man if they start off as they finished, but I realise from experience the number of things that can crop up to influence this. After all, each player is human and not a mechanical engine which, when you press a button, goes through its work every minute of the day. I do wish all followers of football would remember this very important point when a player has an 'off day'.

"However, we must get on to the battle which starts this afternoon. We will all find the pace of the game stepping up, the tackling keener and the teamwork improved with a view to getting back to 1939 standards – which is all to the good of the game. Whether we start on the right foot this afternoon or not, I do feel our boys will provide many happy afternoons for us all.

"When I came here I set out to have a team play methodical and progressive football. Without method a team gets nowhere. Without making progress after creating an opening or a position, the opportunity is lost and the team is back where it started. This will always be my policy, so I leave it to the players to supply the answer, and I hope you will have something good to shout about!"

The new dawn of League football was greeted not with autumn sunshine but with severe storms and torrential rain, although this did not deter over 950,000 spectators from returning to their favourite terrace spot to cheer on their favourites, 41,025 of them in Moss Side, Manchester where they were soon to forget, for ninety minutes at least, the trials and tribulations of the past few years, celebrating United's 2-1 victory over Grimsby Town.

They were not, however, carried away with this initial victory. The *Guardian* correspondent Don Davies reported that United had simply "played well within their powers and staved off the weakest challenge they are likely to meet this season". But four days later they were to brush aside a Chelsea team that had defeated Bolton Wanderers on the opening day by the odd goal in seven, with an emphatic 3-0 victory.

Stamford Bridge had been packed to the rafters, or near enough, for Bolton's visit, with over 61,000 inside, but for United's visit the 6.15 kick-off caused problems for many, and a mere 27,750 clicked through the turnstiles. Although the home support were disappointed with the result and Lawton's failure to beat Crompton from the penalty spot – the United custodian diving full-length to punch the ball away – they had little option but to acknowledge the visitors' superiority, taking a 2-0 interval lead through Rowley and Pearson, with Mitten adding a third which prompted many to begin making their way to the exits for their journey home.

The bright neon lights and the hustle and bustle of the capital certainly appealed to Matt Busby's team, as they returned to London three days later to face Charlton Athletic at the Valley and once again Jack Crompton proved his worth with yet another penalty save in United's 3-1 victory. Three straight victories, eight goals scored and only two conceded had made many sit up and take notice of the homeless Mancunians, with some going as far as to tip them to be there or thereabouts come the end of the season as they sat atop the First Division level on points with Blackpool and Middlesbrough.

The 5-0 hammering of Liverpool at Maine Road on September 11th only endorsed those credentials further and they were soon to be two points clear of their nearest rivals, but a 3-2 defeat at Stoke, despite almost snatching a point having been 3-0 down, proved that there would be a few bad days in the months to come. Winning the League championship could only be achieved over the course of a season, and not in the opening half-dozen weeks.

Attendances for United's 'home' fixtures at Maine Road were certainly more than comparable to those of that last pre-war season at their now-depleted home across Manchester, when the highest had been 42,008 for the visit of Arsenal – although the final ninety minutes of that 1938-39 season had seen a disappointing 12,973 turn out to see Liverpool beaten 2-0. With the new season only a matter of weeks old, there had not been an attendance under 30,000, with Arsenal again proving to be attractive opposition, pulling in 62,718, although the top-of-the-table clash against Middlesbrough saw 65,112 pass through the turnstiles, making a total of almost 250,000 having watched those opening five 'home' fixtures. Such attendances were not simply beneficial to United, but also had City rubbing their hands due to the terms of the agreement between the two clubs. The Arsenal and Middlesbrough fixtures drew over £9,000 between them in gate money.

Individual on-field performances were attracting much praise, from Crompton's safe pair of hands to Delaney enjoying a new lease of life south of the border. Jack Rowley was leading scorer with seven goals, Hanlon was coming on to his game, 'Mouser' Cockburn had sprung from relative obscurity to the brink of international recognition, and stand-in captain Jack Warner even found himself under consideration by the Welsh selectors.

The visit of Preston North End to Maine Road on October 5th saw Jimmy Murphy take over team matters, as Matt Busby was off looking for a goalkeeper, having failed to entice Frank Swift away from Maine Road. But the Welsh understudy could not celebrate the occasion with a victory, the visitors claiming a point in a rather lacklustre 1-1 draw. Busby's away day was equally frustrating, as were the weeks that followed.

Yet another Crompton penalty save gave United a share of the points against Sheffield United at Bramall Lane in a 2-2 draw, but on the Lancashire Riviera at Blackpool, the lights of the illuminations sparkled even brighter in the October darkness as the Seasiders subjected United to their second defeat of the season, hitting them right from the first blow of the referee's whistle, going two in front in under five minutes and never giving the visitors the opportunity to mount anything of a fightback. Seven days later, there was still less fight on display when Sunderland arrived in Manchester and found numerous United players off form, brushing them aside at ease, and scoring three without reply. Without Hanlon and Carey, United were certainly weakened. Cockburn, who had found himself propelled into the international spotlight after only a dozen First Division appearances, while still working in an Oldham cotton mill, must have made the England selectors doubt their wisdom in selecting the former Gosling player, as he endured his poorest performance to date in a red shirt. It was also not a promising return to the fold for Johnny Morris, back in the line-up for the first time since February 1945, having been stationed in India, his welcome re-appearance now landing Busby with a selection headache.

And a headache Matt Busby certainly had as his team made it five games without a win, drawing 0-0 at Villa Park, and slipping to fifth in the table, five points behind leaders Blackpool. It was a fixture that had confirmed his goalkeeping fears with Jack Crompton absent through injury for the first of seven fixtures, his place taken by the inexperienced Collinson, who at least kept a clean sheet on his debut.

A 4-1 triumph over Derby County at Maine Road in early November got the show back on the road, if only briefly, while United were to show some dogged determination in the 2-2 draw against Everton at Goodison Park, twice pulling themselves back into the game. An emphatic 5-2 rout of Huddersfield Town followed though little else had been expected against the division's bottom side.

Despite hitting five against the Yorkshiremen, who had already conceded thirty-five goals in their fifteen fixtures, all was certainly not well. Wolves then took both points in a five-goal thriller despite being twice behind, the inexperienced debutant Worrall being torn apart by Mullen on several occasions. The early-season confidence was gone, injuries had begun to take their toll and the heady heights of topping the table were now little more than a memory.

For many of the supporters, regaining a semblance of normality following the horrors of the past few years was a long and drawn-out process. Although unemployment was relatively low, rationing was still firmly in place, affecting everyone, even footballers. But, even then, they were a privileged species.

A look at the Old Trafford wage sheet for October 1946 reveals ten players – Carey, Chilton, Delaney, Hanlon, Mitten, Pearson, Rowley, Warner, Whalley and Wrigglesworth – on £10 per week, with the likes of Crompton on £8 and Aston and Morris on £7. The 1-1 draw against Preston earned the eleven selected players a £1 bonus. Even then, footballers were considerably better off than the average supporter who paid his hard-earned cash at the turnstile every Saturday afternoon, many of the players also supplementing their income with a second job.

However, like the skilled building craftsman who could earn 2/6d (approx. 13p) an hour, they couldn't avoid rationing, which still blighted everyone's life. Bread was one of the restricted items, a poor wheat harvest, due to heavy rain, not helping matters. Clothing was another commodity that required coupons, a new suit costing around £3 and a shirt 3/6d (approx. 18p). Little wonder that there was a thriving black market, although in their attempt to obtain new playing and training kit, United appealed for any spare clothing coupons rather than exploring those illegal avenues.

Such an appeal could have been considered slightly above the club, as they had published the accounts and balance sheet for season 1945-46, announcing a profit of £10,215.15/1d. United's total income had been £40,083.2/2d, with the following deductions to be taken into account:

Entertainment Tax .... - £22,648.11/-

Bank, Loan and Mortgage Interest	- £2,259.17/10d
Players Benefits	£1,972. –
Repairs, Renewals, etc	£486.18/3d
Hire of Ground	£2,000.
Depreciation	£500.

Summing up that 1945-46 season, the club statement accompanying these figures read:

> "After an indifferent start, the team settled down and finally maintained a satisfactory position in the League table and rounded off the season by winning the Lancashire Cup...
>
> Your directors recommend payment of a dividend of 7½% (less tax) on the Preference Shares for seasons 1943-44, 1944-45 and 1945-46."

If the supporters were only coping the best they could under the current circumstances, the directors were buoyant, as plans had been drawn up for the proposed 'new-look' Old Trafford once permission was given to proceed with its reconstruction. The architects' drawing gave the impression of large covered stands and spacious terracing, accompanied by up-to-date facilities for the players.

It was hoped the capacity could rise to around 125,000 with the railway station, now fully operational alongside the ground, providing quick and easy access. But could the ideas on paper be transferred into brick and concrete? This was certainly something for much debate.

It was back to winning ways with a 4-1 'home' success against Brentford on the first Saturday of December, but despite the scoreline, many observers were critical of United's performance, in particular their squandering of so many scoring opportunities. Seven days later, they were considered 'unlucky' to lose 2-1 at Blackburn, Busby perhaps ruing the fact that he had allowed the Rovers goalscorer Jack Smith to leave United instead of trying to accommodate him in his front line. Had it not been for Jack Rowley and Stan Pearson then Smith's playing career might well have remained Manchester-based, and it was thanks to that prolific duo that United secured three points from the next two games, with Rowley's double at Bolton earning a Christmas Day point in a 2-2, United again showing their fatal flaws having been 2-0 in front. In the Boxing Day return, Pearson's goal was all that separated the two sides.

Alf Clarke of the *Manchester Evening Chronicle*, a seasoned observer of all things red, was neither discouraged nor dismayed by the recent performances, although he stated:

> "Defensive lapses, however, such as were seen at Blackburn, must be eliminated if they (United) are to stay in the running.
>
> "I still have great faith in the team. At least we do see good football from them even if the result has frequently not been in keeping with their football supremacy."

Still, according to the man at the helm, results were not the be-all and end-all, as Matt Busby had informed his players, "I want you to play football all the time. If you do that and lose I won't grumble." Such a philosophy had strengthened the belief of the United support, whilst endearing United to many of the neutrals who followed the game. This was due mainly to the fact that Busby's team were no longer a side that simply booted the ball upfield and hoped for the best, but had instead become one of the classiest sides in the First Division.

Much of the credit for this fell at the manager's door. Despite still being a novice, Busby had managed to secure a rise of £33 1/8d a month by the turn of the year, and had adapted well to the everyday running of the club. He had succeeded in creating his own prototype mainly due to the fact that he was not an 'old-fashioned' manager, one who was rarely seen by the players on a daily basis, with perhaps the only rare sighting being on a matchday, wearing a bowler hat and a suit with a flower in the button hole. Yes, Busby did own suits, but he also had a tracksuit, and a well-worn one at that, as he was an almost daily visitor to the training area, happy to pull on his boots again at every opportunity and enjoy a physical, sweat-staining half hour or so with his players.

During those training sessions, Busby could often be seen deep in conversation with individual players, not cajoling them into putting more effort into their approach; nor was he simply passing on instructions, or simple tips on how they might improve or approach their game from a different angle. Instead, he was forming a friendship, a special bond between player and manager. It was not just first-team players who enjoyed this one-on-one attention, as reserve players were treated little differently. The soft Scottish brogue would tease that little bit extra out of his players, hoping to transform them into mini versions of himself, whilst going on to create a team, and team spirit, that would lead to greater things.

Busby had enthused about his wealth of forward talent, proclaiming that "one of those days the United forwards will find nearly everything they do in the shooting line will come off, and then we shall have a field-day," adding how opposition goalkeepers often enjoyed "international form" when facing his team, but "it won't always be like that".

The visit to Blundell Park, Grimsby, was far from one of those days that Busby had prophesied, although the home goalkeeper George Tweedy had 'one of those afternoons', as once again the United forwards lacked that knockout punch, Rowley missing three ideal opportunities that he would normally have put away with ease, leaving United to cling on for a point from the goalless draw.

Failing to find the net against the mid-table side, Alf Clarke was of the opinion that "United should have won the game comfortably in the first half."

Rowley was to miss the following fixture against Charlton Athletic, perhaps succumbing to an injury that had hampered his performance at Grimsby. This allowed Busby the opportunity to give Ronnie Burke his second first-team outing following his debut against Sunderland back in October. It was a well-deserved recall, as the former Luton Town amateur had scored twenty goals in sixteen Central League appearances, an excellent return that had seen the United second string stride to the top of the table. Burke was perhaps not quite ready for a permanent place in the first eleven, but his performances at the lower level certainly kept the likes of Rowley and co. on their toes.

Although it was four days into 1947, Burke celebrated the New Year in style, scoring twice in United's 4-1 victory, with another youngster, Eddie Buckle, playing in place of Charlie Mitten and marking his first-team debut with a goal. Interestingly, Matt Busby had decided to play John Aston at right-back, although he had featured mainly as a centre-forward toward the end of last season and in the number eight and six shirts in his two appearances this term. Aston showed his versatility in a full-back berth, and enough potential to convince his manager that this was the position where his future lay. Those team changes, normally notified to the rank and file on the terraces and stands by courtesy of a blackboard being paraded around the ground – adequate if you were situated towards the front of the sprawling masses – were brought to the Maine Road crowd by way of a newly installed loudspeaker system. Football was progressing, as were United.

Despite his two goals, Burke found himself back on the sidelines for the FA Cup third round tie against Bradford Park Avenue, as Rowley returned, notching two of the goals in the 3-0 victory. Both Aston and Buckle had retained their places, the latter once again getting his name on the scoresheet, going on to make it three goals in three games after scoring in the 4-2 win over Middlesbrough. With eleven goals in three games, it looked as though United were back on track, the victory in the north-east at Ayresome Park pushing them up to third in the First Division, six points behind Wolves with two games in hand. But no sooner had the fanfare of trumpets heralded the return to form and goalscoring than everyone was brought back to earth with a bump.

Up against Second Division Nottingham Forest – whom the *Guardian* felt United should defeat "without much difficulty" – in the FA Cup fourth round at Maine Road, they were instead back to their infuriating worst, putting the mid-table lower league side under constant pressure on a hard, frozen surface, but failing to gain any advantage. They paid for their inconsistency and missed opportunities with a 2-0 defeat, shattering the beliefs of many, including numerous bookmakers, who felt that Busby's team had everything it took to stride all the way to Wembley and back to Manchester with the cup itself.

Having suffered concussion late in the match against Middlesbrough, playing the final minutes in a daze and having to spend the night in hospital, Jack Crompton was unfit to play against Forest. His place was taken by Bill Fielding, who had played his part in denying United League Cup North success in 1945 whilst with

Bolton Wanderers, for whom he had originally guested before signing permanently in the summer of 1944.

Matt Busby had searched high and low for an experienced back-up keeper, even going to Belfast to try and convince Tommy Breen to re-cross the Irish Sea and return to Manchester. Breen had originally joined United in November 1936, for a £2,500 fee from Belfast Celtic, making seventy-one appearances before returning to his native city on the outbreak of war, where he assisted his former club and Linfield. Strangely, the keeper was in fact still a United player and had a transfer fee of £1,000 on his head, but Breen[4] spurned Busby's advances, as did Belfast Celtic's current custodian Hugh Kelly, forcing the United manager to make the short journey to Bolton to sign Fielding, with Billy Wrigglesworth heading in the opposite direction in a straight exchange deal. Ironically, Wrigglesworth was one of the United goalscorers who had netted against Fielding in the second leg of that War Cup Final.

"Old Trafford Exiles" was the heading above a full-page article by Denzil Batchelor in the January 11th edition of the *Leader Magazine*.

> "It cannot be said that the German bombs pulverised the cobbled streets, imposing squares and massive public buildings that make up Manchester. But fair and square, the incendiary bombs peppered the famous football ground at Old Trafford and reduced most of the seating accommodation on one side of the ground to a desolation of rubble and a jungle of weeds.
>
> "Down below, the workrooms in which the raw material used to be moulded into a team of footballers were reduced to a shambles. The gym, the room for electrical treatment, the players' dressing room, the recreation room – all were gone.
>
> "All this happened years ago, and the scene of the disaster has been swept clear of rubble, but the essential

---

4 Breen held the distinction of being the only goalkeeper to concede a goal direct from a throw-in, when he touched the ball into his own net during an FA Cup tie at Barnsley in 1938.

repairs (except for one dressing room) have not been made, or even promised. The historic home of Manchester United, is used by the reserve team nowadays, who play before a handful of spectators in the barren stands: and the famous Old Trafford roar that used to rouse like sudden thunder when Pearson or Rowley slashed home a goal, now echoes from the home-from-home that hospitable Manchester City have lent the First Division team on alternate Saturdays."

Batchelor also spoke enthusiastically about the current condition of the club's playing side, continuing his article:

"Manchester United have nothing much to worry about. They have been high up or among the leaders of the First Division since the beginning of the season, and they have won this eminence with one of the youngest teams in the first-class game today; and yet without depending on any player juvenile enough to be at the mercy of the call-ups. Two international players, Warner of Wales and Delaney of Scotland, are over 30, but I do not think that the regular side has any other performers over 26, and – this is just as important – none under 22 either.

"A young team and a cheap team. The great Delaney cost £4,000 before Celtic could be induced to let him go, but most of the team were acquired for the minimum £10 signing-on fee apiece. Today, Matt Busby is not in the market for further purchases. He has got all his bargains already – and he is hanging on to them grimly."

It wasn't simply just a case of Busby hanging on to his players, but also keeping them content whilst not in the first team. Charlie Mitten had only recently handed in a transfer request which the board had turned down upon the advice of the manager. "We have no players for transfer," he announced, "we want to keep the players we have."

The request had come as something of a surprise, as Mitten had begun the season as first-choice outside-left, scoring three times in the opening four fixtures, but had recently lost his place to Buckle, who had also netted in each of his two league outings. There may well have been an ongoing problem between the player and club, as the minutes of the directors' meeting of October 21st, contains just one word, 'Mitten', under the heading 'Any Other Business'. His recent transfer request, however, probably arose due to his first-team place falling under threat, Mitten deciding that a move away from Manchester would be more to his benefit than a spell in the Central League.

United may have had nothing to worry about according to Denzil Batchelor, but his opinion came up for debate when the cup exit was followed by a rout at Highbury. Such were the playing conditions in north London that the players had a ten-minute impromptu pre-match kick-about in order to get accustomed to the hard, snow-covered pitch. It seemed, at least in the opening forty-five minutes, that this had paid off, as United took the lead through Stan Pearson and, despite the home side scoring twice, Morris equalised just before the interval.

The covering of snow hampered progressive football, but was thick enough to prevent serious injury when any of the players took a tumble. United had looked fairly comfortable until fifteen minutes into the second half when their game fell apart as the defence slipped and floundered. An ankle injury to Chilton didn't help matters much and allowed McPherson to put Arsenal 3-2 in front, then Rooke scored thrice in six minutes to give the home side a 6-2 victory.

Between the sticks, Fielding was unsteady with Aston and McGlen offering little in the way of protection, while Chilton, following his injury, could do little to keep the on-form Rooke under control.

From a snow-covered Highbury to a heavily sanded Maine Road four days later, where fewer than 8,000 turned up for a 2.45pm kick-off against Stoke City. They watched a disjointed exhibition of football and a tale of three penalties, two scored and one missed – the latter by Buckle, who did make amends with his second effort as the teams shared the points, leaving United without a win in three games.

Now in fifth place, five points behind Blackpool, subsequent fixtures saw them drop to seventh without kicking a competitive ball for seventeen days. In that same period the Seasiders had leaped to second, although the points difference had been reduced by one, making the meeting of the two sides at Maine Road an important encounter, perhaps more so for United if they were to mount any sort of championship challenge in the coming weeks.

The country seemed to be in the middle of a second ice-age and once again it was Arctic conditions for both players and supporters, the attendance again down on average with just under 30,000 present, when early-season fixtures had been attracting over 57,000 on some afternoons.

The conditions again played a major part in the proceedings and a Hanlon goal, five minutes before the interval, seemed to be all that would separate the two teams at the end of the ninety. The visitors continued to press forward, but Chilton and his fellow defenders stood firm. As the game moved into its final three minutes Blackpool looked the better of the two sides. Any hopes of a last-gasp equaliser, however, were soon forgotten as Rowley, returning to the side in place of the unfortunate Buckle, beat Wallace twice to give United a 3-0 victory.

It was a much-needed win, one that would certainly restore confidence, but there was to be no change in position, just points. There were still another five required in order to overhaul leaders Wolves.

A last-minute equaliser at Sunderland for a 1-1 draw and a 2-1 win against Aston Villa kept things ticking away nicely on the pitch, but off it, the goalkeeping situation continued to raise concerns, not least in the mind of a worried Jack Crompton, who was being kept out of the team by Bill Fielding. Meanwhile, the form and non-appearance of certain other players in the side was creating more than a trickle of interest.

Busby had scoured the country for a keeper and had been disappointed not to have signed Bernard Streten, the England amateur international goalkeeper who was playing with Shrewsbury Town. It was hoped that he would move to Manchester upon his demob, but opted to join Luton Town instead, where he was to win one full England cap, forcing the United manager to look elsewhere, his focus now falling on Reg Allen of Queens Park Rangers.

"We are interested and we shall make an offer," proclaimed Busby, having already been rejected by the player earlier in the season. This time he was confident that a deal could be secured, as the player had requested a transfer; however, the offer from United would have to be around £10,000 – a record for a goalkeeper. Despite the two clubs agreeing a transfer fee, the player himself was not fully committed to a move north, with his fiancée's opinion proving the deciding factor, making Busby's hunt for a goalkeeper an ongoing process. The failure to lure Allen to Manchester, however, did little to pacify Crompton, who decided to ask for a transfer – though his request was turned down flat by both his manager and the United board.

Charlie Mitten's future as a United player was also still up for debate as, like Crompton, he continued to find himself out of the first-team picture. The forward was not without his admirers, with Chelsea showing continued interest and prepared to pay a five-figure fee for his signature. Had Reg Allen decided to move north, then his transfer fee could have been reclaimed, in part at least, with Mitten's move in the opposite direction.

Other players who had stirred up interest from other teams were full-back-cum-forward John Aston, a target for Preston North End, while Ted Buckle's recent success had cast him into the spotlight with several enquiries being made as to his availability. On both accounts, Busby dismissed any potential move out of hand.

The season was by now reaching its crucial stage, the period when titles would and could be won or lost, despite the fixture list stretching well into May. United's championship hopes suffered a blow at Derby in mid-March when the advantage was twice thrown away to give the home side both points by the odd goal in seven, despite Crompton being reinstated. This was to be only a momentary setback as the points were soon to be accumulated and an assault on the top of the table commenced.

Everton were comfortably beaten 3-0, but lessons had not been learned, as once again advantage was twice thrown away in a 2-2 draw at Huddersfield, leaving United still six points adrift of leaders

Wolves with the Midlands side due in Manchester the following Saturday – ninety minutes that would either keep the title challenge alive, or leave it to others to pursue the chase.

Wind and heavy rain made conditions far from acceptable for both players and supporters, but the former cast the dismal weather far from the minds of the 66,000 in attendance, as United turned in their best performance of the season to register a notable 3-1 victory.

Hanlon gave United the lead in the twenty-fifth minute, a goal that was considered by many in their half-time chat not to be enough to take the points. And they were to be proved right, as the visitors dragged themselves back into the game nine minutes after the interval through Westcott. Their joy, however, was short-lived as within two minutes they were 2-1 behind, Rowley restoring United's lead, single-handedly splitting the Wolves defence wide open before blasting a shot high into the net, leaving Williams helpless.

Delaney and Rowley kept the Wolves goalkeeper busy, while at the opposite end Mullen, a thorn in many defences' sides this season, was comfortably held by Carey, the duel being the major decisive factor in the final outcome. No lapses of concentration blighted this performance and victory was ensured in the sixty-seventh minute when Rowley notched a second, firing a right-footed shot past Williams, following good work from Delaney and Burke.

Wolves slipped up again two days later, losing 2-1 at Derby, while leaders Blackpool also stumbled to defeat, losing 3-0 at home to Everton. Third-place Stoke City had no problem in defeating Grimsby 3-0, making United's 3-1 victory over Leeds United at Maine Road an important outcome that maintained the challenge at the top, despite being a drab encounter, devoid of excitement and lacking in colour.

The backlog of fixtures on United's calendar could now perhaps work in their favour, as although they were three points behind Blackpool, they had five games in hand. Stoke City had played one more and were level on points, as were Liverpool, while Wolves had a two-point advantage with the same number of games played, making the next few games critical from everyone's viewpoint.

Games played over holiday periods could swing either way, the same opponents being faced home and away on consecutive days. Going back to season 1931-32, for example, United defeated Wolves 3-2 at Old Trafford on Christmas Day, only to lose 7-0, with more or less the same line-up, twenty-four hours later. 1928-29 had a similar outcome with a 1-1 draw at home against Sheffield United on Christmas Day followed by another crushing defeat on Boxing Day, 6-1 at Bramall Lane. But such fixtures were only at the halfway point of a season and ground could be made up. When it came to the packed Easter fixture list, teams at the top and bottom of the table could find a bad result having severe consequences.

For Matt Busby's team there was no slip-up, as Leeds were once again beaten 2-0, despite enjoying the better of the first forty-five minutes. Goals came from Burke, making it three in two games, and McGlen, nudging United into third place, still two points behind Wolves. A disappointing 0-0 draw at Brentford followed, Charlie Mitten's return to first-team action doing little to aid the required push towards the top. So much so, that he found himself back on the outside looking in for the following four games.

After Blackburn Rovers had been hammered 4-0, United were second only on goal average, four points separating the top five clubs. Then a solitary Jimmy Delaney goal saw Portsmouth beaten at Fratton Park; but if one fixture was now going to define United's season then it would be the short bus ride along the East Lancs Road to Liverpool, as the Anfield side sat poised in fifth place, ready to pounce on any slip-ups by those above them.

Henry Cockburn was an absentee due to flu and although replaced by the experienced Warner, his decisive midfield play and ability to direct the flow of the game was sorely missed. United played a defensive formation which allowed the home side to push forward, and they were punished as early as the tenth minute when Stubbins scored after Liddell outpaced Carey to cross into a packed goalmouth, the Liverpool forward acting the quickest to prod the ball past Crompton. Try as they might, United's often free-scoring forward line struggled to find any momentum, and it was only after Delaney moved to centre-forward that the Liverpool defence fell under pressure.

Stoke had also won, with Wolves held to a draw, the defeat leaving Busby's team still two points adrift of leaders Wolves, but now having played a game more. Stoke were a point in front on the same number of games. Liverpool were a point behind, having played a game less. United had three games left. Six points were crucial, as were slip-ups by the trio of fellow challengers.

A 1-1 draw at Preston was better than nothing, but again the forwards let the side down. The only good news of the afternoon was a 3-2 home defeat for Wolves against Everton as Liverpool once again triumphed, 3-1 at Charlton.

Seven days later, those not amongst the 37,614 at Maine Road – a rather poor attendance considering the importance of the fixture against Portsmouth – were tuned into the Light Programme on their radios, eagerly awaiting the 5.30 results service. Some, already having listened to the last half hour of Liverpool's match at Brentford, rejoiced in the Merseysiders' dropped point in the 1-1 draw. With bated breath they sat listening as the last three results from the First Division schedule were read out... Manchester United 3 Portsmouth 0, Stoke City 0 Sunderland 0, Wolverhampton Wanderers 3 Blackburn Rovers 3. Those results put United level on 54 points with Wolves, but they had played a game more. Stoke and Liverpool were both on 53 and like Wolves had played forty games, one less than United.

The following Saturday only Liverpool of that quartet were in action, defeating Arsenal 2-1 and leap-frogging into top spot. Two days later United faced Sheffield United at home, the final ninety minutes of the season and the outcome entirely out of Matt Busby's hands. Nothing he could do, other than cajole his team to victory, could determine where the First Division championship would end up. He had, with the exception of Jimmy Delaney, a full strength team at his disposal, with hope and belief the unseen twelfth and thirteenth men.

Three goals in thirteen minutes gave United the perfect start, but despite the headline above Alf Clarke's *Manchester Evening Chronicle* report reading "United – 6-2 Championship is now within grasp", it was not to be. Stoke and Wolves had also won, and Liverpool's 2-1 victory at Molineux on the last afternoon of the season was enough to clinch the title. Unfancied, except on their own doorstep, they had come from behind, turning in results when it mattered most, snatching the title from United's grasp by a solitary point.

There was disappointment, but no tears. Matt Busby, twenty years after arriving in his adopted city, had given Manchester their best season in the First Division since 1910-11, when they last lifted the title. "There can be no doubt that he has scored a personal triumph in guiding the team through its best season in years," wrote Alf Clarke. "Blackboard and easel methods are not Matt Busby's way; he believes in practical demonstrations. Whatever he expects a man to do on the field he can himself perform, and he does so every week at Old Trafford, where his young players on the staff are amazed at his remarkable skill with the ball.

"He joins in the hurly burly of a hard practice match with the enthusiasm of a youngster, and most of the ability which brought him fame. The players respect him for his skill and knack of encouraging them when things are not running too well.

"The Busby method is never to browbeat a player for some blatant mistake on the field. He takes him to a quiet corner, gives him a fatherly chat and a pot of encouragement. The player is refreshed and unembarrassed at being shown the right way."

Few could have expected such a positive initial post-war season and the outcome, despite the disappointment, was more than encouraging for the future. It gave a solid foundation to be built upon, with a squad of seasoned professionals at the top of their trade, giving hope for the seasons ahead.

Not only had it been a successful campaign on the field, it had also boosted the club's financial situation – not to mention that of neighbours City with gate receipts totalling £71,523 compared with £47,821 the previous season. Even those for the Central League were up by almost £600, obviously boosted by their championship triumph, outdoing their senior colleagues.

Due to the overall performance of the team, bonus payments for the players increased from £744 to £1,568, the extra few pounds being more than welcome in the pay packets. But there were also bonuses for the manager, his staff and secretary Walter Crickmer.

Even today, the figures might raise an eyebrow or two. Crickmer was given £50 for his contribution, while trainer Tom Curry found an additional £10 in his end-of-season wages, and Jimmy Murphy £15. For Matt Busby, however, his push towards the title earned him the sum of £400. Wonder if Murphy knew?

Jimmy Murphy was indeed unhappy as the warm summer days of 1947 approached, but it had nothing to do with money. In charge of the United reserve side, the Welshman had guided his 'lads' to the Central League title, but over a celebratory drink with Busby he confessed that he was far from satisfied.

> "I told Matt that it was all very well winning the reserve team championship but the important thing for the future was to produce young players for the first team.
>
> "And that was the situation – there was just no-one I could recommend as good enough for promotion to the First Division.
>
> "We had won the Central League comfortably by several points, but I was forced to tell Matt 'There isn't one first team player there for you,' to which Matt simply replied: 'Well, Jimmy, we'll just have to make our own players from kids.'"

It was an idea that many clubs were to imitate, but which none would emulate in terms of scale or success.

Chapter Three

Heading For Wembley

AS Denzil Batchelor wrote, the United reserve-team fixtures at Old Trafford never produced 'ground full' notices, or anywhere near it. However, on June 6th 1947, the gates were firmly locked with 36,000 inside, tickets having sold out weeks before for the Salford Schoolboys v Leicester Schoolboys showdown in the English Schools FA Final replay. The Salford boys had been more than happy with their 0-0 draw against the current holders in the first match, but a venue for the replay appeared potentially problematic. Earlier-round ties had been played at United's Cliff training ground but, such was the interest in the final, a larger venue was required and following consultation with the local constabulary, the 36,000 all-ticket limit was put on Old Trafford, with a strong, prominent police presence to ensure that no spectators encroached on the strictly out-of-bounds bomb-damaged areas.

It had been a long time since the hustle and bustle of a matchgoing crowd and the kind of vocal encouragement given to the Salford team had been heard in the vicinity of the Manchester Ship Canal, and the youngsters out on the neglected pitch provided excellent entertainment. The crowd certainly received their money's worth, as the match went into extra time, neither side having scored at the end of the ninety minutes; but in the added half hour, the local boys soon made the breakthrough and went on to add a second, to lift the trophy for the first time. For the captain of that victorious Salford side, the surroundings were soon to become a second home. His name? Geoff Bent.

Salford Schools were not the only group who wanted to use the bomb-damaged Old Trafford, as a look through the directors' weekly meeting minutes shows, with names such as the Cheshire Association, Manchester Youth Organisation League, Manchester Schools and Christies Hospital all writing for permission to use the humble facilities. But more than any local association or minor footballing organisation, it was United themselves who most wanted to play on that Old Trafford pitch – and making at least as much effort as the club's directors to transform that dream into reality was MP Ellis Smith, whose contribution to the cause over the next few months would be immense.

It was back to the Manchester University-owned Firs ground at Fallowfield for pre-season training under the guidance and watchful eye of not just Matt Busby and his faithful backroom team, but also former United goalkeeper Len Langford who was in charge of the summer fitness tuning. The players were more than happy to be back to the daily grind, looking forward to an increase in their wages once the new season kicked in, with the additional supplement of a winning bonus doing much to improve their lifestyles.

For those on the United payroll, their close-season wages were better than most, but that additional couple of pounds a week would obviously make a difference, with the club's summer wage bill making interesting reading. For the weeks between June 1st and August 16th, the average earnings for a United first-team player was £116, with eleven individuals being paid that amount, those earnings being supplemented with bonuses ranging between £20 9/6d, to Stan Pearson, and the £1 9/3d to Bert Whalley due to the fact that he had featured in only three First Division fixtures during the previous season. The likes of Ronnie Burke, whose nine goals in thirteen games did much to ensure that runners-up position, claimed £6 6/9d in bonus payments but was paid only £80 during the summer break. Others, such as Crompton and Cockburn, received £91 with bonus payments of just over £14 and £15 respectively.

Charlie Mitten, who had not enjoyed the best of seasons and was clearly unhappy at finding himself in the Central League side had also seen an increase in his weekly wage from £10 to £12, with his summer pay of £116 increasing by £9 15/- due to his bonus payment based on his twenty league appearances. But for reasons unknown, despite rumoured links of a move south to join Chelsea, he approached the board of directors for financial assistance, the Football League approving the club's doubtless surprising application to extend him a £130 loan.

All the playing staff of the 1946-47 season, except for goalkeeper Robert Brown, who was in the forces, were retained for the following season, with Joe Dale (from Witton Albion) and Tommy Lowrie (formerly with Troon Athletic) being added. Much to the delight of most, they were on new terms, a £2 rise bringing smiles to their faces.

A bigger smile perhaps could be found on Jack Crompton's, as he went from £9 to £12 once the new season got under way. Henry Cockburn, however, was still on £9, as he was only a part-time professional.

There was no fanfare of trumpets to herald the new season following the shortest close season on record, just temperatures of between 74 to 77 degrees and bone-hard pitches – along with an early shock for United who were to find themselves 2-0 behind after nineteen minutes in the opening-day fixture against Middlesbrough at Ayresome Park.

A Fenton double had stunned Busby and his team, and despite one or two near misses at either end, there was no further scoring until the sixty-fourth minute when Rowley pulled United back into the game, heading home a Delaney cross. With fifteen minutes remaining, and having just been refused a penalty when Delaney was brought down, Rowley levelled the score with another header, this time from a Mitten centre. A goal that was to give United a share of the points.

If Busby wanted an early tester for his team it was to come four days later when League champions Liverpool visited Maine Road. Many gave their evening meal a miss, dashing towards Moss Side in the late afternoon sunlight straight from work in order to ensure admission. They were not to be disappointed, and it was the United players who were to show their hunger, determined to gain an early advantage over their Lancashire neighbours.

Liverpool started strongly, but United soon had the upper hand and opened the scoring in the twenty-fifth minute through Morris. Mitten, for the second successive fixture, confirmed his worth and his deserved starting place, coming close on two occasions. Carey, Aston and Chilton stood firm at the back and the home side's superiority was confirmed in the sixty-ninth minute when Pearson made it 2-0. It was still, however, early days, despite having dented the reigning champions' crown.

But the ball was rolling and the momentum was maintained with the visit of last season's FA Cup winners Charlton Athletic to Maine Road, the Londoners crushed 6-2. It was a result that flattered the visitors, as in his *Guardian* match report, Don Davies (writing under the pen name 'An Old International') mentioned that,

> "A colleague with a flair for objectivity carefully put down on paper one stroke for every shot at goal, including headers, made by a Manchester United player from within the 12 yard limit. Between 3.55pm and 4.40pm he collected a sheaf of some thirty strokes, which means that in the second half the Manchester forwards were entirely engrossed in scoring attempts, many from point blank range."

It is worth noting that the goalkeeper who faced this barrage and conceded the half dozen was no novice, but Sam Bartram, one of the best custodians in the country at that time.

In the return fixture at Anfield, Liverpool gained some sort of revenge with a 2-2 draw, but it was United who once again captured the headlines in a mirror image of the season opener against Middlesbrough, coming from 2-0 behind to take a point and consolidate their place amongst the leading pack. But then the wheels came off the wagon with a resounding thump, startling everyone on board as well as those observing from the sidelines.

At Highbury, Arsenal took both points with a 2-1 win, then Burnley snatched a point at Turf Moor in a 0-0 draw. Sheffield United left Maine Road with a 1-0 victory under their belt, while the first competitive Manchester 'derby' fixture since 1936-37 finished goalless, watched by an enthusiastic crowd of 72,000. As September drew to a close, the visit to Preston's compact Deepdale ground brought yet another defeat, this time by the odd goal in three. Stoke City then took a share of the points with a 1-1 draw at Maine Road, followed a week later by one of the shocks of the season when Grimsby Town journeyed to Manchester and scored four, one more than United could manage. Sunderland then made it nine games without a win for Matt Busby's team with a 1-0 victory at Roker Park. Manchester United had plummeted to 18th in the First Division table, only a point above second-bottom Stoke City. Being five points better off than bottom club Bolton Wanderers gave them some sort of safety net.

So what had gone wrong?

Johnny Carey had missed three games, as had Mitten, and Delaney a couple, while Rowley had to move to the left flank, lessening the threat of the United forward line, his place taken by Hanlon. There was certainly no lack of fight from within the ranks, as they continued to come from behind to, in most cases, gain some reward. Even against Grimsby, such resilience and determination had clearly been visible when they found themselves 3-0 behind at half-time, hammering the more defensive visitors in the second forty-five, but getting caught out again when Grimsby decided to re-emerge from their shell. Against Sheffield United the forward line was all over the place, while the visit to Roker Park, marked by five positional changes and the early withdrawal of Warner, was more bad luck than anything. But it was generally accepted that the enforced reshuffling of the pack did little to prevent the downward slide.

The results of late would certainly have affected the players, knocking their confidence, as well as putting a dent in their pay packets, with few of the expected £2 win bonuses materialising. For reasons unknown, Johnny Morris then decided to put in a transfer request, as did Fielding, the latter obviously disgruntled due to being relegated to reserve team football, though the former was a first-team regular. Perhaps it was a decision more rooted in Morris's domestic situation, as a few weeks later he was given the tenancy of a club house in Denton Road. Jack Rowley had already been installed in 6 Briarlands Road, Sale, while Delaney was a bit closer to home, residing at 8 Warwick Road. Rents were modest, at around £2 per week.

But food was once again about to reappear on the kitchen tables and the candles consigned to cupboards, as Aston Villa were beaten 2-0 on October 25th, the first two points since August 30th. Then, as if a weight had been lifted off their shoulders, the first away victory since April saw Wolves hammered 6-2 at Molineux, with 'want-away' Morris scoring twice. Rowley, who had been reinstalled in a more central attacking role, failed to get on the scoresheet, having notched one of the two goals that defeated Villa, but he was to more than make amends the following Saturday, scoring all four at Huddersfield in a 4-4 draw. Twelve goals in three unbeaten games, but both points should have been secured against Huddersfield, as United held a 3-1 half-time lead. Then, at Derby, a one-goal half-time advantage was also relinquished as the points were again shared. Yet another draw followed against Everton, but this time it was United coming from behind to secure a point.

They had now scrambled up to fifteenth, thirteen points behind leaders Arsenal. It was only November, but many felt that it was safe to assume that there would be no First Division title coming to Manchester this season.

As United toiled on the pitch, Ellis Smith did likewise in Parliament, fighting United's corner in their ongoing attempt to get Old Trafford back to some form of normality. In a House of Commons debate on November 10th, he asked the Minister of Works: "How many of the First Division association football grounds damaged by air raids have been re-built; and the amount spent on each, respectively?"

The Minister of Works, Mr Key answered: "Licences have been given for the repair of war damage at ten out of the twenty-two grounds of the First Division Association Football League."

Following is a statement showing the amount in each case:

Club	Amount Licensed
Arsenal	£1,700
Charlton Athletic	£3,771

Derby County	£3,000
Everton	£5,000
Grimsby Town	£875
Liverpool	£3,728
Manchester United ...	£17,478
Portsmouth	£466
Sheffield United	£4,485
Sunderland	£1,743

The funds were there to kick-start repairs. Setting the ball rolling was the major problem.

Morris continued to create interest amongst those clubs aware of his unrest with a hat-trick in the 4-0 victory over Chelsea, but the draws kept on coming – 1-1 against Blackpool and Blackburn Rovers. Carey, a model of consistency throughout the lean spell, had ensured that if his forwards were not going to win games then his defensive colleagues were certainly not going to lose them. Then, suddenly, as if his endeavours were deserving of some form of reward, the front line took command of the situation, scoring fifteen goals in the following five fixtures, triggering a run which was to produce only one League defeat in thirteen games between mid-December and mid-March. Of those fifteen goals, Morris claimed a third, the others shared between Busby's five-star forward line – Rowley (4), Pearson (3), Mitten (2) and Delaney, more often than not the supplier, with one.

Matt Busby now had few selection problems as his team effectively picked itself. Goalkeeper Ken Pegg had stepped in for Crompton on a couple of occasions, Joe Dale doing likewise for Delaney, with Hanlon, Walton and Worrall all leaving the Central League behind as they clocked up first-team appearances. Those, however, were simply fleeting appearances – once an injury was overcome, they were back in the familiar surroundings of the second team – but one debutant successfully consolidated his place in the side.

Johnny Anderson was the son of a former rugby league player, and was recommended to the club by his old schoolmaster while playing for Brindle Heath Lads' Club, having represented Salford in inter-city games. A former inside-forward, he was signed as a sixteen-year-old, became a professional a year later, and it was against Middlesbrough on December 20th that he made that initial appearance at right-half. The *Manchester Evening News* proclaimed: "United 2-1: Anderson Makes a 'Hit'." As Tom Jackson wrote in his report:

> "John Anderson, 25 year-old ex-Salford schools' player, made his League debut for Manchester United against Middlesbrough at Maine Road this afternoon, after a telegram had recalled him from Leeds, where he was en-route to Newcastle with the Reserves.
>
> "He was at right-half – opposing England inside-forward, Mannion – because United captain Jack Carey, had reported ill, Warner was also unfit."

His name continued to feature prominently within Jackson's report, indeed as a candidate for man-of-the-match, with one mention reading:

> "Anderson almost brought the house down with a 20-yard drive which flashed over the top with Goodfellow out of position."

There was some respite from the rigours of the First Division with the third round of the FA Cup. The name 'Manchester United' had been creeping stealthily up the table to within striking distance of the top three clubs, the doubters of a few weeks previous now wondering if indeed the title could still be achieved. United had been drawn away to Aston Villa, not the best of pairings, but on current form, there was every possibility of a victory in the Midlands.

As usual, there were a few shocks as the competition kicked off in earnest, with the so-called 'big clubs' thrown into the mix against those from the lower regions of the Football League and beyond. Arsenal, the current First Division leaders, were beaten 1-0 at home against Bradford Park Avenue, Colchester defeated Huddersfield by the same score, while Crewe defeated Sheffield

United 3-1. Thankfully United had not been drawn against one of those lesser lights, as no-one could have predicted what might have happened during the course of the ninety minutes. Then again, no-one could have foreseen the unlikely events at Villa Park on the afternoon of January 10th.

A large contingent of United supporters made their way south to Birmingham and were stunned into silence within thirteen seconds as Villa scored more or less straight from the kick-off. Brown found Smith on the left and his cross eluded the static United defence, leaving Edwards with the ideal opportunity to open the scoring. So much for the visitors' 'lucky' blue jerseys!

But within six minutes United were level, Rowley heading home a Mitten centre, a goal that ignited a fuse which fizzled away before exploding into a goal frenzy. Morris netted in the 17th minute, followed by Pearson on the half hour, Morris again a minute later and Delaney three minutes before the interval, giving United a 5-1 half-time lead.

After the break, Villa could only throw caution to the wind in an attempt to salvage something, if only self-respect, from the remaining forty-five minutes, and they did pull a goal back immediately after the restart when Edwards scored direct from a corner kick, giving the home support a glimmer of light as the rain fell and the sky darkened.

With twenty minutes remaining a Dorset free kick was diverted to Smith who made it 5-3, then with nine minutes left on the clock, Villa Park erupted as Chilton fouled Ford inside the area and the referee pointed to the penalty spot, Dorset firing past Crompton to leave the outcome now dangling by a fine thread.

Sensing an equaliser, Villa dropped their defensive guard ever so slightly, just enough to allow Pearson to sneak in and turn a Mitten corner into the net for United's sixth with only two minutes remaining.

After fourteen games without defeat, United's name was now propelled to the top of public house conversation topics, as supporters wallowed in the recent performances of their favourites, whilst happily proclaiming in the press: "We don't mind if you win or lose, so long as you play with such quality." In his *Daily Mail* column, Eric Thompson profiled Busby's favoured eleven, who had cost a mere £8,000, valued now at £110,000, with an average age of twenty-six. They had top scorers in Morris with 19 and Rowley with 18, and had been watched by 1,195,457 spectators to date. "… Their secret is dressing room harmony," Thompson wrote, "shrewd talent spotting, manager Matt Busby's high ideals and personal contact."

Louis Rocca, a man associated not just with United but also in their guise as Newton Heath, for over fifty-five years, also spoke highly of Matt Busby's credentials and impact on the club. Writing in the *Manchester Evening Chronicle* he penned:

"No one disputed the talent of the United players, but it was the blending that has made it the successful machine it is today.

"How then has this come about? The answer is that the United manager is also a psychologist. He has imparted his football knowledge to the players by playing with them.

"He goes onto the field in practice games at Old Trafford on Tuesday mornings. You will, if you are lucky enough to be watching, hear his words of advice to one and all, and throughout the game you will see the Busby genius so very apparent.

"He has moulded the United team into the complete model. And I need hardly say, he has the unanimous support of the United directors.

"I have been identified with many managers in my long experience, but I give pride of place to Matt Busby for the manner in which he has undertaken the task and his friendship for every member of the staff.

"The reserve players are just as important to him as the senior stars. And what greater tribute could be paid to him than his selection to manage Great Britain's Olympic Games Soccer team this summer.

"I have studied Matt Busby both on the field and off, and I have never met a player like him in my long experience, one who can put over in practice and theory the points which are essential to harmony and success.

"Not only on the field, but in private pre-match talks is the Busby influence shown. He will go through our opponent's team individually and collectively picking out the weak spots, emphasising the danger points.

"He knows the style of every player of the opposing team; he knows which is his best foot, which way he will try to beat his man. All these points are sorted and sifted.

"So, then to the plan of the campaign by United. Frank discussion by the players he desires – and always gets it. There must be no doubts left about United's plans. Every man knows his job, and Matt is the first to congratulate them when the game is over.

"If defeat has been our lot, there is no bickering. But plans which have not produced the desired results are talked about during the course of the next week.

"Matt Busby believes in making his own stars. Yes, he bought Jimmy Delaney, but was ever there a shrewder transfer? Glasgow Celtic have regretted the day when they accepted United's cheque.

"Now he is there to encourage the youth of the club, and you can take it from me that United have some future stars in the making.

"You cannot rest on your laurels in football; you must think of tomorrow, and Matt Busby has this in mind."

Seven days later came ninety minutes that could be judged as a yardstick as to the credentials of Matt Busby's team. A match under the microscope, when it could be determined if this post-war United were not simply a team who could float from being an attractive, goalscoring machine, to a collection of strugglers, lapsing into defensive failings, when expected to shine. Were this Manchester United side really championship challengers, who could prove capable of surpassing those players of almost four decades before?

Arsenal were in town. The Londoners would certainly be looking to get back on track following their shock FA Cup defeat the previous Saturday, whilst looking to consolidate their place at the top of the First Division table where they held a six-point advantage over Burnley. United sat in fourth, a further three points behind. While not expecting to score another half dozen goals, they would be looking to continue their recent sterling work and to extend that unbeaten run.

Despite the rain, over 80,000 supporters converged on Moss Side on the afternoon of January 17th, eager to witness what had the makings of an epic encounter. Arsenal's Barnes, Mercer, Compton and Rooke against United's Carey and his five-star forward-line colleagues. Such was the ferocity of the spinning turnstiles, had they been connected to a generator, the lights of Manchester could have shone brightly without charge for the rest of the day.

"Gate Records Go in Match of the Year", "Game In a Classic Pattern", "Arsenal Weather the Storm" and "Arsenal Dodge an Impending Rout" were just a quartet of the headlines that preceded the reports of that Maine Road encounter. Ken Abram wrote:

> "All provincial League gate records went with a crash at Maine Road yesterday, when Manchester United and Arsenal drew 1-1 in the match of the season.
>
> "More than 82,000 saw the game – 81,962 paid – which is the best crowd for any League match outside London, falling just short of the 82,905 who watched the Chelsea-Arsenal clash at Stamford Bridge in 1935.
>
> "Manchester City's ground now holds three records. In addition to yesterday's crowd, 84,569 saw the City-Stoke Cup game in 1934, and 80,407 saw the mid-week Cup semi-final replay between Derby County and Birmingham City in 1946."

Had some of the hundreds outside managed to find a way in, then even the above record would have been shattered.

'Old International' with the ever descriptive prose, appreciated by his *Guardian* readership, penned: "Only those who have ever been called to deal with a swarm of rats – artistic rats, intelligent rats, persistent rats – will appreciate the degree to which the Arsenal defence was overrun on Saturday." Desmond Hackett of the *Daily Express* simply wrote "Lucky Arsenal" three times before delving into the match summary that was on a parallel with all the others, telling their readers and reminding all who were in attendance just how fortunate the League leaders were to return south with a point.

It was certainly a creditable performance by the Arsenal defence, on a heavy and mudded pitch, keeping Rowley and co. at bay, although he was the man who secured the point for United with his equalising goal in the twenty-seventh minute, following the opener by Lewis ten minutes earlier. Hackett was of the opinion that United should have tested the Arsenal goal with more shots from outside the area and, perhaps with a little more luck on an afternoon when they hit the post, the bar and Arsenal defenders, both points would have been theirs.

United's overall performance was nothing new to their supporters, or to close observers of the game, but for one visiting guest, Manuel P. Gonzalez, director of the Argentine FA, their performance was impressive. So much so, that after regaining his breath, he made a beeline for the United directors, inviting the club to take a month's tour of his country during the coming summer. Sadly, such a ground-breaking adventure failed to materialise.

Although a rent-paying tenant at Maine Road, United were forced to find new accommodation on Saturday January 24th in order to play their fourth round FA Cup tie against Liverpool, as their landlords City also maintained in interest in the competition and had been drawn at home against Chelsea. Somewhat surprisingly, United decided to take the tie to Goodison Park, a short walk across Stanley Park from their opponents' Anfield home; but it was a move which saw yet another ground attendance record created – 74,721 squeezing into Everton's compact stadium, paying receipts of £8,810.

Now installed as FA Cup favourites, United did not disappoint, with three goals in a seven-minute first-half spell – from Rowley, Morris and Mitten – enough to overcome their opponents. Another three or four during the second forty-five minutes would certainly not have been an injustice, nor would have created a false scoreline.

All good things, however, have to come to an end, and United's unbeaten run bit the dust on the last day of January against Sheffield United. It was a game they should have won, their defeat at Bramall

Lane by the odd goal in three due more to bad luck than a poor performance.

Prior to the team's departure from Old Trafford, goalkeeper Jack Crompton reported unwell with laryngitis, forcing Matt Busby to put a call out for the untried twenty-year-old Robert Beresford Brown, home on leave from the RAF, to make the journey from Huddersfield to Sheffield to make his League debut. The former Durham schoolboy had only made half a dozen Central League appearances, but even with this change in personnel, the visitors should have won comfortably, as the home side were reduced to ten men in the opening minutes when their own goalkeeper was carried off. He was later to return on the wing, simply to make up numbers, but even with United taking the lead, Sheffield scored twice prior to half-time and survived a second-half barrage to earn both points. Unfamiliarity and nerves may have contributed to United's downfall, but no finger of blame for the surprise reversal could be pointed at Crompton's temporary replacement: he made numerous fine saves, including a penalty five minutes before the interval, as United's title aspirations took a dive.

Victories over Stoke City (A), Sunderland (H), Wolves (H), Aston Villa (A), Huddersfield Town (A) and Bolton Wanderers (A) kept United in second place, seven points behind Arsenal, but only one in front of Burnley, who had played a game less. Had points not been dropped against Grimsby Town (A) and Preston North End (H), both 1-1 draws, and in a 2-0 home defeat against Bolton Wanderers, then the gap would have been much narrower and with the hot breath of United on their necks, the Gunners would have felt far from comfortable.

Although it was still only early February, many were of the opinion that the outcome of the First Division title was a foregone conclusion, with Arsenal odds-on to take the honours and Burnley the runners-up spot. But despite the credentials of the London and Lancashire duo, United had captured the attention of many. As one contributor to a contemporary weekly magazine wrote:

> "With the stonewalling success of Arsenal and Burnley, football begins to take a sober 'New Look'. But the side that

stands out most for dash and science, brilliance and drama, is Manchester United, currently favourites for the Cup.

"In some ways, this is an outlandish season. Already the Championship is as good as clinched by Arsenal, who have headed the League table from the first whistle, with Burnley running them up. Both teams have shown themselves hard to beat, and hard to watch. They play as sober and solid and ultimately maddening as a stone wall; and few have found joy in it, except the pool-punters who don't care how the play is as long as their team gets the points. A club working on such a system may win games, but it is likely to lose friends.

"Hence, no doubt, the astonishing popularity of Manchester United, a team which has hung about sixth place in the League for some time, but which is commonly thought of as the strongest and most attractive side at present on the go. United's style is the opposite of Arsenal's in so far as it is an aggressive, positive affair, based on constant methodical attack at high speed. It is not the bull-headed, blaze-away style the Wolves used to have in the days of gland treatments. It is an ingenious, constructive business, centred on no fancy plan, but on the old classical truisms of keeping the ball on the island, and keeping it low, and moving quickly into open spaces that lead to the other fellow's goal. It is a style that endeared the (**Moscow**) Dynamos to us, before they went home and made an unseemly fuss."

Although the scent of the championship was wafting under the noses of the United support, it was the FA Cup that put a spring in their step, as it did with many followers of the game. Having despatched Liverpool to march into the fifth round, they had once again to search for an alternative 'home' venue to take on the cup holders Charlton Athletic, as landlords City also had the benefit of a home tie. They could have returned to Merseyside, taking over either Anfield or Goodison Park for the afternoon, but instead opted to take the tie across the Pennines to Leeds Road, Huddersfield.

The falling drizzle did little to dampen the spirits of the 33,312 crowd or to have much bearing on the performances of those involved out on the heavy pitch, although many of those who had paid admission had to give their watches a second glance, having made their way to the terracing and stands. Only then did they discover the match had kicked off early due to Charlton wanting to catch a convenient train back to London from Wakefield.

Playing against the wind and rain, and at times finding it hard going on the muddy pitch, United failed to display their usual sparkle. They squandered numerous opportunities due to poor finishing and on at least three occasions missed an open goal. They also had the heroics of Sam Bartram to contend with, the Charlton keeper standing between his team and a heavy defeat.

The deadlock was broken in the twenty-fifth minute, when Warner drilled the ball home from all of twenty-five yards. With Bartram unsighted, the Charlton defence waited on the half-back to pass the ball rather than shoot, the Welshman's effort catching everyone by surprise.

Charlton showed some resilience in the second half, but failed to overcome the United defence and at times the conditions. Some unusually lacklustre United forward play kept the tie in the balance until the final few minutes.

It should have been all over when Pearson found himself in front of goal with little more to do than tap the ball past Bartram, but he somehow managed to put his effort wide. Much to the relief of Pearson, his team-mates' and the supporters' relief, Charlie Mitten did not do likewise as Delaney's centre floated into the area with five minutes remaining, his header beating Bartram to ensure United's place in the next round.

Preston North End's 1-0 victory over Manchester City in the FA Cup fifth round left Maine Road free should United capture yet another home draw in the following round. Preston could hardly have been expecting a return journey to Manchester to compete in the sixth round, but their name duly followed that of United out of the velvet bag, to produce a tie that the *Guardian* feature writer saw as "the best match of the round" and one that "is likely to tantalise the critics no less than it excites the spectators". He continued:

"United's brilliant all-round attack, whose strength is its speed, combination, and beautiful positional play, will meet a forward line which is less nicely balanced but which has designed most successful and thrustful offensives round Finney. Today may well go to the team that is clever or lucky enough to score first."

Not only did United score first, after Preston had made most of the early running, Mitten firing home a Morris centre from point blank range in the twenty-third minute; they then took full advantage of Preston's inexperienced stand-in goalkeeper Hindle, who was making his debut, putting four past him with the visitors only managing one by way of reply.

Pearson made it 2-0 in the thirty-third minute and although McIntosh pulled one back for Preston before the interval, United never looked in danger of making a cup exit. An early second-half rally kept United on their toes, but further goals from Pearson with his second in the seventy-seventh minute and Rowley eight minutes from the end put the FA Cup favourites into the semi-finals for the first time in twenty-two years.

Opponents in that semi-final tie at Sheffield Wednesday's Hillsborough ground were the 1946 FA Cup winners Derby County, a team not without their own star individuals, featuring household names such as Scottish international Billy Steel and front-line partner Raich Carter. But they were to be well subdued by the United defence. Although the team did not play well as a whole, they were far superior to their Derby counterparts.

Busby was well aware of Derby's double threat and made plans accordingly. Despite one or two anxious moments at the beginning and end of the game, United were rarely threatened. In fact, it was a game won and lost in the course of the opening twenty minutes. Lost by Derby, as they failed to take advantage of their opening forays, and won by United thanks to their ability to soak up the Derby pressure and step up their game, claiming victory through individual brilliance.

The opening goal came on the half hour, Stan Pearson heading home following an overhead kick from Rowley. Three minutes later

Pearson was again ideally positioned to put United two in front, again with a header, as Wallace in the Derby goal was caught out of position. Steel did manage to pull one back three minutes before the break and although Derby sensed a second half comeback, their dreams were soon to evaporate.

Eleven minutes into the second half Pearson claimed his hat-trick with a strike worthy of winning the cup itself. Morris swung the ball out towards Mitten, whose pass inside found Pearson and, as the United danger-man took the ball towards the goal line and an angle where it looked impossible to score, he shot across the face of the goal and the ball flew past Wallace into the far corner.

United should have increased their advantage and superiority, while Derby spurned opportunities to grab some consolation in defeat, Crompton on three occasions stopping the ball on his line. But there was no further scoring as United strode on to Wembley, where Blackpool were patiently waiting to provide the opposition.

By the end of March, United had overtaken Burnley and claimed second place in the First Division table, albeit only a point in front, having played a game more. Now came the danger that their focus could drift towards the twin towers of Wembley and that meeting with Blackpool in just over a month's time.

On April 3rd Derby County ventured north to Manchester to face United for a second time in a matter of weeks, seeking revenge, but a 1-0 defeat kept their victors within sight of Arsenal. Now there were only five League fixtures remaining, with seven points separating the two sides, so there appeared to be little possibility of United overcoming their disadvantage to pip the Gunners to the title. The odds had lengthened even more two weeks later, following a 1-1 draw at home against City and a 2-0 defeat at Goodison Park.

The team that had practically selected itself over the course of the previous weeks and months now showed changes on a match-by-match basis due to international call-ups, injuries and most probably the visit to north London that loomed on the horizon.

Eddie Buckle re-emerged upon the scene against Everton for only his second outing of the season, while Johnny Ball and Laurie Cassidy both made their League debuts, following in the footsteps of Tommy Lowrie who had stepped into the first-team spotlight the previous Saturday against City. With five regulars missing and the novice Cassidy suffering from stage fright, it was little wonder that Everton took both points.

Against City, in a sometimes over-physical encounter which saw reporters comment on players "losing their dignity, but keeping their tempers", a point from the 1-1 draw was perhaps all that was deserved.

But with the 'big guns' back, the Cup Final warm-up went according to plan, with Chelsea hammered 5-0 at Maine Road. Mitten, Delaney, Rowley and Pearson, the latter with a double in the final eight minutes, sent their opponents back to London with boos echoing in their ears following a rather robust display, which saw Rowley leave the field with an injury ten minutes into the second half.

And so attention turned to Wembley, and no sooner had United triumphed over Derby County in the semi-final than the ticket applications began filtering through the Old Trafford letter box. Long before they were due to go on sale, around 18,000 applications had been received for the 12,000 or so tickets. Both the finalists had around 25,000 tickets to share between them, with some 58,000 going to county associations and the remainder to Football League clubs, on a sliding scale depending on their status.

"It is a heartbreaking task," proclaimed secretary Walter Crickmer. "Members and voucher holders will have first preference. After that our staff will do their best to sift the chaff from the wheat, and, believe me, that is no easy task."

Due to the heavy number of applications, the club were forced to put up a notice on the outside door of the office, stating that 'no further application could be accepted'. This was to little avail, as even with the letter box sealed up, supporters would attempt to push their hopeful applications under the door.

The United party set off for their Weybridge headquarters on the Friday morning prior to the final, sharing their train with numerous supporters for the journey south. Upon arrival at Euston, the boisterous followers gave their heroes a noisy escort along the platform, but before reaching the station concourse, pushing and shoving developed as press photographers jostled in an effort to obtain shots of the United players, asking if they would stop and pose for a group photograph. Having already objected to granting normal access to photographers, the players declined their request, a number of them covering their faces with their arms. An appeal was made by one disgruntled photographer to Matt Busby, but the manager simply replied "An agreement has been reached". When asked if this involved a fee of £10 per picture, he replied "yes".

Throughout the Friday night and Saturday morning a vast army of both Blackpool and United supporters arrived from the north-west. One follower from Manchester immediately commandeered a station porters' trolley upon stepping off his train in order to convey his six crates of beer to the left luggage room which he would pick up later. "United are winning today," he exclaimed, "and there won't be any beer in London tonight. That's why I've brought my own."

From the seaside resort an estimated 10,000 were London bound, ten of whom were in invalid chairs, taking over the guards' van for their journey south. Although they were in possession of match tickets, they were well aware that their chances of seeing the match were slim, as their 'bath chairs' were prohibited from the stadium. If this was indeed to be the case, then they intended going to the main entrance and demonstrating.

The influx of football supporters enlivened London on that bright and sunny spring morning, with many making the most of a rare visit to the capital to take in the sights. But Wembley was their destination and many decided that Buckingham Palace, Trafalgar Square, Piccadilly Circus and the like could wait, and they wasted little time in heading out towards the twin towers.

Those with a ticket kept their precious little piece of card closely guarded. Those without were soon accosted by the 'touts', 'ticket speculators', 'spivs' or 'scalpers' – whatever name you prefer to describe those with tickets to sell at inflated prices. Some felt there were fewer than usual of those members of the underworld lurking in the shadows, while others considered them to be greater in number than in the past. Nevertheless, having been at Wembley since around 7.30am, they had little problem in finding buyers. Not since the 1923 Cup Final had so many ticketless supporters converged on the stadium.

Prices ranged from £25 for a £2 2shilling stand ticket down to £3 for a 3shilling spot on the open terraces. One Blackpool man offered a week's holiday at the Lancashire resort for a ticket, another said he would be prepared to pay £10 for one, while a Manchester woman said that she could get a house if she obtained a ticket for an estate agent. Just prior to kick-off one man offering a 3shilling ticket for £6 was set upon by a gang of ticketless fans, but it was a Blackpool man who had the satisfaction of outsmarting the touts. Asking the seller if he could inspect the ticket before handing over his money, as there were countless forgeries going around, the ticket was handed over, inspected and as quick as a flash, 3shillings was deposited into the tout's hand with the ticket's new owner quickly dashing through the nearby turnstile.

But it wasn't just the rogue ticket sellers who came under fire from the supporters without, as they were also quick to criticise the "retired Army men, lawyers, parsons and schoolmasters, who want in to see their one professional game a year, denying the ordinary fan from obtaining a ticket." A staff reporter from the *Reynolds News and Sunday Citizen* spoke to a Major A. Gillsan from Leicester, who said:

> "I get two tickets for my wife and myself through the County Association. Of course I don't usually go to professional football matches. Rugger is my game. But after all, the Cup Final is different."

His ticket would have been better in the hands of Peter Weeks from Salford, who walked around the ground with a piece of card bearing the words, "Wanted – one Cup Final ticket".

> "I go and see United every week," he said, "but I was just unlucky when the tickets were dished out. I am willing to give a couple of quid for a three bob ticket, but honestly the prices they are asking are too high for me."

It wasn't simply the tickets that were exchanging hands for silly money, as hats in the colours of both the finalists were so much in demand that straight sales were abandoned by the sellers, offering their wares to the highest bidders. Old wartime air raid warning rattles, painted in both red-and-white and tangerine-and-white were on sale for 5shillings. Rosettes were also available at 1/6d to 5shillings.

Tickets, however, were of much more importance and many who were unable to afford the prices asked were not prepared, or content, to simply sit outside and listen to the radio commentary. Another *Reynolds News* staff reporter watched as around eighteen supporters took five minutes to scale up a fifteen-foot drainpipe, surmount a thick hedge of barbed wire and overcome a screen of wire netting before gaining entry into the ground. Two others, clad in the tangerine of Blackpool, climbed a fifty-foot pipe leading up to the stadium roof, before disappearing from view.

But the reporter was not simply to be an observer, scribbling notes as he watched the antics of those around him, as he soon got caught up in the afternoon's early drama. Joining another group of ticketless supporters, they attempted to gain entry via a padlocked gate, watching anxiously as Joseph Bromley from Manchester worked on the padlock with a penknife(!) and a hairpin temporarily borrowed from a Blackpool housewife.

"I have watched the United play every round of the cup and I am going to see the final," Bromley proclaimed as he worked away at the lock, prodding and turning his instruments. After twenty minutes there was a loud click, the padlock fell open and into the ground streamed the delighted supporters. Their timing, or that of Joseph Bromley, was impeccable, as they had no sooner scrambled on to the packed terraces than half of them were leaping up and down celebrating the opening goal of the game.

Kicking off amid brilliant sunshine, the teams having emerged from the newly built dressing rooms at the 'London' end of the stadium, it was Blackpool who looked the more impressive early on and with fifteen minutes gone, it was the Seasiders who took a deserved lead, although in controversial fashion. Mortensen, one of Blackpool's danger men along with the ever-threatening Matthews, surged through the middle, taking the ball past Chilton. As he neared the edge of the United penalty area, the centre-half stuck out his leg in an attempt to push the ball away from the foot of the Blackpool man, but only succeeded in tripping him up. It was debatable as to whether or not Mortensen was actually inside the area when fouled, but the referee had no doubt in his mind and pointed to the spot. Shimwell made no mistake with the penalty.

Pearson headed against the crossbar as United surged forward in search of the equaliser, which was to arrive almost on the half-hour mark when Hayward, the Blackpool centre-half, hesitated in heading clear a Delaney through ball, in two minds whether to leave it to his goalkeeper to collect. Sensing the hesitance of the Blackpool defender, Rowley, sniffing the half chance, slipped in, rounded the stranded keeper and placed the ball easily into the vacant net. Little did anyone in the packed stadium know that Scottish international winger Delaney had, like Rowley, been a doubtful starter earlier in the week due to an injury picked up against Chelsea.

It was a disappointing goal to lose, but it gave Blackpool the impetus to continue the attacking play that had produced the opening goal, and they were rewarded with a second within six minutes. Mortensen latched on to a pass from Kelly before once again evading the attention of Cockburn, leaving him with just the United keeper to beat which he did with ease. Rickett almost headed a third just prior to the interval, but he was denied by a superb one-handed save from Crompton.

Few of the Manchester contingent were concerned that United were behind at the interval, as they expected a fightback during the second forty-five minutes, but were shocked and silenced when it was Blackpool who immediately took up the running, with Ricketts again proving a danger. An exchange of passes with Matthews created an opening for Dick, but he was too hesitant in grasping the opportunity. It was to prove a costly miss, as United grabbed the equaliser in the seventieth minute, against the run of play, when Rowley leaped to head home a Morris free kick.

The inter-switching between Rowley and Delaney had been one feature of United's play that had been missing from the final, but unknown to the man on the terracing, the latter was carrying an injury that could have kept him out of the game altogether. Delaney had been advised not to venture into the crowded central position, but to remain wide on the right.

Mortensen almost restored Blackpool's lead, running once again at the United defence, but Crompton dived to pull off a fine save. It was the beginning of the end for Blackpool, their opportunity of lifting the cup had disappeared in that one instant, and within ten minutes United were in front for the first time. Hayward slipped as he moved in to tackle Pearson, the United man whipping in a shot which beat Robinson, going in off the post.

There was now no way back for Blackpool and, with only three minutes remaining, Anderson hit the ball towards goal from a considerable distance out. To his and everyone else's amazement, the ball flew straight past the outstretched arm of Robinson.

"United won in the end fairly and squarely after being desperately near defeat, and so put the seal on two seasons of good football," wrote Archie Ledbrooke in the *Daily Mirror*. "They were twice behind and yet emerged to victory, a feat recalling to old timers Tottenham's 1901 win when they were a goal down to Sheffield United, made it 2-2, were a goal down again in the replay, and yet lifted the trophy. This is the only comparable case in the history of the competition. Such a performance cannot be minimised by any criticism. The winners kept pegging away confident in the belief that good football would bring results.

"So United are justly labelled the team of the season, taking much of the limelight off Arsenal. If they can only make a better start next August and September, the League championship can follow this Cup win."

It was a proud Johnny Carey who led his team-mates up the thirty-nine steps to the Royal Box to receive the cup from King George VI. The King warmly shook the Irishman's hand and said: "Congratulations, it was one of the most thrilling games I have seen." To which Carey replied: "Thank ye sir and God bless ye." Not perhaps the correct etiquette, but when you have just captained your team to an FA Cup victory, your thoughts would be anywhere but on Royal protocol. In any case, the King did little more than laugh, patting the United captain on the shoulder. As Carey turned away, however, the treasured trophy slipped from his grasp, but thankfully there was no lasting damage. A concerned Duke of Edinburgh stopped the Irishman to inspect the trophy and to help replace the lid.

"I never despaired," said the victorious captain as the victory was toasted with champagne, lemonade and orangeade, "for I knew that good football would eventually bring its own reward and that it was only a matter of time. Blackpool were gallant and clean losers and at times played superbly."

Team-mates Jack Rowley and Stan Pearson were also to reflect on the triumph, the latter saying:

> "When I got my head to that free kick by Johnny Morris and saw the ball go into the Blackpool net for our second goal, I had a feeling that we were on the way to winning."

Pearson, who had put United ahead for the first time added when asked if he had felt overcome by the tense atmosphere replied:

> "No, and I think that my recent experience in the international against Scotland at Hampden Park may have had something to do with it.
>
> "I remember, as I hit the ball, saying to myself 'this is it', but after I had shot, I kept running and as the ball hit an upright and ran along the goal line, I actually saw it veer over the line and enter the net. Believe me, I felt very relieved."

Into central London streamed the Mancunian hordes, eager to celebrate their team's victory, many gathering around the statue of Eros in Piccadilly Circus, "waving colours, ringing bells and twirling rattles." Back in Manchester, all was quiet, but the following day would see much activity around the Town Hall area in preparation for the triumphant homecoming, with poles for flags and bunting put up around the square.

The journey back to Manchester was completed in two stages, as the United party left the train at Stockport and headed for Hale, to the home of chairman James Gibson, who had been unwell for some time. Upon arrival, the players lined up on the front lawn, the chairman appearing at a first-floor window with Matt Busby, Johnny Carey and of course the cup itself. "I'm proud of you boys. This is a moment I have been waiting for ever since I took over." The players were then to go individually to greet the chairman in his room and to receive their personal congratulations.

Their guard of honour into the city began some seven miles outside, with reports telling of "children with red and white rosettes as big as their faces," the reception in Moss Side "as loud and welcoming as that at the Town Hall." Their arrival at this final destination was preceded by the familiar one-legged serviceman, who could be seen hopping around the perimeter on a matchday, who had raced along from Princess Road in front of the team coach.

"We want Carey," chanted the estimated 300,000 squashed into Albert Square, with women and children fainting in the crush. "This is magnificent," said Billy Meredith, proudly waiting to greet the United players. "In 1909, we had a horse coach and no big crowd like this."

One supporter was too young to attend the Cup Final, or indeed the homecoming, but was to get an unexpected close-up view of the famous trophy. Mike Carey, son of the United captain, was only six at the time and recalled:

> "Unfortunately, I never saw dad play for United. In those days young children, or women for that matter, did not tend to go to matches, but on the Monday after the final he woke me up and said 'come and have a look what we've just won.' as he took me into his bedroom of our small semi at 13 Sark Road, Chorlton-cum-Hardy. 'It's under the bed'. It was the actual FA Cup in a big box!! Dad said that Matt Busby had told him that as captain it was his job to look after it.
>
> "I did sometimes go to the ground on a Sunday morning after a match to check up on the injured players and I went with him sometimes. The 'medical centre' at the ground was located at the end of what is now the tunnel and was a bit like a wooden scout hut, as I recall.

"I do remember one day that a massive reserve team goalkeeper ran in, jumped up for some reason and cracked his head on one of the roof cross-members. He did a backward somersault!! All the other players thought it was very funny. They were a hard lot!"

Following the cup success, there were numerous celebration dinners to attend, at the Town Hall, in Eccles, in Salford and even at the Lewis's department store in Manchester city centre. But before the players could rest on their laurels, there were still two further League fixtures to fulfil. The first ironically enough was against Blackpool, and it was to provide revenge of a sort for the Bloomfield Road side, who won an exciting encounter with the only goal of the game.

Rounding the season off was a home fixture against Blackburn Rovers, ninety minutes that could secure the First Division runners-up spot for the second consecutive season. Going into the Maine Road match, they were level on points with Derby County and Burnley, with a superior goal average; but the visitors were not going to make things easy, despite being doomed to Second Division football next season. Blackburn started brightly, forcing Crompton into making two fine saves.

United were just beginning to look like their usual selves when Delaney set them on the road to victory with the opening goal in the thirty-fifth minute. It was then left to Stan Pearson to take control of the match, scoring a hat-trick which rendered meaningless Blackburn's solitary effort.

So, despite the championship still eluding them, United had won their first post-war trophy. The players had earned a £20 per man bonus, with a further £550 'talent money' to be distributed amongst all those who had figured in the season's cup-ties. The 'Team of the Season' could surely only improve and add to this initial triumph with further silverware.

Chapter Four

The Good, The Bad and The Title

1948-49 – 1951-52

AN FA Cup winner's medal in 1933-34 was all Matt Busby had to show for his years in the blue shirt of Manchester City and the red of Liverpool, so there was an inner determination to ensure that, as a manager, he would lead his team to much more in the way of footballing honours. It was hoped that the FA Cup success would be a springboard to even greater things.

In the build-up to the 1948-49 season United undertook a series of local friendlies, but not against the likes of Cheshire League Hyde United or Stalybridge Celtic, or even Lancashire Combination sides such as Bacup Borough or Ashton United. Neither did the red and white shirts have to be laundered, as those pre-season encounters were surprisingly Sunday cricket matches against the likes of Prestwich, Thornham, Stand, Taylor Brothers and Ashton, with two-day midweek fixtures against Longsight and Levenshulme thrown in for good measure.

Even when it did come down to an organised kickabout, Jimmy Murphy decided that it was "too warm for soccer" and cancelled the proposed practice game, instead getting the players involved in a six-a-side 'soccer-heading-tennis' competition.

There were, however, some serious training sessions put in and the team were ready to kick off their First Division campaign against Derby County at Old Trafford. But eager anticipation soon gave way to disappointment come 4.45pm on the afternoon of August 21st, as the visitors headed back to their Baseball Ground home with both points following a surprise 2-1 victory, thanks mainly to an inspired performance from goalkeeper Townsend.

"If Manchester United's supporters were ruffled by their team's defeat in the first match of the Association football season against Derby County, their feelings must have been mollified by United's victory, 3-0 at Blackpool," wrote Don Davies in the *Guardian* three days later. He was also quick to add that the victory at the seaside, although "emphatic", was also "flattering", but his words were simply dismissed by those supporters who read his analysis. The respected correspondent's comments were considered even more nonsensical five days later when reigning champions Arsenal were defeated 1-0 on their own turf. Davies, on this occasion quick to point out that the game was certainly not "a classic", wrote:

> "United's success by the only goal was well merited and by no means reflects their superiority. As in their cup-ties last season, United won through their fine team work, each attacking move being the outcome of shrewd co-ordination."

The result was sweet revenge, not simply because of Arsenal's championship success of last season, as the seven-point gap could not be denied, but for the unjust remarks made by London newspapers prior to the match, saying that the United players were "swell headed". It was a remark which stung Busby, who told his players to ignore the jibes, whilst saying to the press in general:

> "Nothing has hurt me more since I came into football. There is not a word of truth in it. Naturally the team are very proud of their Wembley achievement, but never at any time have they allowed it to affect them in the way described."

But this was Manchester United, masters of their own destiny and a team who could go from sublime to mediocre and back again in next to no time. On their day, they could knock three goals past any team whilst in the same ninety minutes could forsake their good work by conceding four. Such was the case when Blackpool made the journey to Manchester for the return First Division fixture between the two sides. Twice United went behind, only to claw their way back into the game and draw level, before taking a 3-2 lead on the hour mark. At that point, most thought it was game over, but Blackpool fought back, drawing level with ten minutes remaining, before going on to score the winner with virtually the last kick of the match.

And so the season continued. From conceding four against Blackpool to a 4-1 victory over Huddersfield, then four days later conceding three in a five-goal encounter at Molineux against Wolves, before sharing the spoils in a goalless draw against landlords City. The pen of Don Davies was set scribbling frantically once again, indirectly pointing a finger at Busby for dropping Johnny Anderson and replacing him with Billy McGlen, a decision that the reporter felt had destroyed the balance and rhythm of the side. This result left United floundering in mid-table, already six points behind leaders Portsmouth.

As great a concern as the failure to win games, lacking form and consistency, was the on-running saga of repairs to the Old Trafford ground. There had been an overwhelming demand for season tickets, forcing the club to issue 'unreserved seats' at £4.4s in Stand D, but whilst encouraging, it was also disappointing that all this revenue was not finding its way into United's coffers.

By late September, there was still no idea when the ground would be ready again for regular first-team football, despite the club regularly seeking permission to rebuild. Ellis Smith continually brought up the subject with his Parliamentary colleagues and back in January 1948 had asked the Minister of Works if a light alloy could be used for the roofing of the stands. The reply was negative. A month later, following a speech from the Chancellor of the Exchequer, in which he said that "the government desired to encourage all forms of entertainment", Smith quickly seized the point, stating that Manchester United Football Club wanted to "finish the building of the ground so that it would hold 120,000 people". Again the response was not favourable towards United.

A frustrated Walter Crickmer kept in regular contact with the Member of Parliament and in one piece of correspondence bemoaned the state of affairs regarding the ground, in particular the failure to get the stand back to some sort of normality. He almost pleaded with the MP to try and get something done, "if only as a compliment to this great industrial centre, whose people have certainly made a magnificent effort in the export drive."

There was a sudden swing in the right direction come November – although on immediate reading it could have been translated as anything but – when the City directors sent their United counterparts a letter to quit Maine Road at the end of the season. Part of the message stated that City "were not disposed to continuing the tenancy beyond the end of the present season and the directors feel the arrangement which has been in operation for eighteen years cannot be expected to go on indefinitely." City were well aware of United's rising popularity and also financial status, due to their house guests publishing a profit of £22,328 for the previous season – almost double that of the twelve months before, with additional property (player leased houses) of £11,529. This financial factor also saw City try to force United's hand by asking for a change in the tenancy agreement, requesting a percentage of the gate money, rather than a lump sum. To this suggestion, they received the polite but firm reply of "No". In an effort to justify their actions, they were to say:

> "We have always wanted to help United in their great misfortune and we have accommodated them to the best of our ability, but this business would go on for ever unless the City board took a firm stand."

With the notice to quit Maine Road to hand, some suspected, quite wrongly, that the United directors had instigated the situation in order to force the government into speeding up the release of funds to carry out improvements. The onus was now firmly at the feet of the War Committee and hopes for a permit to begin the necessary restoration work were beginning to improve. Many supporters who had stuck by the club through some difficult times over the years, especially those with family fan connections stretching back as far as the Newton Heath days, decided that now was the time to step forward. They sensed that the War Committee were simply dragging their heels and that something, sooner rather than later, had to be done to aid United.

A Salford reader of the *Manchester Evening Chronicle*, a Mr. H. Miller, wrote to the United correspondent Alf Clarke saying:

> "Anyone is permitted to buy £1 worth of wood each month. Why cannot 40,000 or 50,000 supporters buy £1 worth of wood and present it to the club to build a stand and seating?" Unfortunately the suggestion was a 'no-hoper', as Alf Clarke was to point out: "Good idea, if done a year ago, when imported timber was available. Now only 'home grown' timber allowed and this would be unusable."

A Mr H S Thompson of Stockport went as far as to organise a petition, in the hope of persuading the Ministry of Works to expedite the issue of licences for the restoration of Old Trafford, and the signatures flooded in at the rate of around 500 per day. The organiser wasn't simply content to have a large number of signatures on paper, he was also assembling a work-force, saying: "Once the licence has been issued, I can get two or three hundred supporters to lend a hand with the alterations if necessary."

With the ball rolling, albeit slowly, as regards to the necessary repair work, the Football League secretary Frank Howarth announced that it could be possible for United to play at Old Trafford next season. Initially, the club were somewhat concerned that people might stay away from games if there was no, or little, covered accommodation.

It wasn't simply the weather that could keep supporters away, but also the performances of the team which were considered 'below par', despite last season's FA Cup success. Early season fixtures had seen attendances range from 52,620 on the opening day to 57,187 for the visit of Huddersfield, but the defeat against Wolves in mid-

September saw a mere 33,871 turning up, making United's concern of falling gates once the colder, wetter weather kicked in more of a probability than a possibility.

Inconsistency continued to reign as September eased into October with home victories against Wolves (2-0) and Aston Villa (3-1), intermixed with a 2-2 draw at Sheffield United, 1-1 draws at Old Trafford against Charlton Athletic and Burnley and 2-1 away defeats against Sunderland and Stoke City. Such results left United still floundering in 12th position, now eight points adrift of Portsmouth at the top. The draw against Burnley, with both goals coming in the final eight minutes, was simply a case of too many players falling below their usual high standard of play, none more so than Pearson and Morris. An injury to Delaney had seen his 'stand-in', Eddie Buckle, score in the games against Wolves and Sheffield United, only to find himself back on Central League duty as soon as the Scot was fit again. Busby was apt to stick by his 'regular eleven', leaving those in the second string wondering just what they had to do in order to play First Division football on a regular basis.

Those indifferent displays, however, were soon brushed under the carpet when the ninety minutes at Deepdale against Preston North End finally saw the team click and return to something like their old form. Despite taking a three-minute lead, Preston were hit with a tidal onslaught which saw Pearson back on song, claiming a double, as did Mitten, with Morris and Rowley giving United a 6-1 victory.

This was the impetus that Busby's team needed, setting them off on an unbeaten twelve-match run, during which they took a point from second-top Portsmouth one Saturday and defeated the current leaders Derby County 3-1 seven days later. The latter victory left United only five points adrift in fourth place. Perhaps the unveiling of a "Manchester United FA Cup Winners 1948" flag above the Maine Road stand against Everton, seven days after the 6-1 victory over Preston, was the inspiration required to finally put together a successful run of results.

The 0-0 Christmas Day draw with Liverpool was the first time United had drawn a blank since the City encounter in mid-

September, with reports referring to the often free-scoring front line as once again being far below their best form. Most of the home support in the 47,788 crowd accepted it as such, but one individual considered Stan Pearson to be more than responsible for the stalemate, so much so that he waited behind after the game to let the England international know exactly how he felt. Few knew of the individual's behaviour until Alf Clarke brought the matter up in the *Manchester Evening Chronicle*, writing: "Criticism is just part and parcel of a soccer player's life. His friends tell him what they think, the press express their opinions and occasionally the BBC announcers and commentators have a few words to say.

"A man, outside Maine Road on Christmas Day voiced his opinion that Stan Pearson was the cause of the draw." Nothing much wrong with that, but an open letter from Pearson revealed a bit more.

"I was lazy and had never tried during the game and had missed chance after chance," said Pearson, quoting from the letter. "He was entitled to his opinion, but unfortunately my wife overheard him and not unnaturally challenged his remarks about the game. His only reply was a perfectly filthy remark.

"The object of this letter is to give the man the opportunity of repeating this insulting remark to me. I shall be outside the players' entrance at Maine Road on Saturday January 1st from 1.30 to 1.45pm."

The New Year's Day fixture against Arsenal would have attracted a good crowd anyway – 58,688 compared to the 47,788 against Liverpool – but how many now turned up, making a beeline for the players' entrance hoping for some pre-match entertainment? In any case, they were to be disappointed, as Pearson stood alone within a circle of supporters, and no dissenting fan made an appearance. Once inside, they must have been more than content with the 2-0 victory over the reigning champions. It was a victory that kept United in fourth place, but which saw their deficit behind top-of-the-table Portsmouth reduced to just two points.

Prior to the second goalless stalemate of the season against City, the *Manchester Evening Chronicle* enjoyed better-than-usual midweek sales due to its front-page headline: "United Can Build Stand To Seat 3000". Alf Clarke revealed,

"Manchester United will be able to start re-building their
blitzed ground at Old Trafford next week. The Ministry of
Work, I understand, are sending out a licence this week-end
to Manchester United to go ahead with temporary repairs
on the site of the blitzed main stand, and the work should
be completed before the opening of next season."

Clarke went on to say that the temporary construction was to be
built with tubular scaffolding, providing seating for 3,000 under
cover. The whole of the blitzed site would be terraced in concrete
and standing accommodation would be available on each side of
the temporary new stand. It would, however, see the maximum
ground capacity reduced to around 50,000, with cover for around
15,500 – 7,500 of those on the Popular Side, 5,000 on the terraces
at both corners and the remaining 3,000 in the new stand.

The announcement in the House of Commons on January 24th
that the Ministry of Work had given instructions for a licence to
be granted to United had been met by loud cheers, with Mr H.
Lewis of Stretford asking: "Are you aware that that answer will
give a great deal of satisfaction to many thousands of supporters
of the finest team in the country?" Satisfaction not only to the
supporters but to the directors as well, as it brought an end to the
search for accommodation for next season, with Swinton Rugby
League Club's Station Road ground having been proposed as a
possible new home. Capacity there was only 40,000, but 10,000 of
those were under cover, with 5,000 seated.

Now within touching distance of the leaders, United began
their defence of the FA Cup at Maine Road with a third round
tie against Bournemouth, the Third Division South side putting
up little resistance in a 6-0 defeat. But three weeks later Second
Division Bradford Park Avenue were to put up a much sterner fight
in round four.

Drawn at home again, the Yorkshire side were more than happy
to leave Manchester with a 1-1 draw, having repelled the red tide
through one hundred and twenty minutes, and perhaps considered
themselves even more unfortunate to achieve the same scoreline in
the replay. In his match report, Don Davies of the *Guardian* was far

from impressed by the facilities on offer at the Yorkshire ground, writing that it was as if the events had been viewed 'through the bottom of a bucket'. He had been perched on a balcony set so far behind one goal line that,

> "Consequently, to try and get a complete picture of this punishing game, dragging its barren length through two solid hours, one had to add to the incidents clearly seen at the little Horton end, eye-witness accounts brought by runners from the other end; rumours passing round the crowd; attempts, often wildly inaccurate, to interpret noises off; and lastly, new and surprising facts gleaned from the evening papers."

Those members of the press had no such problems reporting on the mid week second replay at Maine Road. On this occasion it was the spectators who had at times to rely on the word of others to determine what was happening.

On the day of the game, as much was made of the possibility of absenteeism from factories as the on-field chances of United progressing or Bradford causing a cup upset. Newspapers had enquired with various companies in Manchester and Bradford as to numbers of how many had stayed away, but were generally met with a firm refusal to comment. Some factories reported there had been no absenteeism as special appeals had been made to workers, along with warnings of consequences for choosing to stay away. Notwithstanding, 101 workers out of the 1,100 workforce at Lancashire Dynamo in Trafford Park went AWOL, and were duly suspended for three days.

Some 5,000 had travelled from Yorkshire and with 70,434 inside Maine Road, it was estimated that around 30,000 (or 7,000, depending on which newspaper you read) were locked out. Finding the gates closed, many rushed a turnstile near to the main entrance, with several hundred gaining entry before the situation was brought under control by the police. Others sought to get inside by climbing a wall, with police having to draw their batons in order to stop them. Another group of supporters, equally desperate to see the game but decidedly braver, climbed on to the roof of a nearby house and sat perched beside the chimney pots watching the action unfold.

As the game kicked off, many were still in the city centre, queuing for the special buses to take them out Moss Side way. The queues had apparently stretched for some six hundred yards, with an estimated 3,000 having waited on the 'match specials'. Many of those later buses that set off failed to get anywhere near the ground due to the congestion. Inside the ground, there were numerous fainting cases, with a sixty-two-year-old man collapsing and dying.

Bradford, perhaps having missed their best opportunity to overcome United in the two previous fixtures, were soundly beaten 5-0. The fifth round draw once again saw United coming out of the hat as the home side, followed once again by lower opposition in the form of non-League Yeovil Town. Although they had previously defeated Sunderland, there were to be no repeat heroics in front of their 6,000 travelling fans, as United showed little compassion, trouncing their visitors 8-0 in front of over 81,000 spectators.

Fourteen days later, in round six, a solitary goal was enough to defeat Third Division North side Hull City, with an estimated 15,000 having made the journey from Manchester. Sixteen special trains left the city, with one breaking down before reaching Hull, its hungry and thirsty occupants deciding to abandon their carriages and get off to walk the two hundred yards to Penistone. Eighty supporters selected a much more dependable mode of transport, hiring five planes for the half-hour journey from Ringway. Without the influential Johnny Carey, United had to dig deep for their victory, with goalscorer Stan Pearson pounding the Boothferry Park turf like a policeman on his beat, guiding his team through yet another successful cup-tie.

The season was slowly developing into a mirror image of the previous campaign. Indifferent League form before drifting practically unnoticed into a challenging position amongst the front runners at the top of the table, coupled with the sweet scent of Wembley in the heavy Mancunian air.

But despite this upsurge in form and the possibility of a second consecutive Cup Final appearance, all was not well within the ranks, though only those within the inner sanctums of Old Trafford were aware of the goings-on.

Missing from the United line-up for the December 18th fixture against Derby County was Johnny Morris, reportedly 'unfit'. He did reappear against Arsenal and Manchester City, and against Bradford in the first match of the FA Cup trilogy, but since then he had not made any of Matt Busby's starting elevens. By the end of February there was only one list that his name could be found on, and that was the transfer list.

Morris was a supremely talented individual, capable of doing anything with a football. "A brilliant inside-forward who knows his way to goal" was how one programme pen picture described him. Morris had joined United as a fifteen-year-old in 1939, but the love affair was to come to an abrupt end, as some romances are wont to do. "He is not happy with the club and that is the reason he is being allowed to move," was the official line behind the transfer, but things had been simmering away for some time.

Busby had struggled to create a harmonious relationship with Morris and had reportedly confessed to another player that he had "tried every angle", "bullied" and "flattered" his inside-forward, but to no avail. A prime example of the love-hate relationship between manager and player is emphasised by a training ground incident following the loss of a goal from a free kick against Blackpool.

Towards the end of the training session, keen to prevent another goal being lost in the same manner, Busby had five of his players line up in a defensive wall, rather than the usual four. The strategy was rehearsed in various positions in front of goal, and seemed to work well. Satisfied, the manager called time on the session and the players were happy to be going for their lunch. Johnny Morris, however, thought otherwise.

Defiantly, Morris suggested that despite adding an extra body to the wall, it was still possible to score, irritating his manager and doing little to appease his hungry team-mates. Annoyed at being contradicted, Busby turned to the player and asked him to demonstrate the frailty of the five-man wall. Calmly, Morris took a ball, stood in front of the wall and with seemingly little effort lofted a shot into the top corner.

This was only one incident, but Busby was the manager and was certainly not happy about his authority being questioned in any manner. He decided it would be better for the overall stability and well-being of the club if Morris were sold.

His availability alerted numerous clubs – twenty, according to some reports – with Everton, Blackpool, Middlesbrough and Chelsea all mentioned as possible suitors, but on March 2nd, it was announced that Liverpool and United had agreed a fee of £25,000. "I don't think anything of it," said Morris when asked about his record-breaking move. "It will not make the slightest difference to me. Strange isn't it that I cost United a £10 signing-on fee and now my value is £25,000."

But it did bother him, inasmuch that the fee was agreed, he had spoken to Liverpool, but still requested more time to think things over. "I must give the matter serious consideration. There are one or two things I must think about – personal matters." A week later, his move to Merseyside was off and he was now joining Derby County for £24,000, which was still a world record fee.

Somewhat strangely, Morris continued to train at Old Trafford following the move to the Baseball Ground, due to his wife having recently given birth and having to wait for a club house in Derby. "I am very happy to go to Derby County," he was to say following the move. "I shall do my best for them and I hope to win a championship medal with my new club." But he had to deny reports that his transfer was due to having fallen out with his team mates. "It is a lot of nonsense. I got on very well with my team-mates and every United player was my friend. There is no discontent in the United camp at all."

This followed rumours that he had fallen out with Stan Pearson and had hit Johnny Carey. Carey did have an eye injury, but said that it was the result of a clash of heads with Trevor Ford of Aston Villa during a recent match.

With the imminent departure of the wayward Morris, Matt Busby had already pencilled in his successor – Johnny Downie, a twenty-three-year-old Scot who had impressed in the three FA Cup ties against Bradford Park Avenue. An £18,000 fee took him over the Pennines to Manchester.

It was a transfer that many players failed to come to terms with, feeling irked that Busby had ventured into the transfer market to sign a replacement for Morris instead of giving a regular first team place to someone within the ranks. Eddie Buckle had scored twice in five outings this season and once in three last term, while Ronnie Burke was another capable replacement who had netted five in six games this season and nine in thirteen during 1946-47.

The conveyor belt of talent that United had hoped for was still in the process of being finely tuned and oiled, but it was certainly in motion despite Busby having commented on the shortage of schoolboy talent due to the lack of coaching at that particular level. His scouts had their work cut out, but still brought teenagers to the club with signings of young, promising players often tucked away in the bottom corners of the local papers. Eighteen-year-old Frank Clempson had been signed in September, while many, too engrossed in the news of the impending transfer of Morris to Liverpool, missed a more modest report: "Manchester United have signed on professional forms nineteen-year-old Roger Byrne, left half-back, who has been playing as an amateur in the 'A' team." Byrne, like Johnny Carey, had slipped into the Manchester United bloodstream virtually unnoticed.

Johnny Downie was, to be fair, no Johnny Morris and he was also obviously cup-tied. Although Busby was relieved to see the back of a potentially disruptive influence, Morris's absence caused the United manager some concern, forcing him to organise a 'trial match' behind closed doors, prior to the FA Cup semi-final against Wolves.

There was also the distinct possibility that Johnny Carey could miss the all-important semi-final, and the remainder of the season as well, following an anonymous letter received at Old Trafford saying that if the United captain played for Ireland against Wales in Belfast he would be "beaten up".

It was certainly something to be taken seriously, as another letter had recently been sent to a player prior to a fixture at Linfield's ground which had been ignored and the player in question was attacked and left with a broken leg. When asked about the letter, Matt Busby said:

> "It is obviously a letter from a fanatic. Religion appears to
> be at the bottom of it, but we are not concerned with any
> religion at Old Trafford."

Carey, although from the Republic of Ireland, was also eligible to play for Northern Ireland, and the thought of a Republican playing for and captaining the north in Belfast was of some concern to certain factions. It was of no concern to the player, who travelled across the Irish Sea, along with Vernon of West Bromwich Albion who had received a similar threat, and played his part in the 2-0 defeat, returning to Manchester unharmed. Much to the relief of many.

Unflustered, Johnny Carey led his United team out of the Hillsborough tunnel to face Wolverhampton Wanderers in the FA Cup semi-final, looking for a victory that would take them back to Wembley and the opportunity to retain the cup, a feat last accomplished by Blackburn Rovers way back in 1889-90 and again in 1890-91.

The outcome, however, was far from guaranteed as an eighteen-match unbeaten run had come to an end at Villa Park on February 19th, while a return trip to the Midlands the week before the semi-final had also seen a 1-0 defeat against Birmingham City. But, on their day, United were a match for anybody, even though they would miss the artistry of Morris; although new signing Downie was cup-tied, and half-back Johnny Anderson was entrusted to fill the vacant inside-right slot.

Fourteen corner kicks to their opponents' three emphasised United's attacking play, but a mistake in the twelfth minute by Chilton – considered by many the weak link in the United team – saw his attempted pass-back pounced upon by Pye, who in turn found Smyth, the Wolves inside-right having little difficulty in beating Crompton to give his side the lead. Thankfully for Chilton, his error was not to prove decisive, as Mitten snatched an equaliser eleven minutes later. Pearson was to shun a glorious opportunity to claim the winner, but with both sides suffering injuries, Cockburn for United and Pritchard and Kelly of Wolves, perhaps a draw, at the end of extra time, was a fair result.

In the Goodison Park replay, 74,000 witnessed what would be claimed by some as a robbery; but, in the cold light of day, the winners were perhaps deserving of their Cup Final place.

The opening twenty minutes belonged to United, whose forward line attacked their opponents at will. But under the leadership of Wright, who was guiding his two reserve full-backs through the game, safe in the knowledge that goalie Williams was capable of stopping anything that came his way, Wolves sustained the barrage and could claim the advantage in the second half.

Chances were missed, defences were stretched and the game looked to be once again looming towards extra time. Then, with five minutes of normal time remaining, Hancocks picked out Pye who looked suspiciously offside, but was waved on by the linesman as Carey raised his arm in protest. Drifting past Chilton, his shot was fumbled by Crompton, bouncing off the goalkeeper's chest to enable Smyth to move in and head the ball into the net. There was little time left even for United to grasp a match-saving equaliser, looking to extra time to salvage the dreams of a second final appearance. Their march towards history had come to a halt.

Alf Clarke questioned the approach and the tactics employed during the game. "Where is the nip of last season?" he asked. "The interchange of positions, the ball on the ground and so forth? And why did United go on the defensive in the second half?" All those tactics were an integral part of the current United side's success, and yet were so obviously missing in that Goodison Park semi-final.

With the vision of Wembley's twin towers having disappeared from view, attention could now be focused on the First Division title and, although there were still a dozen games to play, the majority of those would need to be won. Despite leaders Portsmouth dropping points, nine points still separated the leaders and fifth-place United, who had two games in hand. Hopes of claiming that initial post-war League success took a nosedive as the first two fixtures in April brought a 2-1 defeat against Huddersfield Town at Leeds Road and a 1-1 draw against Chelsea at Maine Road. Many loyal fans believed that the defeat against the Yorkshire side was, in its own right, enough to destroy any hopes of challenging Portsmouth for the title.

If points could be clawed back, then results would certainly have to better those of Portsmouth, as goal average would definitely not settle the title: the south-coast club already claimed a superior haul even before they hammered Newcastle United 5-0 while United toiled at Huddersfield. But Portsmouth were far from invincible, losing 1-0 at Blackpool and 3-0 at Birmingham City as Busby got his team back on track with victories against Bolton at home and away (3-0 and 1-0), and at Burnley (2-0). Could an improbable triumph still be achieved?

Sadly, the answer was no, as the first 'home' defeat since September 1st, 2-1 at the hands of Sunderland, brought an end to any outside hopes that were still held at Maine Road, Old Trafford or wherever. Even Newcastle United, who also kept Portsmouth looking over their shoulder, failed to maintain their challenge. It was certainly disappointing from United's point of view, as their final fixture was against Portsmouth at Maine Road, and had they managed to get within touching distance it could have seen a 'winner takes all' scenario.

But it was to be nothing more than 'winner takes runners-up spot' as United defeated the newly crowned champions 3-2 in a notable finale. A victory that prompted Don Davies to write in his match report for the *Guardian*:

> "Manchester United's rousing victory over Portsmouth by 3-2 at Moss Side provided three items for debate during the summer months – that Cockburn's best position is at left-half, that Manchester United's best available half-back line is composed of Anderson, Chilton and Cockburn and that in dropping Anderson in September and ignoring him until the end of the season someone made a bad blunder."

Disappointment all round, with the only cause for celebration being captain Johnny Carey being named as 'Footballer of the Year' by the Football Writers' Association – a fitting accolade for Busby's leader on the pitch, yet only a consolation prize compared with the League championship medal he had yearned for.

So, three times the bridesmaid. It seemed the opportunity to become the bride, to make that final push to become First Division champions, was simply something lacking from United's make-up. It annoyed Busby that the ultimate step could not be taken, but he possessed the determination to get there. Only time would tell if he would succeed and, if so, with which club, as overtures had already been made by Tottenham Hotspur, who were keen to lure Busby towards the bright lights of London. "Yes, there have been some indirect approaches to me," he admitted, "but I am quite happy at United and I have no intention of leaving, having started a job I want to complete." There was even an offer from Bob Smith, the Manchester City chairman, and another to take over the Italian national side, accompanied by a huge salary; but Busby believed that contracts were signed to be honoured and all approaches were rejected out of hand, and soon forgotten.

Having defined his position with United, he could now concentrate on laying down the plans for the club's future, whilst looking forward to finally having a stadium to call home.

Season 1949-50

There was very little wrong with Manchester United. The great majority of clubs would have been more than content with an FA Cup success and three consecutive First Division runners-up spots. But it had been thirty-eight years since the championship trophy had resided at Old Trafford, the Second Division triumph of 1935-36 not even worth thinking about, as it was finishing at the top of the First Division to which everyone aspired.

So it was back to the drawing board during the close season, another crack at that elusive title eagerly anticipated along with the club's long-awaited return to Old Trafford after what had seemed like an age in exile across town.

Having defeated Derby County on the opening Saturday of the 1949-50 season, a solitary Jack Rowley goal all that separated the two sides, August 24th was approached with a vast wave of excitement. It was a date that had been circled on countless calendars since the start of the year. No one cared that it was something of a local 'derby' with near neighbours Bolton Wanderers in opposition. It could have been against any team. Simply returning 'home' was all that mattered.

By the end of 1949, the final remnants of war damage had been removed and the levelling and concreting of the stand area had got underway. Some wooden cinema-type seats were procured to accommodate around 3,000, all without cover, but who cared? Being back in the environs of the ship canal would be enough for club and supporters alike. Shelter was only provided for a select few, such as the directors and the press, with a corrugated iron awning constructed over their respective boxes in an attempt to keep out the elements.

A fifteen-foot red and white banner proclaiming "Welcome Back to Old Trafford" was prominently placed, but many paid it little attention as they scurried toward the turnstiles, having been held up in a mile-long traffic jam with vehicles bumper to bumper and three deep. Fans abandoned stationary buses in droves as the football traffic melted into the evening 'rush hour' traffic coming from the nearby White City stadium, and yet more sports devotees poured out of a cricket match at 'the other' Old Trafford.

Having managed to get inside, many were then unable to see the action due to poor crowd control, partly caused by volunteer stewards having been delayed by the volume of traffic on Chester Road and other approaches to the ground. Some who had paid between 1s 3d and 3s 6d for a lower-priced seat found it too packed and moved into the Stretford End, while others realised they were not going to be able to see much of the ninety minutes, and were allowed to leave the ground through a specially opened gate.

In the club programme for the match, chairman Mr J. W. Gibson wrote:

> "Dear Friends, At precisely 6.30 this evening one of my greatest wishes will be gratified. Yes – it is the kick-off at our opening League match which will really be 'at home' for the first time since just before the outbreak of war. You remember – it was the Grimsby Town game on August 26,

1939. After ten years it will be a wonderful sight to see our supporters back at Old Trafford, and, as Chairman of the Club, I offer you all a warm and cordial welcome.

"It grieves me to know that I cannot welcome you back to a properly restored ground, let alone the fully developed stadium which I had in mind many years ago. However, we must do something about the grandstand before next season and I hope the powers that be will see fit to grant the necessary permission.

"You know, of course, that plans are being formulated, and when the work is finally carried out, your ground will compare with the best in the country. We are patiently waiting on that day."

So, at 6.30pm on Wednesday August 24th 1949, United ran out on to the Old Trafford lush green turf for the stadium's first Football League fixture in a decade. As it transpired, it was a rather untidy ninety minutes, with both sides scorning easy early opportunities to add to the scoreline.

It was not until the 40th minute that United took the lead, after Downie had come close with a shot against the post. A Lynn free kick was contested by Pearson and Gillies, the latter reaching the ball first, only to see it glance off his head and past his own advancing goalkeeper. Mitten added a second from the penalty spot after Rowley had been obstructed in the box by Gillies and Roberts, and the third came from a Rowley header following another free kick.

Midway through the second half came a curious incident. The referee awarded a free kick against United, and as Bolton prepared to take the kick, a spectator walked on to the field of play, heading in the direction of the referee, near the centre circle. Players and officials stood still in amazement, uncertain what was happening, possibly thinking that the interloper might have an important message for the referee (other than what was on his mind). But before he reached the centre of the pitch, the trainers of both clubs and a policeman caught up with the errant fan and escorted him off the pitch and out of the ground.

The League programme saw United get off to a promising start, with four wins and a draw in the opening five fixtures, but three consecutive draws in early September – against Liverpool and Chelsea away, and Stoke at home – kept them three points behind early leaders Wolves. Sunderland, however, made them look relatively average as they claimed both points in a 3-1 victory at Old Trafford, just as had Burnley seven days previously in their 1-0 victory at Turf Moor.

Up until that Sunderland reversal, Busby had kept faith with his regular eleven, albeit bringing in 'want-away' Chilton at wing-half in place of Cockburn and then Warner, the centre-half having lost his place in the starting line-up to Sammy Lynn. However, with Carey and Cockburn both on international duty, Busby was forced into making changes for the visit of Charlton, bringing in Ball and McGlen, with Bogan taking over from Buckle. The latter turned in a promising display on his debut, doing enough in the 3-2 win to cement his place in the side, temporarily at least.

Victory over Charlton headed a run of nine games unbeaten, although it was studded with unexpected draws, one of which was a thrilling 'Big Dipper' ride for the supporters at Blackpool, where a 3-0 lead was squandered, the Seasiders grabbing an equaliser two minutes from the end. United remained three points off top spot.

The search for a goalkeeper came back into focus when Sonny Feehan took over from Jack Crompton for a couple of outings in November; then a new signing, eighteen-year-old Ray Wood, stepped into the spotlight in the 1-1 draw against Newcastle on December 3rd – only for his raw inexperience to send him back into the juniors for the time being.

As autumn began to turn to winter, conditions at Old Trafford became as much of a focus as the actual players and fixtures. With crowds of between forty and fifty thousand, it was not unusual to see supporters making their way towards the exits before the final whistle. This wasn't simply due to results, but to the lack of cover, many now heading for home if heavy rain persisted. In the *Evening Chronicle*, Alf Clarke attempted to assist their cause by asking: "When is the United ground going to be put into a state of repair which the public continue to demand?" He added that it was a bit much to expect people to pay 5/- to be rained on, but did also mention that it was not entirely the club's fault as an application was in place to continue with improvements.

Attendances fluctuated considerably, with 30,343 watching the 1-1 draw with Newcastle United on December 3rd, while 10,000 more had witnessed the 6-0 hammering of Huddersfield Town a month before. The irregular performances of this period were clearly illustrated before and after the Huddersfield rout with goalless encounters against Portsmouth and Everton. Consecutive 1-0 defeats against Fulham away and Derby County at home in early December added to the inconsistency that seemed to blight every campaign.

1949 came to an end with a 2-1 New Year's Eve victory over Manchester City, leaving the gap between them and leaders Liverpool at two points, but it was edging towards cup time and yet another two-pronged assault on the English game's major trophies.

In the third round, Southern League Weymouth put up a token resistance in their 4-0 defeat, though Third Division Watford did much better in round four, holding out at Vicarage Road until the 89th minute, when Jack Rowley managed to prod the ball home.

Having enjoyed some good fortune in the early round FA Cup draws in the past couple of seasons (coming out of the maroon velvet bag alongside the likes of Bournemouth, Yeovil and this season's two lesser lights), the competition took on a different perspective when paired with reigning league champions Portsmouth in round five. The home draw was eagerly anticipated by supporters and ticket touts alike, though the latter found it hard work to shift their tickets despite considerable numbers being turned away when the 40,000 had gone on sale the previous Sunday. Prior to the match, touts with handfuls of tickets offered them for sale at various prices, no two sellers quoting the same price. As kick-off drew near, they were all forced to lower that price considerably in a frantic attempt to sell what would soon become a worthless piece of paper.

Portsmouth, currently three points behind second-placed United (who were in turn a point behind leaders Liverpool) brought a sizable following north, but they were to endure a disappointing opening forty-five minutes as Mitten and Pearson gave United a comfortable

2-0 lead. But with Lancaster in the United goal "not inspiring confidence" and the forwards misfiring – "it would perhaps be kinder to say that they had an off day" – it was no surprise when the visitors fought back, drawing level through Clarke and Parker. Only then did a rousing six-minute spell see a Mitten penalty restore United's advantage before a Chilton handball gave Portsmouth a penalty, allowing Ferrier to take the game to a replay on the south coast.

Most would have taken Portsmouth to progress into round six with their home advantage, but United then turned in their best performance of the season. Sonny Feehan replaced the unsteady Joe Lancaster in goal, but was seldom troubled due to a sterling performance by Chilton in front of him, atoning for his error in the first match.

Mitten gave United a twelfth-minute lead following good work from Delaney and Rowley, with Downie adding a second. Although Harris pulled one back for the home side prior to half-time, the visitors looked comfortable. Portsmouth had little time to work the stiff breeze on their backs to their advantage, as three minutes after the restart Rowley centred from the left, Bogan flicked the ball on and Delaney scored a rare goal, which would send United into the sixth round.

Ten days later United were First Division leaders following a 2-1 victory at Charlton, a position they were to maintain until April 15th when a 0-0 draw against Liverpool at Old Trafford saw them replaced by FA Cup opponents Portsmouth.

Neither Sonny Feehan nor Joe Lancaster were the answer to Busby's ongoing goalkeeper problem, and it came as a real surprise when the United manager cast his eyes across Manchester and made City an offer of £5,000 for thirty-six-year-old Frank Swift.

Although he had retired in 1949 to take up a career in journalism with the *News of the World*, Swift remained on City's list of retained players, so any enquiries regarding his services had to made through them. Busby approached their chairman Robert Smith in order to sound out the possibility of signing the out-of-contract Swift, if only on a temporary deal. "Personally, as always, I was quite agreeable to helping United in their extremity," said Smith, "and I said I would put the matter before the board meeting.

"But, the majority were against it and there was nothing I could do. I told Matt Busby of our decision when he returned from Portsmouth." Swift himself was to say: "I do not intend to play in first class football again." That particular avenue was now a dead end.

The need for a new goalkeeper was emphasised in the FA Cup sixth round tie against Chelsea when Jack Crompton looked to have well covered a Campbell shot from twelve yards out, but the usually reliable keeper allowed the ball to slip from his arms and roll over his back and into the net to give the home side a sixth-minute lead. It was a goal that knocked the confidence of United players and although they managed to keep Chelsea at bay for a considerable time, a second goal, from Bentley, confirmed to those in red shirts and their travelling support in the vast 70,362 crowd that there would be no semi-final appearance this season.

On the evening of Wednesday March 8th Aston Villa travelled north to Manchester, hoping to catch United in subdued mood following the home side's weekend FA Cup defeat, but little did the Midland side know what lay in store for them amid the industrial sprawl of Trafford Park. Had Villa goalkeeper Joe Rutherford experienced any premonitions about that evening's match, then he would never have made the journey north from Birmingham.

The 7-0 scoreline actually flattered the Midlands side, with the *Guardian* correspondent writing: "Indeed, such was the superiority of the Manchester side that had the score reached double figures it would not have been surprising." The match was a headline writer's dream, featuring a 7-0 scoreline, a meagre crowd of 22,149 and a hat-trick of penalties.

The outcome might have been completely different had Goffin scored from the penalty spot following a foul by Aston on Smith; but Crompton, having had his confidence helped by numerous early pass-backs from his fellow defenders, saved well. It was not until the fortieth minute that the floodgates opened with the first of Mitten's spot-kicks.

Two minutes into the second half Mitten made it 2-0 with another penalty, claiming his hat-trick with a header almost immediately from the restart. United teased their opponents unmercifully without increasing the score and it wasn't until midway through the second half that Villa were put to the sword with two goals in under a minute from Rowley and Downie. The latter made it 6-0 from a position that looked suspiciously offside, before Mitten rounded off the scoring with two minutes remaining. It was his fourth, making a hat-trick of spot-kicks, and he even had the impudence to inform the Villa keeper which side of the goal he was going to place his kick.

A week after that emphatic victory over Villa, the 0-0 draw against Liverpool proved to be the turning point of the season, as United were to win only one of their remaining nine games, drawing three and losing five. These performances were enough to see them finish fourth, surprisingly only three points behind champions Portsmouth. Looking back, it is easy now to pick out the games where the championship was lost – or thrown away – in that fateful nine-match sequence.

On April 7th, second-bottom Birmingham City travelled to Old Trafford, twenty-four points behind their hosts, and proceeded to conjure up the surprise of the season with a 2-0 victory. The diminutive Johnny Berry ran the United defence ragged after switching from the left side to the right, supplying the cross which allowed Stewart to open the scoring. Then he scurried off on a fifty-yard run which took him through the heart of the United defence, leaving him the easy task of beating Feehan from close range. It was a defeat that knocked United off top spot.

The second definitive ninety minutes came eight days later, again at Old Trafford, when Portsmouth came to town looking for revenge and points that would maintain their own title challenge. Three thousand fewer fans than had endured the Birmingham defeat made their way to the ground, and were to witness United's eighth game without a victory. Their downfall was complete, although both of Pompey's goals were not scored until the final five minutes of the game, United's attacking force reported as being "non-existent".

Back in February 1949, Matt Busby had come under fire in the *Manchester Evening Chronicle*, in a letter from a Gorton-based supporter who asked if he were afraid to drop players who were under-performing. "Players are seen to make unforgivable mistakes, passes go astray and open goals usually go where rugby teams welcome them," wrote the critic. Twelve months down the line, the United manager once again came under scrutiny when another missive to the *Chronicle* stated that the club were selling too many youngsters. The letter cited the likes of Burke (sold to Huddersfield in June 1949 for around £16,000), Buckle (sold to Everton in November 1949 for £6,500), Anderson (sold to Nottingham Forest in October 1949 for £9,000) and McMorran (who never even made the grade with United), all of whom had been allowed to depart, leaving the club with one of the weakest teams in the Central League. It was certainly a justified point, as a look at the Central League table would reveal the name of Manchester United in its lower regions, having lost half of their fixtures. The author of this second letter, however, did admit that the club were giving some of its youngsters a game at this level despite their age and inexperience, mentioning the likes of Dennis Viollet and Jeff Whitefoot, not long before the latter was propelled on to the sports pages of the national newspapers on April 15th.

"Office Boy Picked – 16, he will play for the first team" was the headline in the *News Chronicle*, with their reporter writing:

> "There was a party last night at 8 Platt Street, Cheadle, Cheshire – to celebrate the selection of 16-year-old Manchester United office boy, Jeffrey Whitefoot, to play for the First Division leaders against Portsmouth at Old Trafford this afternoon.
>
> "Jeff, who played for Stockport and England schoolboys last season is a half-back of great promise.
>
> "Since he signed amateur forms for United last August and became an office boy at the Old Trafford ground, he has graduated from the 'Colts' to the reserves for whom he has played ten games."

The article also revealed that Manchester City had approached the youngster's City-supporting father in an attempt to coax him over to Maine Road; but despite him being agreeable to the move, the lad himself wanted to remain with United.

With Whitefoot having spent the Friday night in a 'secret location' in order to escape publicity, Matt Busby told reporters: "I don't want to say where he was because we may want the same facilities again." In the circumstances, the teenager seemed unconcerned by the fuss surrounding his selection, going for an early-morning walk before opting to give the pre-match dinner at Davyhulme Golf Club a miss. Prior to kick-off, a battery of photographers surrounded the mouth of the Old Trafford tunnel awaiting his arrival on to the pitch – in fact, they actually made their way out towards the centre circle, before they were asked to leave by stand-in captain Stan Pearson.

Despite the 2-0 defeat, the youngster enjoyed a favourable ninety minutes, receiving hearty congratulations from members of the opposition at full time. An invitation to take part in the Saturday evening *Sports Special* radio programme was politely declined as Whitefoot said he wanted to go to the cinema.

Whitefoot's debut overshadowed that of another youngster, as twenty-year-old, Salford-born Tom McNulty replaced Johnny Carey at right-back, and also enjoyed a promising first-team baptism.

Youth was slowly beginning to seep through. Sixteen-year-old Cliff Birkett had been on the verge of a call-up into the senior side the previous month, and with Busby's regular post-war starting eleven beginning to age, the time was now right to be looking towards the future and justifying the comments regarding the youngsters of promise who were lurking in the levels below.

It was with much relief all round that the 1940s had finally drawn to a close, the upheaval of the Second World War allowed to fade slowly into memory. The new decade had dawned discouragingly in those fatal few weeks towards the end of season 1949-50, proving to Matt Busby that his side were perhaps just not good enough to be crowned First Division champions; but now it was hoped that the 1950s would herald a new era.

The 1949-50 close season did not disappoint, as Manchester United ventured further afield than normal on a transatlantic trip. European tours had been made in 1908 to Switzerland, Czechoslovakia, Austria and Hungry, while 1927 had again seen

United visit Switzerland, but normally a foreign trip meant Scotland or Ireland. The likes of America and Canada were certainly an adventure, and the United management never envisaged anything other than a pleasant, relaxing break. However, this early trip to distant shores produced one or two on-field problems. Sixteen players, Matt Busby, Tom Curry and directors Dr William McLean sailed across the Atlantic on the *Queen Mary* for the eleven-game tour, but not all would return.

The standard of football in Canada and America was well below that of the First Division, akin to the English Third Division according to Johnny Carey. It was of little surprise that United found the net on a regular basis, registering scores such as 5-0, 9-2 and 7-1, although there were the odd low-scoring ninety minutes as well as defeats against an FA XI (4-2) and Jonkopping (3-1). There was even a 6-6 draw against Mexican side Atlas.

Goals galore, plenty of time to relax in the New World surroundings, but lurking in New York was Englishman Percy Wynn, a representative of the Colombian side Bogota, hoping to entice one or two United players into making their fortune in South America.

"If he comes anywhere near or is found hanging around trying to entice the men, he'll end up with a smack on the nose," said the US Soccer Association executive secretary Joseph Barraskill. Matt Busby, however, was slightly more diplomatic, saying: "Neither I or any of the team has yet been contacted by Mr Percy Wynn. In any case, from the club's point of view, I should have no 'truck' with him. But I could not prevent him talking to the players if he did contact them. At the same time, I have no fear of losing any of our players. My impression is that they are simply not interested in such offers." "£3,500 a year does not tempt us," added Johnny Carey.

Little did the United manager, or his captain, realise that their opinions were about to be proved quite wrong. Having previously rejected South American advances, the close of the tour saw Charlie Mitten make a midnight dash to Bogota, leaving the United team hotel in a pre-arranged secret departure plan. He stressed that it was simply a 'look and see' visit and that he would fly back to Manchester to speak with his wife. But it turned out to be more than a flying visit to Colombia. It was soon reported that Mitten had signed a £40 per week, two-year deal, following in the footsteps of Stoke City's George Mountford and Neil Franklin – despite being contracted to United, and without consulting with his wife.

The player had been warned that he was treading a dangerous path, risking the possibility of finding himself in trouble not only with United, but also the Football Association. Matt Busby tried his best to dissuade Mitten from heading off into the unknown, but was always aware that his pleas were falling on deaf ears. In his parting shot, however, he informed the player that should he ever return to England, silently certain that he would, that his career as a United player was at an end.

Season 1950-51

For fifty-five years Louis Rocca had served Manchester United and Newton Heath football clubs, from tea-boy at 6d a week, to chief scout and a hundred and one other positions in between. His death on June 13th was mourned by all within the football club and those on the outside who knew the man "with a thousand transfer secrets", whom club secretary Walter Crickmer had dubbed "the encyclopaedia of the club".

Rocca, who in his younger days reportedly thought nothing of travelling to United away games decked out in a pair of red and white pyjamas, is believed to have secured the signing of some thirty-two players for a sum of only £4,250 and three freezers of ice cream. His pre-war captures alone conjure up a list of legendary names. Charlie Roberts, a mere snip at £750; Billy Meredith, an even bigger bargain at £150; then throw in the likes of George Wall, Alec Bell, Dick Duckworth, Sandy Turnbull and Johnny Carey. The ice cream? That was what Rocca used to persuade Stockport County to part with a talented youngster named Hughie McLenahan. Post-war, Rocca and his faithful band of scouts, schoolmasters and priests were responsible for bringing seven of the 1948 FA Cup winning team to the club.

But despite the absence of Louis Rocca around the club, the conveyor belt continued to revolve, and the summer of 1950 brought, at long last, a new goalkeeper of some repute to the club.

Prior to setting off across the Atlantic, Matt Busby had finally agreed terms with Queens Park Rangers to sign Reg Allen, who had first been targeted three years before. A fee of £10,000 was to bring the twenty-eight-year-old former commando, and prisoner of war, north.

Having returned home from their 16,000-mile working holiday, there were only days rather than weeks for the players to spend relaxing with their families before the big kick-off. The new First Division campaign began with Fulham's visit to Old Trafford. The journey back across the Atlantic had given Busby time to consider his options with the departure of Mitten, but as per the past four seasons, his team practically picked itself.

Jack Crompton found himself in the Central League side as Reg Allen immediately became the first choice keeper. Carey, having finished the previous season at right-half, returned to his familiar right-back role, partnered by Johnny Aston. Chilton and Cockburn made up two-thirds of the half-back line, the trio completed by another new addition in Eddie McIlvenny, a former Scottish junior player who had joined Wrexham in 1947 before moving to the States two years later to live with his sister. It wasn't long before he was again pulling on his boots, teaming up with the Philadelphia Nationals, and it was while playing against United for his new team that he had caught Matt Busby's eye.

Delaney, Downie, Rowley and Pearson remained the mainstays of the front line, but somewhat surprisingly Busby decided to play Billy McGlen in the vacant outside-left spot. A position totally alien to him, but one to which he soon adapted and indeed held on to for the opening seven games. McIlvenny, however, was not so fortunate, disappearing from view after only one more outing.

Beating Fulham 1-0 on that opening Saturday brought smiles all round, although the headline in the *Manchester Evening Chronicle* Saturday 'Pink' read – "United Miss Mitten and Fulham Miss the Goals". But three defeats in the opening seven games soon knocked the team's confidence and prompted Matt Busby to look for a competent winger – a player who would never bear comparison to the departed Mitten, but who would offer something in the way of stability to his beleaguered team.

In the third game of the season, Bolton had recorded a 1-0 victory at Burnden Park, the Lanarkshire-born Harry McShane enjoying an excellent afternoon on the home side's left flank. It was a performance which nudged Busby into enquiring about his availability, before stepping in and securing his signature with full-back Johnny Ball moving in the opposite direction.

Whether it was all down to McShane's presence is debatable, but there followed an immediate improvement in form, with only one defeat in the following nine outings. Whilst not exactly turning in headline performances, the 3-1 victory over Sheffield Wednesday, in which McShane scored his second goal for the club, kept United only a point behind leaders Arsenal.

Since the return to League football after the war, United's form had received much praise, so it was inevitable that international recognition would be awarded to a number of the first team regulars. Carey, Cockburn, Pearson, Aston, Chilton, Rowley and Delaney all received call-ups from their respective countries. Being selected for international duty was an honour to the club as well as the player, but it wasn't without its problems, as international fixtures would often be played on a Saturday afternoon. International weekends caused havoc with a manager's team selection, but did at least allow members of the Central League side the opportunity to grab a rare ninety minutes of first-team football.

Against Sheffield Wednesday, with Aston and Chilton on international duty, Busby blooded another two of his talented youngsters, twenty-year-old Billy Redman and seventeen-year-old Mark Jones, neither of whom showed any signs of nerves. The Barnsley-born, former England schoolboy international Jones caught the eye more than his fellow debutant, but both young understudies proved capable of stepping into the spotlight and holding their own. It was a sight that augured well for the future, as those current first-team regulars were certainly not getting any younger.

A 3-0 defeat by Arsenal at Highbury offered a clear hint that Busby had still not found that elusive formula that would deliver the title – a fact underlined by a calamitous December which saw only three points obtained from the six fixtures played. Christmas itself was nothing short of disastrous, with little in the way of goodwill and festive cheer. Santa Claus by-passed Old Trafford altogether as back-to-back fixtures against Sunderland both ended in defeats, 2-1 at Roker Park on Christmas Day and a calamitous 5-3 Boxing Day reversal at Old Trafford.

Busby was clearly in a quandary, not simply seeking a run of victories but also the players to enable him to obtain those results. An influx of new blood was perhaps the answer. Whether it came via the cheque book or from the reserve and junior sides was immaterial, as the Manchester United first eleven was now beginning to show one or two cracks, and something had to be done before the matter became more serious.

Jimmy Delaney, the bargain buy who had proven he was far from 'past it', had left the club in November, returning north to join Aberdeen for a fee of £3,500 – £500 less than Busby had paid for him back in 1946. It was a move that had been in the pipeline for some time, as Delaney had hinted to 'Waverley' of the *Daily Record* the previous year that he would not be averse to returning to Scotland, the wheels being set in motion for the actual transfer following a friendly between United and Aberdeen in September. The Scottish journalist had only recently recalled the chat with Delaney, Matt Busby and Derby County's Billy Steel following the opening fixture of season 1949-50 when he said that all three had admitted that they would be happy to return north (Steel later joined Dundee). Apparently Busby had also hinted that Dundee and Celtic were two clubs that interested him. The latter was strenuously rejected by chairman Bob Kelly, although the mere hint of Busby's interest was enough to cause a family rift between those in charge at Celtic Park.

'Waverley' was one of the old-school football journalists from a bygone age, who were light years away from their modern day counterparts who have access to so much more than a shared telephone and a notebook and pen. But those essayists of yesteryear converted the ninety minutes of a football match into a literary art form. One such member of the press box crowd who followed United around the country was Eric Thompson of the *Daily Mail*. Thompson took the 'art form' part to heart, and being a gifted cartoonist would often add a caricature to his reports. But when it came to prose description of the action, few could touch Don Davies, who wrote under the pen-name of 'An Old International' for the *Guardian*.

Davies was a keen observer of the game, with Manchester United often under his microscope, while he also found Matt Busby a character worthy of study. Of the United manager, he was to write:

"Assuming that success depends on the following factors: 1. Personal qualities, 2. First-hand knowledge of the game at top level, 3. Ability to instruct, 4. Ability to handle men, 5. A reasonable share of good fortune, then Matt Busby would appear to be singularly well-blessed on all counts.

"He is readily accessible to the humblest of his playing staff as to his Chairman of Directors and treats everyone, even press men, with patience, courtesy and good humour, yet, oddly enough, ever since he came to Old Trafford he has been known to the players as 'The Boss', a striking example of inherent persuasiveness being known by its opposite.

"A willingness to experiment has been one of Matt Busby's characteristics from the start. Mr Busby is no indoor manager glued to his desk. He prefers to don his tracksuit and join in the practice session with his players, criticising, encouraging and instructing. His chief assistant, Mr James Murphy, is a man of the same mould.

"From observations made, it would appear that these two mainly concern themselves with field tactics and match strategy, since a good deal of the practice is gained under the match conditions, leaving the training in basic skills to the club coach, Mr Bert Whalley, who takes the players in hand as soon as they are accepted for the youth team. The fact that Matt Busby as a player was not immediately successful, and had to pass through years of keen disappointment and bitter struggle, has probably added to his value as a manager. His shrewd psychological insight into the trouble of his young charges, coupled with his depth of understanding and generosity of nature, made him the ideal father confessor.

"But he makes it clear that while he is ready to pay generously for loyal service, he puts the interests of the club before that of any individual, and that no player, however eminent, will hold his place in the side unless he can be said to deliver the goods."

All well and good, and having replaced Delaney with Tommy Bogan and then seventeen-year-old Cliff Birkett, Busby almost immediately had to find a replacement for the injured Jack Rowley. He surprised everyone by switching left-back John Aston to centre-forward and moving Billy McGlen, who had begun the season at outside-left, into Aston's defensive slot. Strangely enough, Aston flourished in what turned out to be a permanent move until the end of the season, scoring fourteen goals in his twenty-two League outings. His performances prompted suggestions that he could even add to his international caps with appearances in his 'new' position, whilst he also picked up a *News Chronicle* player of the month award in January.

Aston's switch did not go down well in all quarters, however, as the letters page in the *News Chronicle* was to show. Upon his return from injury, Jack Rowley now had to be content with the outside-left spot. While praising Busby's foresight, many were quick to point out that due to the player's absence at the back, goals were being leaked. It was also felt that there was a distinct lack of cover in the reserve side, which continued to flounder in the bottom half of the Central League. One of those who wrote to the paper summed up the situation perfectly: "We have the best crop of youngsters ever, but until they are ready for first team duty in a season or so, we need at least two experienced forwards to hold the fort."

If those youngsters of promise were needing some encouragement as they strode along the stony road to the professional ranks, they were certainly given it on the evening of Thursday January 25th 1951 when instead of their usual training session at the Cliff in Lower Broughton, they found themselves lining up alongside, or against, Matt Busby, now aged forty-two, together with Jimmy Murphy. The manager and trainer had donned their boots for a ground-breaking fixture – "what was probably the most important football match seen in the North since the war" wrote George Follows of the *Daily Herald*, as it was played under floodlights. "Although it was not the first floodlight football match in the North, it was the first with powerful backing. It may be regarded as the real opening of the floodlit era," continued Follows, who quoted Busby as enthusing "Perfect. No playing difficulties at all," when asked his opinion at full time. Busby also exclaimed, "I think this is the way that football will be played in the future. It speeds up the game for the spectators, gives practically everybody the chance to watch midweek matches."

Installed on eight 35-foot poles evenly spaced along each side of the pitch and about twenty feet back from the touchline, each pole carried two pairs of £500, 1,500 watt lamps. It was estimated that the cost of powering them over the course of the ninety minutes was 7/6d. Certainly money well spent.

The United manager was not the only one to speak enthusiastically about the venture, as referee Gordon Gibson said it was, "much better than many Saturday afternoon matches I have had. A big help to the players I should say, as because with the ground blacked out behind the lights disturbing crowd effects are lessened." While from a spectator's point of view, "the white ball was easy to follow, easier than in the average Saturday afternoon match, except when a very high ball passed 'through' a light. It would also cut out many press-box inquests on 'who scored?'"

The disappointments of December were soon forgotten as the New Year kicked off with a 4-1 FA Cup victory over Oldham Athletic before moving into an unbeaten twelve-game run in the League, propelling United from eleventh at the end of December 1950 to second at the end of March 1951, four points behind leaders Tottenham. The run was kick-started with a 2-1 victory over the League leaders, and saw only one draw. It was augmented by FA Cup victories against Leeds United (4-0) and Arsenal (1-0), but the sixth round was to bring a surprise 1-0 defeat at Birmingham City, leaving the championship as the only avenue open to success.

Sadly, any hopes that the championship could be snatched from Tottenham's grasp were shattered on April 7th with a 2-0 defeat at Stoke. Even twelve goals in the following three fixtures were rendered meaningless, as that defeat in the Potteries was to prove crucial – especially as the leaders slipped up seven days later with a 2-0 defeat at home to Huddersfield, coupled with a 4-1 final day home defeat at the hands of Blackpool.

United brought down the curtain with a 1-1 draw at Blackpool, leaving them four points behind Tottenham and cursing, once again, the failure to capture that elusive First Division title due to a poor run of results over a four-week period. Matt Busby still had much work to do if he was to capture the title he so craved.

Season 1951-52

Although the 1950-51 campaign had only just disappeared over the horizon and been confined to the records books, Manchester United continued to look to the future. As the *Manchester Evening Chronicle* revealed: "United Sign Five Boy Stars: Summer Coaching Plan", this alongside photographs of the five hopefuls, three Salford schoolboys – Colman, Marsden and McLoughlan – and two Manchester schoolboys, Lowry and Beale. Alf Clarke reported:

> "Once again Manchester United have swooped on star members of the local boys' teams and are the only club in the country operating a close-season coaching school. This development of youth is the answer to the big transfers.
>
> "'We established a team off the field as well as on it' enthused Jimmy Murphy. 'People like Joe Armstrong our chief scout and Bert Whalley our chief coach. God was with us and soon the kids started coming through as if off some conveyor belt. It was like seeing little apples grow.
>
> "'When I started as a youngster you had to stand on your own two feet and you got precious little help from anyone. It was a man's world and professional soccer was largely the survival of the fittest.
>
> "'My method was always to allow a youngster to play quite freely for the first four or five months after he joins, to give him time to develop his own talents. His style must not be cramped by immediately demanding of him that he should do this and not do that.

135

"'I always insisted on free expression in that initial settling-in period. That doesn't mean I ignored the boys. Far from it, I was always watching very intently and then after a period I would have assessed exactly what line to take with each individual.'"

But the net wasn't simply cast across Manchester and its environs, as what was taking place at Old Trafford was being noticed around the country – including Jimmy Murphy's old Midlands stomping ground where one Vic Homer[5] contacted Murphy regarding a promising youngster he had come across on his doorstep.

Stan Dunn was a 'Black Country' boy who had progressed from his schools side to Quarry Bank Celtic. His performances at inside-right had caught Homer's eye, which had taken him to the verge of becoming a Manchester United player.

"There was a football scout known to us all who lived in the area and although I have no idea what his links were to the big clubs or how he came to be 'authorised' to scout for players, it transpired that he was a 'recognised' scout for Manchester United. His name was Vic Homer. At the time he noticed me I was also noticed by Stourbridge Football Club.

"Vic was a local man who had an air of superiority about him. He worked for the local car company so probably got this attitude from the fact that he earned more than the average man in our area. Anyway, he got me a trial with United and I travelled up there with another local youngster called Alan Dunn, whose father drove us up to Manchester. Upon arrival we met with another youngster up for a trial – David Pegg – and were taken to a boarding house not far from the ground where Mark Jones was also lodging.

"Eventually we got to play a match. I remember I played inside-right and Dennis Viollet was on the right wing. Matt Busby himself was watching the game.

---

5 Possibly the brother of former United player Tom Homer, as he hailed from the area.

"At the end of the game Matt Busby told me I played well but, in effect, he had younger lads who were as good. Two years in the Forces had set me at a disadvantage from my fellow players. I returned home, but a series of correspondence ensued between me and Jimmy Murphy.

"He wrote to me in April 1951 saying: 'Heard from Vic today. He told me you had started work. I'm just returning from Ireland, have been there just a week. Unfortunately Stan, we have no fixtures left this season. However Stan, you can sign the enclosed form and I'll send for you in July or August, whichever suits you. You have a grand chance here and great opportunities. All good wishes, Jimmy Murphy'.

"Shortly afterwards, in response to my letter voicing my concerns over signing on the dotted line and committing myself, Jimmy wrote: '...You don't want to have any fears Stanley about this signing forms etc. If you don't come up to our expectations I'll very soon tell you and your form will be cancelled immediately. August will soon roll round and you can have a few games with us as I've said before there is an excellent chance for you here – I mean this.'

"I didn't take up my place in the squad. My dad had died when I was just 15 and my place was with my sister and my mum. I had, as Jimmy mentioned in his letters, taken up a position working at the local Co-operative Mutual Society and was earning money in an assured job and our lives were secure.

"Alan Dunn, the young player who I had travelled up to the trial with, was taken on by United and I believe played up to Central League standard – eventually returning to his local side Kinver Harriers.

"I look back on those years with mixed feelings. What if my dad had been around to push me when I went for the trials at United? What if I hadn't had to be the bread-winner? What if I hadn't had to do national service and could have done those trials when I was 18 instead of 20? What if I had given it a go...taken up that opportunity that Jimmy presented to me in those letters?"

Regrets! And there were even more at Old Trafford as the failure to claim the First Division title was becoming much more than a frustration: the runners-up spot, achieved in four of the last five seasons, was like an itch that would not go away. Age was now going against many of Busby's first-choice starting line-up, with the opportunity to claim a championship medal growing fainter with each passing season. But despite those concerns, the first match of the 1951-52 season against West Bromwich Albion saw virtually no change from the eleven compared to the team that had kicked the last ball of the previous season against Blackpool. Only John Aston was missing, as he recovered from a cartilage operation.

There was one individual who would have liked to have been included in that opening fixture, but Charlie Mitten had accepted the money on offer from South America and was now paying the price for his decision, having returned home to find himself fined £250 and banned from playing until the end of the year. Unable to earn a living from kicking a ball anywhere, he wasn't even allowed to train with United or any other club until November 1st.

"The only reason I decided to return was the education of my children," said Mitten. "The Santa Fe club were very disappointed when I told them I was leaving and immediately offered me £1,000 on top of my £5,000 contract to remain." He was also to admit that he would like to play for United again, stating: "I know the rest of the players would welcome me back, but what the club decides is another matter." Whether Busby would have taken him back was another question altogether.

Had Mitten rejected the advances of the South Americans, he would have been in line to join his fellow United players in receiving a wage increase as the maximum wage rose from £12 to £14 (although the close season wage remained at £10 per week). Some clubs were aggrieved at this addition to their weekly expenditure, but were quick to claw back at least some of their outgoings, agreeing by "an overwhelming majority" to an increase in general admission charges.

West Bromwich Albion stated that if player benefits and other add-ons were taken into account, then players could actually receive nearer to £17 per week rather than the stated £12. Meanwhile

Cardiff City bemoaned the fact that only a very small part of the extra three pennies taken at the gate would actually go towards the wage increase. Sunderland, on the other hand, wanted to increase bonus payments from £2 to £6 for League wins, with £3 for a draw instead of the current £1. Needless to say, no-one else was interested in this suggestion.

But who needed Charlie Mitten when they had Jack Rowley? Reinstated to the number nine jersey, he snatched a hat-trick in the opening day 3-3 draw with West Bromwich Albion. Having given United the lead after nine minutes, he was as stunned as his team-mates when the home side took a 3-1 lead just after half-time. His second goal offered some hope, and the third in the 81st minute gave the visitors a hard-earned point.

Another Rowley hat-trick four days later, along with a Stan Pearson goal, gave United a 4-2 win over Middlesbrough, the deadly inside-forward going on to make it nine goals in four games with a single in the 2-1 defeat of Newcastle and a double in the return against Middlesbrough. The latter 4-1 win left United level at the top with near neighbours Bolton. The Burnden Park side were, however, to edge in front three days later courtesy of a controversial Lofthouse goal in United's first defeat of the season. A *Guardian* correspondent wrote that the "high expectations of a great match were not realised", going on to say that although both defences were on top, United were unfortunate not to grasp a point.

Missing for that short trip to Bolton was Harry McShane, his place taken by a rare United signing in Johnny Berry from Birmingham City. Twenty-four-year-old Berry, a former cinema projectionist, had been a thorn in United's side on more than one occasion, in particular scoring what he considered to be his "finest goal" at Old Trafford on Good Friday the previous year. Although he had only joined the professional ranks six years before, his career was halted due to national service in India with the Royal Artillery, and he had soon made a name for himself as one of the fastest wingers in the game. Since losing the services of Jimmy Delaney, Matt Busby had been on the lookout for a replacement and with Berry's name already pencilled into his notebook, enquiries were made and a fee of £15,000 took the player to Old Trafford.

But that 1-0 defeat at Bolton was nothing more than a minor setback as the following four games produced victories over Charlton Athletic (2-1 at Old Trafford), Stoke City (4-0, also at home) and 2-1 against City at Maine Road, along with a 2-2 draw against Charlton at the Valley. The victory over City gave United a one-point advantage at the top over Aston Villa.

It was, however, only mid-September and consecutive defeats at Tottenham and at home to Preston North End saw them tumble back down to sixth, and by the end of November they had also lost against Sunderland and Portsmouth at Old Trafford and against Chelsea at Stamford Bridge. Only the goals of Downie, Pearson and Rowley now kept them within touching distance of the top.

The two consecutive defeats against Chelsea (4-2) and Portsmouth, the First Division leaders (3-1), forced Matt Busby into reassessing his first choice eleven, both in the long term, and more immediately for the visit to Anfield on November 24th. After much deliberation and consultation with Murphy and Whalley, out went Billy Redman and Don Gibson and in for their League debuts came another two youngsters from the Central League side, twenty-two-year-old Roger Byrne and eighteen-year-old Irishman Jackie Blanchflower. Jack Crompton also returned to the fold in place of Reg Allen.

"New boys win spurs" proclaimed the headline in the *Evening Chronicle*, and from the pen of Alf Clarke came: "Blanchflower was playing soundly and his first-time tackling was effective." But it was Byrne who had really caught the eye, the reporter from the *Guardian* telling his readers: "No one in the Manchester defence did better than Byrne, who in his first big match kicked admirably with both feet, positioned himself well against the speedy Jackson and in at least one instance showed the coolness of Carey himself." For Blanchflower, it was a one-off appearance, but Byrne had consolidated his place in the side for the remainder of the season.

Although it was nothing to shout about, the goalless draw at Anfield heralded the start of an unbeaten sixteen-game run, albeit augmented with a further five draws. It was enough to haul United to the top of the table, holding a point advantage over Arsenal, who United had defeated 3-1 at Highbury on December 8th, a victory that cemented their credentials as title challengers.

"When the mud-soaked Manchester United players walked off the pitch at the end of the game against Arsenal at Highbury, they received and deserved the ovation from the home spectators for their 3-1 victory" wrote the *Guardian* correspondent, who went on to use up more ink in writing: "At times, however, the football was as tempestuous as the weather and when the referee twisted his ankle he was replaced by a linesman who had to keep a firm hand on the game and one or two players, one of whom distinguished himself only by his rudeness.

"The dominating factor, however, was the leadership of Carey. The crash and thunder of attacks left Carey serene and undisturbed: shrewd in anticipating a pass or going cleanly into a tackle, he invariably obtained possession of the ball, then cool, poised and debonair he would glide past opponents and drive or flick adroit passes neatly to the feet or heads of his forwards. His effortless style, intelligent moves, and good manners stamp him as an aristocrat of the game."

Despite the first team's championship challenge, the reserves struggled aimlessly in the Central League, although those who attended such fixtures wallowed in watching those teenage prodigies learning their trade. But as the season moved towards the home stretch there were to be no further debutants as Busby now had a relatively settled side, in personnel if not in actual positions. There was also a clear run ahead due to the surprise 2-0 FA Cup defeat against Hull City at Old Trafford.

That defeat is best summed up in the words of Don Davies:

"Hull City gave a display of all-round excellence, marred, perhaps, by a few excesses due to cup-tie exuberance. To say that the Cup favourites met their Waterloo would be both trite and trivial. Say rather that they met their Marathon, their Arbela, their Hastings, their Pultowa, their Blenheim, their Saratoga – their anything and everything you like up to the limit of the fifteen decisive battles of the world.

Not since United merged as one of the great club sides of the post-war era have they been seen to such grievous disadvantage."

On a snow-covered Old Trafford on January 26th an own goal by Alf Ramsey and a Stan Pearson strike five minutes from time saw reigning champions Tottenham beaten 2-0, a result that lifted United into top spot on goal average. A week later, they were a point in front following a 2-1 win at Preston, with a 3-0 victory over Derby seven days later being proclaimed as 'championship form'.

A 1-1 draw at home to Aston Villa rocked the boat, but created no lasting damage and failed to dislodge United off the top as the campaign moved into its final two months. Could Matt Busby finally guide his team to that elusive title? If they were to fail, it would certainly not be for the lack of determination which was clearly displayed in the 2-1 victory at Roker Park on March 8th.

After going a goal behind to a Ford penalty in the 14th minute and then being futher handicapped by a Rowley groin injury, the game was played out mostly in the Sunderland half. Yet despite numerable opportunities it began to look as though the 'lucky' blue shirts of the visitors would have to be binned upon their return to Manchester. Then, with ninety seconds remaining, Rowley managed to scramble an equaliser to the delight of the numerous travelling support, who were still in the throes of celebrating when a Rowley corner swung into the goalmouth and Cockburn hit the winner.

With many now predicting that it was finally going to be Busby's year, opinions were swiftly revised after the ensuing successive defeats. A misunderstanding between Chilton and Crompton gifted Huddersfield both points in a 3-2 defeat, while on the south coast fellow title challengers Portsmouth won 1-0.

Six games remained and despite those two defeats United remained on top with 47 points from 36 games. Arsenal sat second with 47 from 35, with Portsmouth in third on 46 points from their 37 games. The stage was set for a rousing finale.

But Busby was now concerned, worried that once again the title was about to slip through his fingers. He craved the title, not simply for personal satisfaction, but for the players who had given so much over the past five or so years and also to dedicate it to the memory of James Gibson, the late chairman who had died back in September. Gibson had steered the club through some troubled times following his appointment in 1932, plunging his hands into his own pockets to come up with the necessary cash, free of interest, to tide things over. He was also a close ally of Busby's, as would be his successor, the astute Harold Hardman.

Looking for that cutting edge, the vital spark that would ignite the push for the title, Busby decided to make three positional changes to his usual starting eleven for the game at Burnley on Good Friday. He switched John Aston back to his more familiar left-back position for the first time since he had returned to the side at centre-forward in mid-January; Jack Rowley moved from the wing into the centre, and Roger Byrne moved down the left flank to take over the outside-left berth. This wasn't an entirely alien position for the Gorton lad, having played further up the field as a youngster; although not exactly a skilful attacker, he was quick on his feet and would cause any defender problems.

This he certainly did with a headed goal earning United a point at Turf Moor, followed by a double in the 4-0 home defeat of Liverpool twenty-four hours later. "The game was a personal triumph for Roger Byrne," penned Henry Jones of the *Sunday Express*, "a boy who should become one of the team's brightest stars if he has not already arrived." Byrne's star rose considerably higher in the Mancunian sky with another two goals in the Easter Monday 6-1 hammering of Burnley in the return fixture at Old Trafford.

United were now two points ahead of Arsenal, the Londoners having slipped up with a 0-0 draw at Blackpool on Good Friday, followed by a 2-1 defeat at Bolton twenty-four hours later, although staying in contention with a 4-1 win over Blackpool on Easter Monday. They were soon to pull within a point after drawing their game in hand with Newcastle, their fourth game in six days. By teatime on the Saturday they were level after defeating Stoke 4-1, as United could only scramble a point in a 2-2 draw at Blackpool, where Byrne was once again on the scoresheet.

So, with two fixtures remaining it was level pegging. United had to entertain Chelsea at home on the penultimate Saturday, while Arsenal travelled to West Bromwich Albion. Then came what could well be the title decider with the Gunners travelling to Old Trafford on that final afternoon of the season.

Against Chelsea, United were anxious at times and wasteful, with passes going astray and long-range shots failing to hit their target. For twenty-three minutes they stuttered along before Rowley, falling from a tackle by a Chelsea defender, managed to flick the ball into the path of Pearson who blasted the ball past Robertson from twenty-five yards. Prior to the interval, a rare Carey goal gave United a 2-0 lead. With Arsenal losing by a similar scoreline, everything looked rosy.

A ferocious shot from Cockburn hit McKnight on the head and spun into the Chelsea net to make it three, then Byrne blotted his copybook with a penalty miss three minutes from time. Thankfully it mattered little as Arsenal had slumped to a 3-1 defeat at the Hawthorns. United were all but champions.

To prise the League championship trophy out of United's grasp, Arsenal had to win 7-0 on their visit to Manchester, an impossible task, with little need for the home support to ransack drawers and cupboards for lucky charms and talismans. The Londoners had already thrown in the towel, their manager Tom Whittaker and captain Joe Mercer both sending Matt Busby telegrams saying, "All at Arsenal send you congratulations on a worthy championship win," as the players, backroom staff and directors celebrated the victory over Chelsea in the Old Trafford boardroom.

Much to the surprise of many, there were indeed seven goals at Old Trafford on that last Saturday afternoon of the 1951-52 season, but as the *Manchester Evening Chronicle* Saturday 'Pink' headlines revealed – "Six Goal United Thrash Arsenal, to Make Sure of the Title" – the Londoners were to return home with only a Cup Final appearance to look forward to.

Attacking the Stretford End, it took only eight minutes for Rowley to open the scoring. Byrne, clearly relishing his new found lease of life on the left wing, was quickly into the action and within eight minutes of the kick-off, any hopes that Arsenal and their followers had of snatching the championship were thrown to the wind when Carey lobbed the ball into the visitors' goalmouth, where Pearson rose to head it backwards to the feet of Jack Rowley who fired home. It could quite easily have been Arsenal who had taken the lead, but after having dribbled some forty yards down the left wing, Roper's long ball into the United area went behind before Cox could get to it.

Moments later, the crowd were again screaming "Goal!" as Rowley pounced on a deflected shot from Carey, but his effort cannoned off the underside of Swindin's crossbar, bouncing precariously on the goal line. Appeals were made that the ball had crossed the line, but the referee waved play on and the ball ended up being kicked into the side netting.

Rowley was denied by Shaw, Downie was upended by Mercer before he could shoot and another Rowley effort flew across the face of the Arsenal goal. It was surely just a matter of time before United would score a second.

But it wasn't until five minutes before the interval that the second goal came. Forbes, having taken a knock, was lying injured as the ball was quickly moved forward towards the visitors' goal. Pearson gained possession and his shot seemed to take a deflection off Mercer as it flew past the stranded Swindin and into the net.

Two minutes later, it was 3-0. Rowley collected the ball on the byline midway between the corner flag and the Arsenal goal and, through sheer determination, dribbled past one white-shirted defender, then another, and as Swindin moved forward to block his route to goal, he unselfishly pushed the ball back to Byrne, who had nothing more to do than side-foot it into an unguarded net.

A suspected fractured wrist kept Shaw in the visitors' dressing room as the second half got underway, but despite being reduced to ten men, it was Arsenal who enjoyed the best of the play in the opening minutes with a shot from Roper going narrowly wide. But United soon regained their poise and only a double save from Swindin, beating down a Byrne centre before grasping the ball as both Rowley and Cockburn moved in, prevented yet another goal.

Both keepers were kept busy, while Downie and Rowley were denied goals by a raised linesman's flag. Byrne and Carey both spurned good opportunities, but the crowd were brought back to life in the seventy-fourth minute when Rowley scored United's fourth, running on to a forward pass from Carey before calmly lifting the ball over the advancing keeper's head and into the net.

Two minutes later, there was a fifth goal, but this time it was for ten-man Arsenal, Cox beating Allen from close in after Holton had created the opening. The goal brought polite applause from the home support.

With eight minutes still to play, Rowley claimed his hat-trick with a rather dubious penalty award for his record-breaking thirtieth goal of the season – and in the final minute, with Arsenal depleted further, the nine men conceded a sixth goal, man-of-the-match Rowley setting up Stan Pearson who slammed the ball home.

As the final whistle blew, there was an enthusiastic pitch invasion by a vast number of supporters, both young and old, and amid the confusion and chaos, the Beswick Prize Band struck up "See the Conquering Heroes Come", which was obviously note perfect, as they had been practising it now for a considerable number of years! As the players struggled through the throngs of supporters, the band rounded off with "Auld Lang Syne", before being almost trampled underfoot by the ever increasing numbers.

"We want Carey!" shouted the crowd congregated around the mouth of the tunnel; but they were to be disappointed as neither the United captain nor any of his team-mates appeared. Disappointed, they then drifted off in the direction of the station, to the long line of buses on Chester Road and Trafford Road, or simply to the nearest pub to celebrate United's first post-war championship success. The United players, having got scrubbed and changed, were later to make their way to Manchester Town Hall, where the Lord Mayor held a civic reception in their honour.

"A marvellous job," proclaimed Matt Busby. "After many disappointments they've at last got there. They've never stopped driving straight for that title. They've never let up."

But what was the major factor behind the success, other than the manager? In the *Sunday Express*, Alan Hoby wrote of:

"...their phenomenal, almost incredible cycle of success, is the consistency and collective coolness of their more seasoned players such as Rowley, Pearson, Chilton and the human atom bomb Henry Cockburn. With United lucky in possessing one of the greatest players of all time as captain and leader – 33-year-old Johnny Carey, who looks older than he is.

"At the season's start, a few terrace morons barracked Carey when he was playing full-back before manager Busby moved him to right-half 'to give the team more construction' and if there is a footballer living who can pull the ball down, kill it cleanly and roll it on to a colleague as beautifully and meticulously as can the cool, classical and cultured Carey, I have yet to see him."

Hoby added that Busby's ability to switch players around was United's secret weapon, while at the same time keeping the players mentally alert.

If there was a downside to the season it had come back on September 11th, when chairman James Gibson died, sadly not living to see the realisation of his dream: Manchester United finally reaching the summit of the Football League. Had it not been for Gibson coming to the club's rescue with much-needed finance back in those dismal days of the early 1930s, who knows where they would have ended up. But despite his absence from board meetings since the summer of 1950, it would have given Gibson much satisfaction and pleasure to hear that, through his astute business management, the club had finally become debt-free.

Into his shoes stepped Harold Hardman, a noted footballer himself, the task of continuing Gibson's good work an opportunity he relished.

Chapter Five

Sow and Ye Shall Reap –
Seasons 1952-53 – 1955-56

'MANCHESTER United – First Division Champions' had a nice ring to it. The latter three words were a perfect complement to the first two; but could that 1951-52 success be the first of many title triumphs in the post-war era? Could United throw aside the inconsistency that had blighted the recent past? Had all those odd, silly points not been unexpectedly dropped, the Old Trafford honours board could have read quite differently. Matt Busby, whilst glowing in that hour of triumph, still had numerous concerns.

At the 1952 Annual General Meeting he admitted that despite gaining the title, "The club's future left no cause for optimism unless radical changes were made." It was obvious not only to the manager but to those who passed through the Old Trafford turnstiles. His team was ageing, and United were now facing a transitional period. Busby confessed:

> "The depressing thought which used to trouble me day and night, was the great Manchester United side was getting old. Chilton, Cockburn, Pearson and Rowley, all these wonderful footballers, and others besides, were reaching the age when I had to think about replacing them. Had I not been so honest with myself, I might have been content to rest on my League laurels, play the over-thirty stars for

a few more seasons, hoping that something would turn up in the meantime."

For the time being at least, Busby began the defence of the title with the same squad of players, replacing Crompton and Cockburn with Wood and Gibson for the opening fixture against Chelsea at Old Trafford. The 2-0 victory, against a ten-man opposition for all of seventy-eight minutes, was far from notable with United considered "awkward" by one member of the press. They soon found that everyone wanted to prove something against the champions, and that defending their crown would be a considerable task: only one point was taken from the following four fixtures. A draw and a defeat against Arsenal were augmented by further defeats against City and Portsmouth. The results left United fourth from bottom.

That early season gloom was lifted with victories over Derby and Bolton, where Jack Rowley spent seventeen minutes as a stand-in keeper following a finger injury to Reg Allen, with a draw against Villa and the 4-2 FA Charity Shield victory over cup-winners Newcastle United putting a smile back on the faces of the Old Trafford faithful. But a 7-3 defeat at Easter Road, Edinburgh, in a benefit match for Hibernian winger Gordon Smith soon re-opened those so obvious cracks, albeit amid some 'remarkable' refereeing decisions.

Sunderland left Trafford Park with both points following a 1-0 win, as did Stoke a fortnight later, having won 2-0 – while sandwiched in between was a harrowing 6-2 defeat at Wolverhampton, where Alf Clarke of the *Evening Chronicle* stated that "United threw the game away through some of the weakest defensive work I have ever seen." Busby certainly had problems, both on and off the pitch, as he was then confronted by a transfer request from Roger Byrne.

Despite having finished the previous season in a blaze of glory on the left wing, this season had failed to produce any goals from the left flank, amid average performances hampered by the player's annoyance at continually being played up front. Although more than happy as to be involved in the first team's success, Byrne did not enjoy playing out of what he considered his natural position. After much deliberation, he decided that a transfer request was the only solution to his unhappiness at having to wear the number eleven shirt.

To the surprise of many, the club agreed to his request, bringing cries of derision from the terraces. "Have the management taken leave of their senses?" queried one supporter. "Here we have United's best left full-back up for sale because he is dissatisfied with being played out of position. Byrne does not want to play on the wing and rightly so. After all, he is a full-back." Alf Clarke, on the other hand, agreed with the club, citing John Aston's centre-forward escapades as an example to Byrne. The majority, however, sided with the player.

Matt Busby had previously shown his strength in management, standing firm on his beliefs when he felt himself being questioned, by moving Johnny Morris, an integral part of that 1948 side, on to pastures new. But with Byrne, who he left out of the side for the games against Wolves and Stoke, he clearly saw something in the player and the person that he felt he could not do without. Ultimately, he decided to restore the Gorton boy to his preferred left-back position, resulting in the transfer request being withdrawn.

Playing Byrne on the wing was always just a temporary measure, despite the player seeing it differently, and Busby's search for an outside-left had taken him to Easter Road in the hope of persuading Eddie Turnbull to leave Hibs. But just when it looked as though a deal was about to be agreed the player decided that he wanted to remain in Edinburgh. Davis of Sunderland and Henderson of Portsmouth were other noted targets for the number eleven shirt, which would allow Rowley to be moved back into the centre, but the former's part-time job stalled any move and the interest in the latter disappeared into thin air.

Although Byrne's return coincided with a 5-0 victory at Preston, Burnley left Old Trafford seven days later having won 3-1 and performances continued to be unimpressive, particularly at home, despite scoring some victories. Results at Central League level, like those of previous seasons, continued to be indifferent with the foot of the table never far from view. This in reality bothered no one as it was considered little more than a stepping stone between the juniors and the first team, a queue forming to see who could be the next to take those testing steps.

Seventeen-year-old Eddie Lewis was first to be given the nod, claiming the number nine shirt against West Bromwich Albion on November 29th and marking his debut with a seventh-minute goal. Although he did not retain his place following that favourable debut, he was soon to get further opportunities to prove his worth, going on to notch up seven goals in his ten outings.

Lewis had joined United in 1949, having taken part in a summer coaching school, before joining the MUJACs set-up. However, he soon found himself playing for Bolton Wanderers as his father felt that his progress at Old Trafford was too slow – a point emphasised when he scored the winner for his new club against United. A couple of days later, Jimmy Murphy and Bert Whalley were knocking on the Lewis front door, persuading the father to let his son return to Old Trafford. "I was happy to return," said the youngster.

There was now a scramble to reach the door of the first-team dressing room and, seven days later against Middlesbrough, both John Doherty and David Pegg found their names on the seniors' teamsheet for the first time. The former had a hand in Aston's goal in the 3-1 win, but it was the appearance of Pegg, a former England schoolboy international, that brought some relief to Busby: the emergence of the Doncaster-born winger meant the end to his problems trying to fill the outside-left spot. A further seven days down the line came the debut of twenty-year-old Bill Foulkes at Liverpool and, although up against Scottish international Billy Liddell, he settled well, doing enough to show that he also had a future at the club. But what was life like for those young wannabes? Eddie Lewis recalled:

"In the summer months we trained on a Tuesday and Thursday at the Henshaws Blind Institute. During the season, however, Sunday was for treatment for injuries and any player who did not turn up got fined and was dropped for the next game. Monday was generally our day off, but we were so unbelievably keen that we'd go to Old Trafford in the morning and play a game of six-a-side for a couple of hours before going to Davyhulme Golf Club for an often amusing round of golf. We'd pass by the adjoining orchard and pinch some apples.

"Tuesday, there would be a practice match – a kicking fest at each other. Wednesday would see a run along the banks of the canal and back which was about ten miles in total. One day a flock of geese attacked some of us, I have never seen the lads run so fast."

The introduction of those youngsters brought an improvement in results and it was only a 2-1 defeat at Bolton that prevented a two-month unbeaten run, with the 'Babes' headline appearing for the first time in the *Evening Chronicle* of December 20th following the 3-2 victory over Chelsea. The 'Busby' prefix had to wait for another few months yet.

A corner may have been turned, but three consecutive defeats in the latter half of February cancelled out any hopes of retaining the title along with any dreams of a Cup Final appearance. In the FA Cup United had struggled to beat Millwall and Walthamstow Avenue to reach round five where 78,000 watched Everton triumph. But it was 3-0 and 3-1 defeats at Wolves and Stoke respectively that destroyed their hopes of retaining the championship.

February had also seen Johnny Carey prove his versatility and his worth to the club, by playing the whole ninety minutes at Sunderland in goal. An illness to Crompton prevented him from playing and Carey had no qualms about pulling on the keeper's jersey, turning in a commendable performance in the 2-2 draw.

Goals were not exactly the common commodity they had been, mainly due to Rowley being missing from first-team action for some three months, but Messrs Busby, Murphy and Whalley were seeking to amend the problem. They were looking for a long-term successor to the centre-forward-cum-outside left berth, watching Barnsley in action on numerous occasions – mainly in disguise – casting their watchful eyes over the Clarets' centre-forward Tommy Taylor. Even Johnny Carey was sent to Yorkshire to assess the player.

United were not alone in their admiration of the twenty-one-year-old, as numerous other clubs (as many as seventeen, according to some sources) were interested in taking him away from his native Yorkshire. Cardiff City and Sheffield Wednesday were quoted amongst the early front runners when news of the player's possible availability had broken. Barnsley certainly didn't want to sell and Taylor himself had little inclination to leave. The matter was soon to be taken out of his hands, however, as following a Barnsley board meeting it was announced that they were ready to open negotiations, while emphasising that the decision to put the club's leading scorer on the transfer list was purely financial.

Busby knew that if he was to snare the player that Jimmy Murphy had watched fourteen times, he was going to have to break the bank, a figure of £34,000 having already been mentioned; but he was unperturbed and had persuaded his directors that it would be money well spent.

According to Busby, his early discussions with the player had been far from fruitful, with Taylor telling the United manager: "Not now; perhaps some other time," as he was in no hurry to leave Yorkshire, happy to remain at Oakwell. Even when United returned, Taylor was still unsure about the move, asking for six weeks to think about it, whilst promising he would not sign for anyone else. Busby, however, was aware of Cardiff City's interest and wanted to push the deal through sooner rather than later, telling the player that putting the move off would still leave him undecided. Once the Barnsley directors had explained the necessity of the move, Taylor agreed to sign, but the Yorkshire side were not to get the £30,000 they had hoped for, as Busby did not want to saddle the player with such a large fee – and managed to get £1 knocked off. The odd pound apparently went to Barnsley assistant secretary Lily Wilby, who was keeping those involved in the negotiations supplied with tea.

Taylor, who arrived in Manchester with his boots wrapped up in brown paper, was thrown into the fray against Preston on March 7th, a game that saw seven changes in personnel to that of the previous encounter against Stoke City. And he began repaying his transfer fee immediately with a double in the 5-2 win, going on to score a further five goals in the remaining ten fixtures. Strangely, following his move, he continued to live in Barnsley for the time being, training with his former team-mates.

On the debut front, goalkeeper-cum-play-anywhere assistant secretary Les Olive and forward Dennis Viollet, currently serving in the army, had their initial outings against Newcastle in mid-April, but of all those awarded a first team opportunity none made anywhere near the impression as that of Duncan Edwards against Cardiff City on April 4th at Old Trafford.

The Dudley youngster had yet to turn seventeen, but had caused ripples of excitement at junior level, standing out amongst the other youngsters due to his impressive physique, as well as his forceful play. He had been brought to the attention of *Guardian* readers back in December in a match report for a 4-3 defeat at the Cliff training ground against Northern Nomads, where the reporter wrote:

> "The most encouraging thing about the game was that it showed a player of real promise in Edwards, aged 16. Edwards is remarkably strong for his years, is fast, and tackled well, but best of all shot with real power with either foot."

Against Cardiff City in the Easter Mancunian sunshine, he "played a very useful game, holding his own against more seasoned campaigners, doing as well as any other player." An encouraging start for someone who had only played nine Central League games. The result itself, however, failed to lift the impending gloom, with the visitors winning 4-1.

The boy from the Black Country had been a much-sought-after individual, with Bolton Wanderers thought to be favourites for his signature due to his cousin, Denis Stevens, being on their books. But Busby, thanks to his scouting system and his friend Joe Mercer, was well aware of this prodigious talent, as was Edwards of United's interest. No move, however, could be made until June 1st 1952, a day that produced a frenzy of activity.

A telephone call from Reg Priest to Old Trafford brought the news that Bolton Wanderers were rumoured to be close to making one final attempt to capture the youngster. Priest reckoned that if United did not make a counter move, then the youngster might think they had lost interest, and could opt to join Bolton.

United coach Bert Whalley was summoned and instructed to drive down to Dudley to speak to the Edwards family and reassure them that United were indeed interested. Setting off on his errand, Whalley got nowhere near the West Midlands as his car broke down, forcing him to telephone back to Old Trafford stating his unfortunate predicament and that he was going to hitch-hike home.

Upon his late night return, he was met at Old Trafford by an anxious Jimmy Murphy who informed him that it had been decided to hire a car, and that they were both going to go to Dudley that night. To leave the trip to the following day could be too late. The tired Whalley had no complaints as he knew how important the signing of Edwards was to the long-term future of the club, so off the pair went.

Fortunately, there were no further delays or hiccups on the return journey south. The United pair breathed a sigh of relief as they drove into Elm Road, Dudley, to find the place in darkness, with no cars or representatives of other clubs encamped outside the Edwards' house. Although it was now the early hours of the morning, there was nothing else for Murphy and Whalley to do except awaken the sleeping household. Making as little noise as possible, hoping not to awaken the whole street, Bert Whalley knocked on the door.

There were a few agonising moments before a noise could be heard from inside the house, and Gladstone Edwards could be imagined stomping down the stairs muttering 'Who the bloody hell is knocking on my door at this hour of the morning?' Slowly the door was eased open and the half-awake features of Duncan's father peered round the edge.

An apologetic explanation was quickly made by the United duo as they were ushered into the family living room, where Sarah Edwards was already seated. Minutes later a pyjama-clad schoolboy was standing alongside his similarly attired father and he rubbed the sleep from his eyes and signed for Manchester United.

Somewhat unmoved by it all, Duncan was quick to ask his nocturnal visitors what all the fuss was about, as he had already told manager Matt Busby that Manchester United was the only club he wanted to join. It was at 2am on the morning of June 2nd 1952 that Duncan Edwards became a Manchester United player.

The curtain came down on the domestic season with a humiliating 5-0 defeat at Middlesbrough, leaving United a distant eight points behind champions Arsenal. "This season has been the most uneventful since the war. The team has given more indifferent displays than in any other post-war season," wrote Alf Clarke, "though we must not overlook the weakening of resources from time to time." But it wasn't all doom and gloom, as the first team were overshadowed by the club's youngsters who lifted eight trophies ranging from the inaugural FA Youth Cup to the Altrincham Service of Youth League.

Winning the FA Youth Cup in particular was a gigantic step for the club. Such a triumph was a reward for the time and effort that had gone into putting the initial youth structure in place, but few could have been aware of the long-term effect that it would have on the club as a whole.

In the first round of the competition, Leeds United had been brushed aside with a 4-0 defeat, while the likes of Bobby Harrop, Ronnie Cope, Eddie Lewis, David Pegg, John Doherty and Duncan Edwards took the tournament by storm less than a month later. They left the 2,600 crowd at the Cliff speechless and mesmerised with a 23-0 victory over Nantwich. Many lost count as the goals flew past the unfortunate Thorley in the Nantwich goal, and few could name all the United scorers as they made their way home through the dark Salford streets. For the record, Pegg, Doherty and Edwards all claimed five, Lewis notched four, Morton two, while Scanlon and Edwards, the Nantwich left-back, rounded it up to twenty-three.

Spirited attempts were made to subdue the talented United youngsters, but none were able to match their fluent, attacking football. Wolves came close in the second leg of the final, holding their visitors to a 2-2 draw, but the damage had been done in the first leg in front of 20,934 at Old Trafford, where the red-shirted home side had won a 7-1 victory, ensuring their Midland counterparts would earn nothing more than runners-up medals for their endeavours.

The future certainly looked bright, but those youngsters who were to be entrusted with the club's future were going to have to seek guidance from other sources, as thirty-four-year-old club captain and father figure Johnny Carey called time on his career. He said:

> "I have decided not to re-sign as a player because I do not feel capable of playing the United brand of soccer for another year. My 17 seasons at Old Trafford have been very happy ones and my thanks are due to the directors, manager, secretary, players, trainers and other staff for their help.
>
> "My future is undecided. United have offered me a position."

But it was an offer he chose not to accept. "I appreciate it, but I feel it is in my own interests to seek a manager's position with some other club." Carey's walking away from Old Trafford would leave a huge void.

Season 1953-54

United got off to their worst start since season 1930-31, failing to win any of their opening eight fixtures. Five draws, including an eight-goal thriller at Anfield, did little to instil confidence for the winter months ahead. "United's Errors On Defence", "Oh Dear, United" and "United Crushed" were only three of the headlines that hinted towards the problems.

It wasn't until September 16th that the first victory of the season materialised, a 4-1 win at Middlesbrough, but still the team stuttered along, losing to Burnley at home and away to Wolves, defeats that left them twelve points behind leaders West Bromwich Albion.

Although debatably average and unable to match the silverware of the likes of Arsenal since the 1930s, or even Portsmouth who could claim two post-war titles, United had nevertheless managed to conjure up a charisma, attracting attention outwith the First Division and becoming a sought-after commodity when it came to friendlies and testimonials in Britain and beyond. A request to play a game in Zurich on a blank Saturday last season was turned down, but another gruelling eight-week North American tour had taken place in the immediate close season of 1952.

Although crowds across the Atlantic were often sparse, goals were in abundance with four of the dozen fixtures producing thirty-five alone. Montreal All-Stars conceded ten without reply, while Fall River were beaten 11-1; however, the two fixtures against more familiar opponents Spurs saw the Londoners win 5-0 and 7-1!

But it was not the goals for and against that captured all the headlines, as a 2-0 victory over the Atlas Club of Guadalajara in Los Angeles produced a near riot. A trip on Roger Byrne saw United awarded a penalty, a decision that the Atlas players did not take well. One of their number knocked the referee over, and as he was sent off, some of the 1,000 Mexican supporters in the stands, along with Atlas substitutes and coaching staff, began to invade the pitch. As a result, the referee was once again attacked, before five deputy sheriffs intervened. As pushing and shoving developed, continuing for fifteen minutes, another Mexican was sent to the dressing room. Thankfully, on this particular tour, all the headlines were related to the games themselves, and the squad returned to Manchester intact.

Those requests for ninety minutes of United's time were closely scrutinised, and many politely declined, but one which wasn't turned down took Busby and his players across the border to Kilmarnock on October 28th, for the Scottish side's inaugural match under floodlights. With an eye on avoiding injuries, the United manager juggled his side a little, giving the likes of Crompton, McNulty and Gibson some playing time, also bringing Blanchflower and Viollet into the first-team picture.

According to the *Evening Times*, the new lighting was "adequate, although could be better due to darkened spots around both goal mouths." Mentioned in dispatches were complaints about the stand seats costing 5/- with many regulars deciding to stand on the terracing and in the enclosure rather than pay what they considered over the odds.

United found little resistance from the Rugby Park outfit. Cockburn opening the scoring after only two minutes, but soon afterwards the England international had to leave the field with an injury, allowing Duncan Edwards to join the fray – giving the

Scottish public a view of their opponents' strength in depth. As the *Evening Times* reported:

> "Young Duncan Edwards, a 17-year-old reserve, was fielded as a substitute and gave a grand display."

The 3-0 victory, with polished performances from the trio of youngsters, gave Busby much to contemplate on the way home, eventually deciding that it was perhaps time to push ahead in the direction that he saw the club taking. He would now allow Blanchflower, Viollet and Edwards (who had only signed professional the previous month) to retain their places against Huddersfield at Leeds Road.

Their inclusion failed to bring any immediate effect, the game finishing in a goalless stalemate, but it gave birth to the legend that became the 'Busby Babes' courtesy of the *Manchester Evening Chronicle*'s headline above Alf Clarke's match report in the Saturday evening 'Pink' – "Busby's Bouncing 'Babes' Keep All Town Awake". It fitted the scheme of things well, but those youngsters and their stablemates were more Jimmy Murphy and Bert Whalley's prodigies than Busby's. From their arrival at one of the city's railway stations to those tentative steps at senior level they all fell under Murphy's guidance, the Welshman taking on the role of their surrogate father, preparing them for a future at the club. But then, 'Busby's Babes' did have a better ring to it than 'Murphy's Mites'.

Was it indeed Clarke who coined the immortal name, plucking it from thin air as he relayed his match notes down the telephone line to his copywriter? Who knows? But the name was born.

As for the game itself, it was United who took the initiative, almost taking an early lead when Berry sent a tantalising cross into the Huddersfield penalty area, Mills just managing to pluck the ball off the head of Taylor. Continuing to press, further crosses from Byrne and Rowley ensured that the home defence were kept fully occupied.

At the opposite end, Chilton kept Glazzard, Huddersfield's major goal threat, under close scrutiny, although he did manage to get the better of the United man on one occasion – only to find the veteran defender's reactions were still 100%, and an outstretched leg managed to divert the ball to a colleague. Staniforth also had the United support holding their breath as he broke through unchallenged, but a sigh of relief could be heard around the ground as Crompton dealt comfortably with the Huddersfield full back's shot.

United almost made a breakthrough in the fourteenth minute when Viollet gained possession in midfield. Lobbing the ball through towards Taylor, a slip by McEvoy gave the former Barnsley centre-forward the time and the space to control the ball. But, with the goal at his mercy, he somehow managed to steer the ball over the bar.

Edwards and Blanchflower combined well in midfield, the former in a more defensive role, while the latter just failed to connect with a Berry free kick; but it was the Dudley youngster who was really catching the eye, with Alf Clarke writing in his report: "Edwards was coming more into the game the longer it went on. His stamina for a seventeen year old is something terrific."

Huddersfield's play confirmed their favourable League position, displaying a wide array of talent, swiftly moving from defence into attack, although at times they were quite content to send a long ball towards centre forward Glazzard in the hope that he would get the better of Chilton or else force the United centre half into making a mistake.

Both sides proved inconsistent in front of goal in the opening forty-five minutes, during which Ray Wood even tried his luck at goal on a couple of occasions, using the wind to his advantage, with two of his clearances travelling the length of the field. His aim, however, was slightly out, as the ball bounced out of play nearer to the corner flag than the Huddersfield goal. At least he did not suffer any embarrassment from his efforts, unlike Byrne, who sent the ball out of the ground with one attempt as the first half drew to a close.

Huddersfield were beginning to enjoy much of the play, putting the United goal under siege, but to their credit, the visitors defence stood firm and somehow managed to prevent the ball from finding its way past Wood, although he was beaten by a Davie header and could only watch as the ball flashed inches over the crossbar.

Wartime Luftwaffe reconnaissance photograph taken over Salford Quays and Old Trafford. The ground can be seen towards the top right hand corner.

Matt Busby Signs as United Manager

By A STAFF REPORTER

COMPANY SERGEANT-MAJOR INSTRUCTOR MATT BUSBY, Liverpool right half-back and Scotland captain, to-day signed an agreement to become manager of Manchester United when he is demobilised.

Only a few years ago Busby (now aged 34), who has proved himself one of the great half- has appeared for Scotland in eight games, several times as skipper.

Manchester Evening News *reports the signing of United's new manager.*

Cigarette card showing Jimmy Murphy as a West Bromwich Albion player.

Matt Busby in his days as a City player.

Louis Rocca, involved in the club in one capacity or another since the days of Newton Heath and the man who wrote to Matt Busby regarding the job vacancy.

The single sheet programme from Busby's first game in charge against Bolton Wanderers on October 27th 1945.

A skeletal main stand at Old Trafford, with the Stretford End in the background.

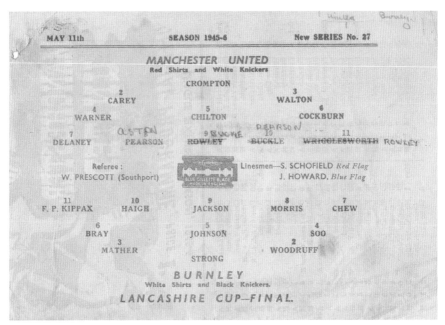

The single sheet programme for the Lancashire Cup Final against Burnley on May 11th 1946.

Salford Boys v Leicester Boys – English Schools Trophy Final second leg, June 7th 1947. First game at Old Trafford after the war. The Salford team was captained by future United player Geoff Bent.

Evening Chronicle
Souvenir Picture of Manchester United
(MAY, 1947)

Manchester Evening Chronicle *souvenir photograph of United from May 1947. Standing (left to right): Mr W Crickmer (secretary), Aston, Tom Curry (trainer), Warner, Walton, Crompton, Chilton, Murphy (coach), McGlen, Matt Busby (manager). Front row: Rowley, Burke, Morris, Carey, Hanlon, Pearson, Mitten. Inset: Cockburn, Delaney, Fielding, Buckle, Whalley.*

Jack Rowley – Guested for hometown Wolverhampton club during the war, scoring eight goals in one game, while in 1943-44 was leading scorer with Tottenham Hotspur when they won the League South. Was to go on and score a United club record 30 League goals in season 1951-52.

Jimmy Delaney – Matt Busby's first signing for United, a £4,000 fee bringing him south from Glasgow Celtic, where he had won both League and Cup winners' medals. Although considered 'past it' by many, he was to prove a bargain buy.

Johnny Morris – Radcliffe born. A hugely talented individual who progressed through the United ranks.

Stan Pearson – A Salford lad, who joined United as an amateur aged 16. He was to lose six years of his playing career due to his army service during the war.

Jack Crompton – Born in the Newton Heath area of Manchester and a product of the famed Goslings club. The only player who could claim to have played on all of United's home grounds during his career.

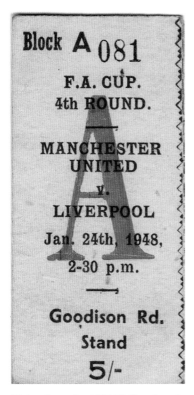

Ticket from the 1948 FA Cup fourth round tie against Liverpool at Goodison Park.

Programme from the 1948 FA Cup semi-final against Derby County.

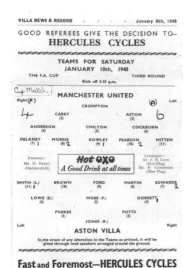

Team pages from the programme for the 6-4 win over Aston Villa on January 10th 1948.

A rosette from the 1948 FA Cup Final.

Manchester Evening Chronicle *'Football Edition' with coverage of United's 3-1 FA Cup semi-final victory over Derby County.*

Ticket for the 1948 FA Cup Final.

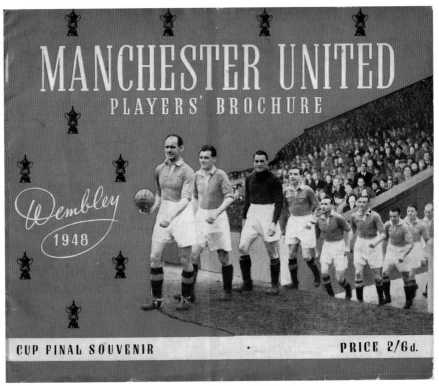

The United player's' brochure produced for the 1948 Final.

The triumphant United captain Johnny Carey on the shoulders of his team-mates.
Carey was to play in every position except outside left during his United career.

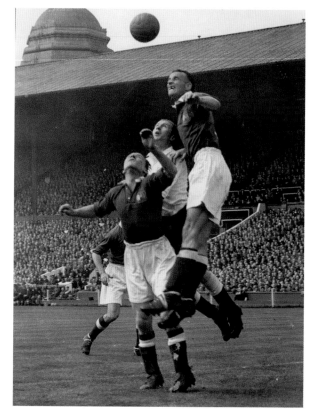

Centre-half Allenby Chilton rises above a Blackpool forward to head clear in the 1948 FA Cup Final.

The Manchester *Evening Chronicle 'Football Edition' with coverage of that afternoon's FA Cup Final between United and Blackpool.*

RETURN OF MANCHESTER UNITED ASSOCIATION FOOTBALL CLUB
FROM THE F.A. CUP FINAL.

THE LORD MAYOR and the CORPORATION of MANCHESTER
request the pleasure of the company of

Mr. J. Anderson and Lady

in the Town Hall, on Monday, 26th April 1948,
Reception 7-0 to 7-30 p m.

Music.   -   Light Refreshments.

TOWN HALL,   R.S.V.P.
MANCHESTER, 2.   Ordinary Dress.   (Card enclosed)
Please observe notes on the back hereof.

Invitation card for the 1948 FA Cup celebration dinner at Manchester Town Hall.

Manchester United, 1948 FA Cup winners.

Manchester United 1949-50. Back row (left to right): T Curry (trainer), A Chilton, J Warner, J Crompton, H Cockburn, J Aston, Matt Busby (manager). Front: J Delaney, T Brogan, J Carey, J Rowley, S Pearson, C Mitten.

The United Review for the first League match back at Old Trafford after the war against Bolton Wanderers on August 24th 1949.

Johnny Berry – A talented winger who was born in Aldershot, rising to prominence with Birmingham City before joining United in August 1951 for £15,000.

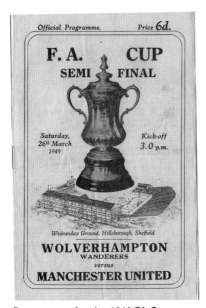

Programme for the 1949 FA Cup semi-final against Wolverhampton Wanderers which ended in a 1-1 draw after extra-time.

Ticket from the FA Cup semi-final tie against Wolves.

The United and Spurs players line up prior to their game in the USA.

Mitten joins Santa Fe for £40 a week

COMING HOME FIRST

CHARLIE MITTEN, Manchester United outside-left, was to-day reported to have signed a two-year contract with the Sante Fe club in Bogota (Colombia) at £2,050 sterling a year, almost £40 a week.

But when his 29-year-old wife, Betty, at her home in Royston Road, Davyhulme, was told of the report, she declared: "I can't believe it. I still maintain he won't sign without first coming home and discussing it with me

"I am still going ahead with plans for a holiday at Scarborough in two weeks' time.

Mitten, who has already signed for Manchester United for next season, told Reuter's Bogota correspondent that he would leave for England on Tuesday, and hoped to return to Bogota in the middle of July with his wife and children.

BOGOTA, COLOMBIA, Saturday.

CHARLES MITTEN, Manchester United outside left, said here to-day that he had signed a two-year contract with the Santa Fe club at £2,050 sterling a year.

He left the Manchester team at New York after their tour of Canada and the United States and arrived in Bogota by air last night. He said he had been impressed with the welcome he received in the Colombian capital.

Mitten is staying with Neil Franklin, Stoke City and England centre half, who recently joined the Santa Fe club along with his clubmate George Mountford.

Mr. Walter Crickmer, Manchester United secretary, had nothing to say. He is awaiting the return of manager Matt Busby and the touring party now on their way home from the United States.

Men with the American air

[in Rio.

Jack Aston and Henry Cockburn, Manchester United players who have flown down to Brazil to link up with the England team after playing with Manchester United in America, have certainly brought with them the air of the United States.

Near-riot for United: Referee hit

"Evening Chronicle" Special Representative

Atlas Club 0. Manchester Utd. 2

THE Bery Atlas Soccer Club of Guadalajara, Mexico — a near-international team—lost to Manchester United in Los Angeles after causing a near-riot on the ground last night.

It all started in the second half when Juan Gomez, the Mexican right full - back, tripped Roger Byrne, the Manchester United outside left, in the penalty area.

Glasgow-born referee A. Thompson, immediately signalled a "spot" kick — and then fireworks began. Mexico's right half - back, Tony Varrillo, showed such violent disagreement with the referee's decision that he charged him, knocking Thompson to the ground.

Pearson goal

There was only one sequel to this—marching orders for Mr. Varrillo. But, as the referee signalled for this, the Mexican substitutes and coaching staff all raced on to the field and began to pummel the referee. For 10 minutes confusion reigned, with some onlookers in the stand even leaving their seats and trying to join in the melee.

"Call out the Guard" cry went

(Left) Newspaper report relating to Charlie Mitten signing for Santa Fe. (Right) Report on the 1952 near 'riot' match v Atlas in the USA.

Charlie Mitten – Born in Rangoon, Burma, but brought up in Scotland. Turned down offers from both Rangers and Hearts before joining United. Was to score a hat-trick of penalties against Aston Villa in March 1950. A talented harmonica player.

Eddie McIlvenny – A Scot from Greenock who played with Morton and Wrexham before heading for America. Whilst with Philadelphia Nationals, he captained the USA national side to a 1-0 victory over England in the 1950 World Cup at Belo Horizonte.

The United team of season 1951-52. Back row – (Left to right) Tom Curry (Trainer), Carey, Gibson, Chilton, Allen, McGlen, Aston. Front row – (Left To Right) Delaney, Downie, Rowley, Pearson, McShane.

The Manchester Evening Chronicle 'Football Final' from Saturday April 26th 1952 covering United's title winning 6-1 victory over Arsenal.

Newspaper cutting saying that
United had signed England schoolboy
international Duncan Edwards.

The programme for Duncan Edwards'
League debut against Cardiff City on April
4th 1953.

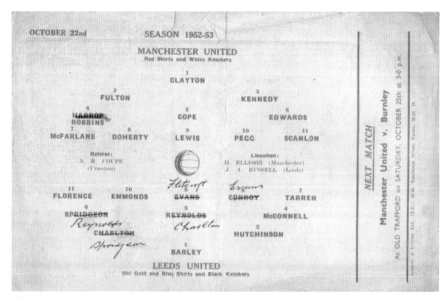

Single sheet programme for United's first ever FA Youth Cup match against Leeds
United on October 22nd 1952, a game United won 4-0. Note the Leeds No.5 – a certain
Jackie Charlton.

Jimmy Murphy and Bert Whalley –
Integral parts of the United management
team and a duo who were responsible for
the stars of the future.

Bill Foulkes – A miner from St
Helens, who thought nothing of
putting in a shift at the pit before
heading to Old Trafford for training.

David Pegg – A Yorkshireman from
Doncaster. The former England
schoolboy international made his
United debut against Middlesbrough in
December 1952.

Dennis Viollet – Born in the City
heartland near Maine Road, but the
captain of the Manchester Schoolboys
side was persuaded to become a Red. A
hugely talented individual with a distinct
eye for goal.

The United players in a relaxed mood outside Old Trafford prior to setting off for an away match. From left to right – Jones, Berry, Taylor, Edwards, Foulkes, Byrne and Whelan.

Mark Jones – Something of an unconventional footballer off the field, who smoked a pipe and bred budgerigars. But on it, the Yorkshireman was a hard tackling centre-half.

Eddie Colman – You couldn't get a more local player, coming from the Ordsall Estate on the opposite side of the Ship Canal from Old Trafford. The Teddy Boy of the United side.

Programme for the Coronation Cup tie against Rangers at Hampden Park, Glasgow.

Programme for the FA Youth Cup Final against Wolves at Old Trafford.

Jackie Blanchflower – Younger brother of Danny who joined United in May 1949, making his debut against Liverpool in November 1951 on the same day as Roger Byrne.

Match report for the game against Kilmarnock in October 1953 that is considered the birth of the 'Busby Babes'

Manchester Evening Chronicle *report for the match against Huddersfield Town on October 31st 1953 with the first 'Busby Babes' headline.*

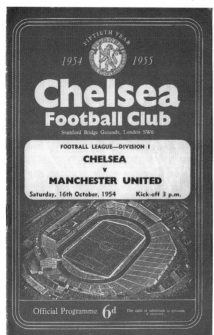

Programme for the 6-5 victory over Chelsea in October 1954.

Duncan Edwards – The Dudley legend. Made his debut as a 16-year-old against Cardiff City in April 1953 whilst still an amateur. Took over the number six shirt from Henry Cockburn.

The FA Youth Cup winning side of 1955. Back row – (Left to Right) Edwards, Beckett, Brennan, Hawksworth, Rhodes, Queenan. Front Row – (Left to right) Jones, Fidler, Colman, McGuinness, Charlton.

The United team prior to a match at Villa Park in October 1955. Back Row – (Left to Right) Whitefoot, Foulkes, Wood, Jones, Blanchflower, McGuinness. Front Row – (Left to right) Berry, Webster, Byrne, Taylor, Pegg.

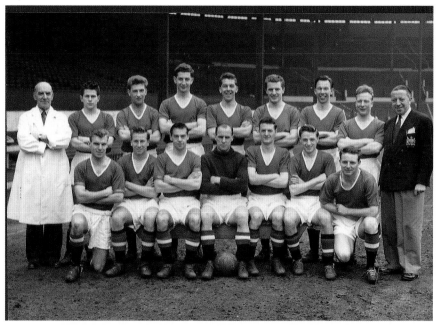

Central League champions 1955-56. Back Row – (Left to Right) Bill Inglis (Trainer), McGuinness, Kennedy, Goodwin, Cope, Bent, Whitehurst, Whitefoot, Jimmy Murphy. Front Row – (Left to Right) McFarlane, Charlton, Webster, Crompton, Whelan, Scanlon, Doherty.

Match ticket for the FA Youth Cup tie against Bexley Heath in 1956.

Roger Byrne lifts the First Division championship trophy at Old Trafford in 1956, surrounded by jubilant team-mates.

Manchester Evening Chronicle *from Saturday April 21st 1956 proclaiming United as First Division champions.*

A muddied and bloodied Tommy Taylor and Roger Byrne celebrate United's 1956 championship success.

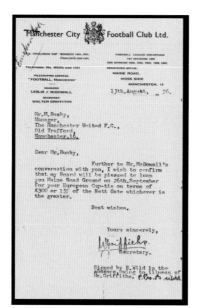

Letter from Manchester City relating to United using their Maine Road ground for the European Cup tie against Anderlecht in September 1956.

Match report for the 10-0 victory over Anderlecht in September 1956.

Match report for the memorable 3-0 victory over Bilbao at Maine Road on February 6th 1957.

Newspaper article relating to Bobby Charlton's debut against Bury.

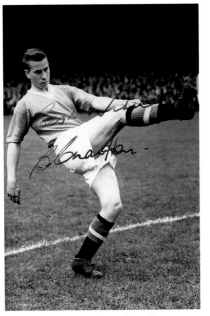

Bobby Charlton – Born into the famous Milburn football family, and much sought after as a youngster before moving south to join the ever-expanding youth set-up at Old Trafford.

Pre-match v Bilbao on January 16th 1957 in a far from sunny Spain.

Viollet scores against Bilbao at Maine Road in the second leg of the European Cup quarter-final tie on February 6th 1957.

Match ticket v Real Madrid at Old Trafford in April 1957.

The programme for the game against Real Madrid.

Newspaper article following United's 4-0 championship claiming victory over
Sunderland on April 20th 1957.

May, 1957

The Chairman and Directors
wish to acknowledge with grateful thanks
your kind message of congratulation on the team's
success in winning the League Championship
The host of communications is significant
that we are in the thoughts of our countless friends
and has created added warmth
to the happy atmosphere which abounds the Club
in it's hour of triumph.

Old Trafford,
Manchester 16.

Card sent out to supporters who wrote to the club congratulating them on winning
the 1956-57 First Division championship.

Match ticket for the 1956 FA Charity Shield match against Manchester City at Maine Road.

Match ticket for the 1957 FA Cup tie against Hartlepools United.

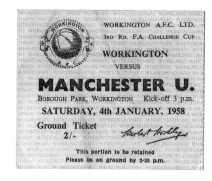

Match ticket for the 1958 FA Cup tie against Workington.

Match ticket for the 1957 FA Cup semi-final against Birmingham City.

Match ticket for the 1957 FA Cup Final against Aston Villa.

Manchester Evening Chronicle *covering the 1957 FA Cup Final defeat against Aston Villa.*

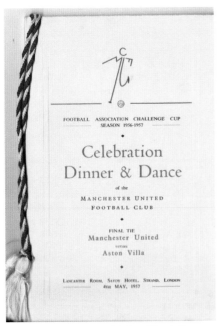

Menu from the 1957 FA Cup Final dinner.

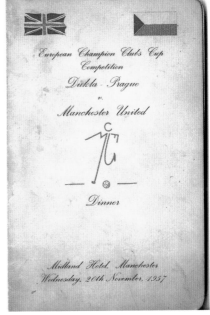

Menu from the after match dinner against Dukla Prague in November 1957.

Harry Gregg – A fearless goalkeeper who had joined Doncaster Rovers from Coleraine. His performances saw United pay a record fee for his services in December 1957.

Kenny Morgans – A Swansea schoolboy player who joined United in January 1955. Made his debut against Leicester City in December 1957.

Dressed to fly – A smartly kitted out United squad pose before flying out on yet another European adventure. Left to Right Bert Whalley, Taylor, Clayton, McGuinness, Colman, Jones, Viollet, Webster, Charlton, Byrne, Pegg, Foulkes, Whelan, Edwards, Bent.

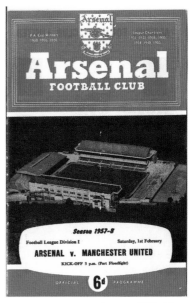

The match ticket and programme for the game against Arsenal in February 1958. The last League game played by the 'Busby Babes'.

Roger Byrne leads out United at Highbury for the memorable 5-3 encounter.

Programme for the game against Red Star in Belgrade.

Pre-match against Red Star.

Back row – (Left to right) Duncan Edwards, Bill Foulkes, Mark Jones, Ray Wood, Eddie Colman, David Pegg. Front row – (Left to right) Johnny Berry, Liam Whelan, Roger Byrne, Tommy Taylor, Dennis Viollet. Insets – (Left to right) Geoff Bent, Jackie Blanchflower, Albert Scanlon, Harry Gregg, Kenny Morgans, Bobby Charlton.

There were opportunities at either end, but with Rowley subdued and Edwards failing to get any power on a shot after being teed up by Viollet, the game petered out with the scoreline remaining blank.

Despite that goalless draw at Huddersfield, the club suddenly came alive, awoken from a slumber. Blanchflower opened his scoring account in the 2-2 draw with Arsenal, notching another in the 6-1 defeat of Cardiff City as Viollet claimed a double, going on to make it three in two games in the 4-1 win over Blackpool. The duo scored a further nine in the next seven games, with the team notching five goals on successive Saturdays against Liverpool and Sheffield Wednesday.

Given the turnaround in fortune it is perhaps surprising that attendances did not follow suit. In those indifferent early season days, only 18,161 witnessed the 2-2 draw with Middlesbrough, while the 4-1 victory over Blackpool attracted the largest crowd of the season to date with just short of 50,000. The two recent five-star performances were not reflected by numbers through the turnstiles as Liverpool's visit saw a mere 26,074 turn up, and Christmas Day family duties were obviously taking priority to many as the Sheffield Wednesday fixture was watched by only a thousand more.

Whilst happy with his mix of experience and youthful enthusiasm, Busby knew in the back of his mind that there would be a few hiccups along the way, the first of those materialising in the FA Cup Third Round at Burnley where any 'Eight goal Thriller' headlines were true to the point. Sadly, from a United point of view, five of them were scored by the home side. In the *Daily Herald*, George Follows wrote of the "finest cup game I ever saw", stating that United didn't lose due to fielding five youngsters, but because "the boys were let down by the men." He added: "There were times, especially when they (United) drew level at 2-2 and then equalised again, when it seemed that United could win despite the handicaps of weakness on the wings, wanderings at centre-half and uncertainty in goal. But for me the final memory will be of the boy Edwards striding through the mud in hopeless battle, the bravest man on the field."

It was all part of the learning curve, as was a further five-goal defeat, with only one in reply on this occasion, against Bolton at home a fortnight later. But George Follows could be found once again singing the praises of Busby's team in their 2-0 defeat of Spurs in mid-February. 'Great days ahead for Busby boys' echoed his headline under which he was quick to say that he was a Walsall supporter, but added that "from now on, until further notice I'd like to watch Manchester United every Saturday. For Matt Busby's young men make a great adventure story, just as exciting as Biggles or Dan Dare and certain to get more and more astounding."

It was certainly going to be a rollercoaster ride, but it would be a while before United were again challenging for honours, the Tottenham victory still leaving them some nine points adrift of leaders West Bromwich Albion. A trio of defeats against Arsenal (3-1), Cardiff (3-2) and Blackpool (2-0), as March rolled into April, did little to improve matters despite a further flurry of goals from Blanchflower and Viollet. The duo netted a combined eight in the final eight fixtures – nine if you throw in a behind-closed-doors, thirty-minute practice match against England at Old Trafford, where a 1-0 victory was recorded by a United side which included four reserves, thanks to a John Aston goal.

Despite losing three of those final eight fixtures, a respectable fourth place was achieved, nine points behind champions Wolves. This could be accepted as a more than satisfactory outcome considering the reshuffle that had brought in the youngsters. And there was a further glow of satisfaction as that conveyor belt continued to drive along with the FA Youth Cup won for a second consecutive season along with the prestigious Zurich Blue Star competition.

The inaugural FA Youth Cup competition saw Murphy's boys brush aside all comers, recording scorelines such as 23-0 against Nantwich and 6-0 against Brentford before beating Wolves 9-3 on aggregate in the final. The Midlands side smelled revenge in the air this season, but with the likes of seasoned First Division campaigners Pegg and Edwards (now an England 'B' international) in the side and scores of 5-0 v Wrexham and 6-0 v Bradford Park Avenue, they once again proved too strong for Wolves, claiming the trophy again by the odd goal in nine.

It was on the European front that the hard work being done by Murphy and Whalley, along with the countrywide scouting network, was shown to be coming to fruition, as the United youngsters won the Zurich Blue Stars tournament in some style.

'Manchester beats the world at soccer,' boasted the *Manchester Evening Chronicle*, with Alf Clarke writing:

> "The United juniors played five games against the pick of youth clubs from Switzerland, Germany, France and Denmark and won four of the five games, drawing the other. Their goal aggregate was eight against none."

In the final, a Duncan Edwards hat-trick and another from Albert Scanlon saw off the hosts.

In the *Manchester Evening News,* Tom Jackson wrote about what made a Busby boy.

> "Firstly the young footballer must have ability and the determination to carve out a career in the game. Secondly he must be ready to listen to the advice of the United manager and his coaches, Jimmy Murphy and Bert Whalley, and thirdly (and this is an essential at Old Trafford), he must be imbued with team and club spirit.
>
> "United have discarded several boys in the post-war seasons whose soccer ability has been good, but whose behaviour in the camp has not come up to the high standard set by the club.
>
> "There is something 'magical' in the name of Manchester United which made all the difference between an outstanding boy player throwing his lot at Old Trafford and joining another League club.
>
> "The Old Trafford nursery from which last season Busby remoulded United's First Division side, is bristling with talented youngsters who are being put through a hard apprenticeship after winning their preliminary spurs at schoolboy level.
>
> "It has now become such a high-powered and efficient organisation that Matt Busby and Manchester United are the envy of managers and clubs throughout Britain."

Jimmy Murphy was also quick to throw some light on the lengthy process that had finally reaped rewards.

> "We had this conviction that long term, the best results would be obtained by finding our own schoolboys and then bringing them up to the Manchester United way of playing the game. I think we have been proved overwhelmingly right.
>
> "Joe Armstrong is the expert with the schoolboys. Not only is he a good judge of character, he has the happy knack of being able to talk to parents and convince them that their sons will be well looked after.
>
> "Bert Whalley does a tremendous job. He is a great judge of players and a first class coach."

Season 1954-55

The foundations for the 'new' Manchester United had been well and truly laid with Whitefoot, Blanchflower, Foulkes, Viollet and Edwards all retaining their places in the starting line-up against Portsmouth at the start of season 1954-55. The average age was pushed further down with Ray Wood coming into the side in place of Jack Crompton and Welshman Colin Webster, who had made his initial and only appearance to date against Portsmouth last season, appearing at inside-right. Throwing Roger Byrne into the mix, that made seven home-produced youngsters in the side for that opening day fixture.

Of the old guard, only Jack Rowley and Allenby Chilton could find a seat in the dressing room against Portsmouth, happy to lend a guiding hand, while perhaps enjoying a new lease of life with the youngsters around them. Henry Cockburn, whilst happy to assist in aiding the progress of the boys, felt that he still had something to give to the game whether it be at Old Trafford or elsewhere, and had handed in a transfer request last season. Like Jack Crompton, he ended up remaining at the club, although both players must have known in the back of their minds that their first-team days were numbered.

Due to the impact the youngsters had made during the previous season, Manchester United was suddenly the name on everyone's lips. The new campaign had hardly come around quick enough as supporters and media alike wanted to savour more from Busby's fresh-faced charges. Extended articles in the popular magazines of the day were quick to feature the team whose last two campaigns could be considered little more than average, with John Arlott writing in one such publication:

> "Manchester United are the outstanding eleven of post-war British football. Others – Arsenal, Newcastle, Spurs, Portsmouth, Blackpool, West Bromwich, Wolves, in Scotland, Hibs and Rangers have had good runs, extending at times over three or four seasons. None, however, can point to such a sustained record as Manchester United."

Having extolled the virtues of their administration, planning strategy and spotting of players, Arlott went on to write:

> "No side in the country is more tactically flexible. They carry the ball very little, for their football rests upon making the ball do the work – putting it into the best place, relying on the man who should go to that place to be on his way there before the ball. Today's Manchester United side is one which, at its peak, plays football as brilliantly thought-out and as swiftly executed as the Hungarians'. At times its combination of speed and precision is almost breathtaking. There seems little doubt that the present young Manchester United side could emerge as one of the greatest combinations in the history of football. Certainly for the next five seasons they must be the best bet in the country to win Cup, League – or both."

Many would have laughed at Arlott's assessment on the opening day of the new season when Portsmouth, amid thunder, lightning and torrential rain, left Old Trafford on the back of a 3-1 victory. "Rain and Goal Flood Hits United", proclaimed the headlines on the front page of the *Manchester Evening Chronicle*'s 'Football Pink' for that particular Saturday evening, telling of a tropical rainstorm over Old Trafford which saw many vacate the wide-open terracing for whatever cover they could find, while others simply left for home. Women and children were caught up in the stampede, with the police and ambulance men standing helpless.

Such were the conditions that the referee had to inspect the pitch prior to the second half commencing, and unfortunately for United, he decided to let play resume, allowing the visitors to improve on their 1-0 lead. The defeat, however, seemed to kick-start Matt Busby's team as the red machine suddenly clicked into action with six wins in the following eight games, drawing the other two, as United stormed to the top of the table. But it was a run that ended as quickly as it had begun, with five defeats in the next eight fixtures, conceding twenty-four goals in the process, prompting a drop back down to fifth.

Despite this downturn in form, United were still only two points behind leaders Wolves, leaving everyone associated with the club despondent and deep in their thoughts of how far in front they could have been.

A day at the seaside as August was drawing to a close gave the 31,855 Bloomfield Road crowd who witnessed United's 4-2 win further insight as to what was taking place at the Manchester Ship Canal end of Warwick Road – along with countless others who perused their morning newspapers over a cup of tea. In the *Daily Herald*, 'The Fan' (a correspondent who took in a different match each weekend) made the journey to Blackpool for the visit of United, and found them far more appetising than the shrimps, cockles and sticks of rock on offer along the seafront. "When you go to watch a team like Blackpool and see they have eight internationals playing you can expect to see something," he wrote. He continued:

> "We saw something too – but not from Blackpool. It came from those Manchester United babies who, perhaps because they aren't old enough to know better, set about Matthews and company with the confidence of a mock auctioneer giving away diamond studded egg timers.

"The one-and-nine pennies generally say their teams of days gone by were the best ever. The Manchester brigade round me didn't think that at all. They say that left alone, this United team will soon be the finest they have ever had."

But, in reality, United's performances were more akin to the big dipper at the Blackpool Pleasure Beach, and Manchester City were allowed to kick-start that indifferent run with a 3-2 victory at Maine Road – before Wolves, League leaders Everton, Sheffield United and West Bromwich also claimed United's scalp. But whilst leaking goals, their all-out attacking play ensured that they also scored a few. Three in the 4-3 defeat by Wolves, five against Cardiff and six in an epic 6-5 victory over Chelsea at Stamford Bridge, all ensured that the plaudits continued.

Was it United's pre-match meal that had helped produce the goals and the current run of form, as reported by Frank Taylor in the *News Chronicle*? "The Busby Babes re-staking their claim for soccer honours this season," he penned punfully, "on steaks... For years clubs have been taking their players for a meal of dry toast and anaemic looking boiled fish before the game. That's no diet for warriors... and now the Manchester United lads have a steak before a game, if they fancy it.

"Says Duncan Edwards, United's young man-mountain of a right half (**sic**) 'With my appetite I feel just grand. I feel as though I have something to play on.'"

In the *Picture Post* magazine of November 20th, Denzil Batchelor wrote:

"The Busby Babes are Babes no longer, but front line warriors trained as a team for any emergency. Indeed, last season Busby's brilliant tactic of introducing one young player after another to restock his thinning battle-line of veterans is one of the chief reasons for our confidence in the young side thoroughly blooded in their job today. Matt Busby explains their current success with a shrug, a smile, and 'I feel we're just trying to play football.'"

Busby didn't have much of a smile when asked about a comment he made at the annual AGM, lamenting the name 'the Busby Babes'.

> "That is a phrase I never invented and I was serious when I remarked that they might have become the 'Busby Blunderers'.
>
> "But what is more important, I said that without the presence of the experienced players like Chilton and Rowley my team might not have been as successful as they have proved so far."

Having shrugged off the 2-0 defeat against West Bromwich Albion at the Hawthorns with victories against Leicester City (3-1) and Burnley (4-2) it was straight back to mediocrity and an unhappy Christmas, salvaging a point from a goalless draw at Portsmouth before losing to Aston Villa home (1-0) and away (2-1) on consecutive afternoons. Those back-to-back defeats left Busby to once again ponder over his starting eleven, debating sentimentality and proven ability against boyish enthusiasm and the need to move forward.

Deciding that he really had nothing to lose, Busby dropped Jack Rowley, a decision that effectively ended his United career, as he was told that the club would not stand in his way if he decided to move on. As the club's highest goalscorer in any one season (with 30 in that 1951-52 championship winning campaign) and highest aggregate scorer with 211, Rowley did not want to leave. At the same time, he did not want to be considered a 'has-been', and was realistic enough to see that his days were numbered. A few weeks later, he was installed as player-manager of Plymouth Argyle. Only two members of the 1948 cup-winning side now remained – goalkeeper Jack Crompton, currently lending his expertise towards bringing the youngsters through the Central League side, and centre-half Allenby Chilton who, like Rowley, was about to see time called on his career as a Manchester United player.

United's title hopes were also about to come to a sudden end, although it was still only February, following a humiliating 5-0 hammering by City at Old Trafford, a 4-2 defeat against First Division leaders Wolves, again at Old Trafford, and a 3-0 reversal at Cardiff, which saw them tumble to eighth, five points adrift. Any hopes of a cup run were also extinguished by neighbours City with a 2-0 defeat at Maine Road. The dismissal of Chilton in the latter fixture, with the score at 1-0, did little to help the cause, although the performance of Duncan Edwards as a stand-in centre half brought much praise, as had his ninety minutes during the 5-0 defeat by their cross-town rivals. Busby had made his bed and now had to lie in it, and despite the disappointing defeats, he was not alone in sensing progress on a learning curve, and was determined to persist with his vision for the future.

Against Leicester, Colin Webster had shown he was capable of holding down a regular starting spot, some even hinting that on current form he deserved to be selected before Taylor. And there were others in the Central League side champing at the bit, ready to step in and grasp their opportunity at the expense of others.

Rowley's place went initially to David Pegg, but he in turn was ousted by another teenager in the shape of Hulme-born Albert Scanlon, who had made his debut in the 2-1 win over Arsenal back in November. Into the number five shirt in place of Chilton came Mark Jones, a veteran of a handful of games since 1950-51, followed against Preston North End by Dubliner Liam Whelan, who made his debut at the expense of a disappointed Webster.

As the season worked its way towards its finale, results continued to bemuse the United faithful as they resembled a mirror image of the previous season, with only three wins gained in the final eight games. Having defeated Sheffield United 5-0 at Old Trafford on April 2nd, they then conceded four at Sunderland in a 4-3 defeat six days later. Oddly enough, one of those three victories came on the final day of the season, when they defeated the newly crowned champions Chelsea 2-1, but it was a result that still left United floundering five points behind the Londoners in fifth, an outcome that did not go down well within sections of the fickle United support.

In an answer to the critics, Matt Busby wrote in his *Evening Chronicle* column:

> "A few years ago we could do no wrong. Manchester United were on top of the Soccer world.

"Now, despite the fact that we still occupy a position in the top half of the First Division, there isn't much that we can do right for some people.

"They agree that youth is a good thing in Soccer, but say that, like other good things, it's possible to have too much of it. And that is where they accuse United of having slipped up.

"They say we're overweight with Busby Babes, as the press have christened United and that there will be no balance until we put more maturity and experience into the scale.

"Well, I don't mind their criticism, indeed, I welcome it. At least it shows that they're interested. Now let me reassure them. I have great confidence in our young players. I am convinced that raw though some of them are at the moment, they are going to turn out all right.

"We no longer have such international stars as Johnny Carey, Allenby Chilton, Henry Cockburn, Stan Pearson, Jack Rowley or John Aston (for the time being, anyway). Into their shoes have stepped players making our team perhaps the youngest in the country.

"Our great team of 1948 grew old together. It was only natural that it would start to disintegrate. We had to find players to fill the gaps. I realise the value of experience, but the youngsters did so well that we could afford to wait and see how things developed.

"If, however, events should suggest that an experienced player is needed to blend with the young team, you can rest assured we shall look into it. At the moment, however, I feel we have the right material to make Manchester United a team to be feared – even next season."

The club had turned full circle in the space of a decade, the initial post-war side being slowly dismantled, practically player by player, and replaced by newer, younger models. Equally importantly, this new-look side could boast of more strength in depth, not appearing wanting when injury or loss of form forced a change in personnel.

Individuals were now looking over their shoulders: it wasn't just the threat from the fast-improving Central League team, but also from the junior ranks, who were once again FA Youth Cup winners. The conveyor belt of talent remained finely tuned and in perfect working order.

Selecting those untried youngsters and throwing them into the First Division cauldron was not a decision Busby made lightly, conferring at length with Jimmy Murphy, the man who worked with the teenage prodigies on a day-by-day basis. Initially, the Welshman was simply 'a coach', dedicated to his job, but toiling away without an official title. However, that changed following the directors' meeting on March 22nd, when it was agreed that Murphy would be conferred the title of 'assistant manager', which was fitting for such an insightful workaholic.

Murphy was certainly no nine-to-five man, as he regularly put in a seven-day week, supported without complaint by his understanding wife Winnie. His son, Jim Jnr, said:

> "He was in Africa when I was born and my mother knew there was a chance that he would not survive the war. As it was he returned home via Tunisia, Sicily, Bari (where he met Matt), Rome and Split. I was always told by my mother that I was about three and a half years old when I first saw Jimmy – Phil would be just six and John almost eight…Nick would be born that December, so I presume he was home early 1946!
>
> "Upon joining Matt at United for the 1946-47, he moved to Manchester WITHOUT the family…it would be over two years before Winnie and her five kids moved to Whalley Range. During the first six years of my life I only saw Jimmy on the weekends when he travelled back to West Bromwich and that wasn't every weekend…he had no car and NEVER drove in his life. For Phil this was the same or worse as he was too young to remember his dad before his army service and 'missed' him until he was eight; similarly with John.
>
> "In Manchester we rarely saw Jimmy for long periods. He was a workaholic, known to put in 70 to 80 hours a

week in a job he loved. Coaching Monday to Friday, Under 17s Tuesday and Thursday evenings, matchdays always out, Sunday lunch a meeting with Matt, Bert Whalley and others to go over the week's games, scouting youngsters and meeting with their parents, 'trial matches', summer soccer schools and training camps. Later, there would be trips abroad with the youth team.

"He also seemed to know everything the youngsters were up to. Albert Scanlon related to me a story: 'I had only just signed for United not long after leaving school and I had always attended a junior football tournament in Wythenshawe in May/early June. One afternoon I got off the bus and as I walked along the road, a gruff voice from behind me said "what do you think you are doing, you are a Manchester United player now". It was Jimmy of course who had been waiting near the bus stop, he knew I was coming but how did he know? He crossed the road with me and put me on the next bus back to Manchester, telling the guard "don't let him off until you reach Piccadilly". Jimmy seemed to know everything that was going on and not just with me but everyone!'

"I cannot recall EVER playing in the back garden with Jimmy and neither can Phil or John. We saw him most days at breakfast and if we were lucky in the evenings UNLESS it was a Tuesday or a Thursday or he was interviewing parents and their talented sons! He was usually home late at night. Saturdays out all day. Sundays early morning and late afternoon and evening he would normally be at home.

"Despite all that, I never felt I was 'missing out' on anything. Jimmy was a stern character but good fun when we would play games or cards on Sunday evenings. Winnie was a terrific mother figure, very much a home person. I think she only went to two or three matches in the whole of her life, nor was she one to go to the pub for a drink or to a nightclub or to a show. Monday night trips to the cinema were her 'nights off'. She spent most of her time in the cellar washing for a husband and six children.

"As I said, Jimmy never drove, but it was never a problem. On one occasion I remember him getting the bus from Whalley Range – it went down Seymour Grove and instead of turning right at the traffic lights towards Manchester, the driver turned left into Talbot Road, right into Warwick Road then dropped him off as he turned right into Stretford Road. That also reminds me that once when he was rushing to get a train from Piccadilly, the station master waved his flag and shouted to the train driver 'hold the train for Jimmy.'"

Jimmy Murphy led a full life with his two families, relishing his role as a surrogate father to all the boys who came under his guidance at United, gaining their unwavering loyalty, despite his reputation as a hard taskmaster. He would ask them testing questions from day one, not to test their general knowledge, but to evaluate how much attention each individual would require. He was often blunt and to the point, but his message always found its way home, leaving his listeners completely aware of the standards that they were expected to maintain.

A perfect example came at half-time during that record-breaking 23-0 FA Youth Cup victory over Nantwich: cock-a-hoop at leading 8-0, players were greeted by a stern-faced Murphy as they arrived back in the dressing room at the end of the first forty-five minutes. They were told to roll their sleeves up and win the match as decisively as possible.

Like the man on the terracing, in particular those who took an interest in not just the senior side but the reserves and juniors as well, Murphy could not deny having a favourite. Not that he had to spend additional hours coaching and grooming this young player, as everything came naturally to Duncan Edwards, the boy from Dudley who had honed his skills on the mudded park playing fields and school pitches, often against boys considerably older – much to his mother's concern. Edwards's rapid rise through the Old Trafford ranks threw him towards international recognition, and he made his full England debut in the 7-2 hammering of Scotland back in April.

Edwards, along with his young team-mates, was United's future. Despite the past three rather indifferent seasons which had produced League placings of eighth, fifth and fourth amid the dismantling and re-construction of first team, the future looked bright – although nothing in football must ever be taken on assumption.

Season 1955-56

Relaxed and refreshed, Manchester United and its supporters now looked forward to the new season with a growing sense of optimism. It had been a mere four seasons since the League championship trophy sat proudly in the Old Trafford boardroom, but they had been four long years of indifferent, sometimes embarrassing results. An ageing team had been dismantled and replaced with numerous youngsters. United bore as much resemblance to a local youth club as a First Division football club, but it was on these young shoulders that the future depended.

Indifferent starts to the season were par for the course for United, so three defeats and a trio of draws in the opening ten fixtures of season 1955-56 came as no surprise, neither did they raise cause for concern amongst the Old Trafford regulars. But attendances had been as unimpressive as the team's performances, and only one of the four home fixtures saw more than 33,000 click through the turnstiles. Satisfactory to many clubs, but it was certainly a downturn for United, over 18,000 down on the corresponding fixtures of last season, losing around £400 per game.

Not all of the missing bodies could be put down to the on-field performances, as the summer of 1955 saw League clubs decide at their AGM to increase the minimum admission charge by 3d to 2/-, professing falling attendances and higher running costs. The previous season had seen gates slump by more than two million, the biggest drop since the war, with bad weather being cited as one of the reasons behind the decrease. Meanwhile, players' earnings continued to rise with more than double the previous number earning £800 a year or more. Against that, many clubs reported takings of over £250,000. Not all clubs, however, were in favour of the price increase, with seven clubs voting against it. United were not one of that group.

While gate receipts represented a club's sole source of income, chairman Harold Hardman made light of United's downturn in fortune, for the present at least. He stressed that,

> "...the club coming from comparative poverty and obscurity such as we experienced in the 1930s to a sound and respected place in the football world is something akin to a fairy-tale romance." Classing United as "a one-time 'Cinderella' club, but could now point to total assets in the region of half a million pounds," he went on to add: "This does not mean that United have this sum at their immediate disposal. But if we were to include a full assessment of our up-to-date ground at Old Trafford, the 'A' team and junior training ground at the Cliff, Broughton, a valuation of our playing material, cash in hand and houses loaned to players, then that estimate would not be far off the mark.
>
> "Considering United's remarkable recovery in recent years it is worthy of note that total profits in the past 13 seasons amount to £212,000. That's a remarkable achievement if you bear in mind that in May 1940, the club sustained a loss of £6,539 on that season's working and, in addition, owed the bank just over £30,000 and was mortgaged to the extent of £25,000 on the ground, as well as having other considerable liabilities.
>
> "From 1940 until 1942 we continued to show a loss until May 1943 when for the first time for years we were able to show a profit. It is true it was only a modest sum of £701, but it marked an important stage in United's recovery – one which has since seen every debt cleared off and, even more important, put the club on a sound financial level."

Hardman went on to explain how this had been achieved in a relatively short period of time, beginning a couple of years before the war with the encouragement and development of boys straight from school. The cultivation of promising footballing material was a long-term plan, highly developed by Matt Busby and his scouting network. He was also quick to admit that,

"The club were not always right, having made mistakes in buying players who did not fit in with the new ideas, hence money being wasted and lost in the sell-on deals.

"Much of the current success has been achieved in the face of a difficult rebuilding process, necessitated by a gradual change-over in first team playing personnel, but it speaks volumes for the way youth is being encouraged at Old Trafford that big-money signings of players have been an exception rather than a rule in the last few years.

"A mere glance at the present make-up of our first and second teams will prove that the policy of coaching and developing the young ideas is one that will pay dividends."

On the subject of players, Hardman said:

"There are no sliding scales of wages at Old Trafford, and there's not a player who has qualified for a benefit after five years' service that has not been paid. Not so long ago we created something of a surprise in football by handing out £750 benefit cheques to five players who were 21 years of age or under. Loyalty is a great asset in any football club. It's no use being able to point to financial successes if there's disharmony among the staff or in the dressing rooms. But I know I am speaking for all within the Manchester United organisation when I say from the merest junior to the highest executive there's a fine spirit which augurs well for the future."

The season had kicked off against newly promoted Birmingham City at St Andrew's. The visitors, hampered by a thigh injury to Taylor ten minutes prior to the interval, twice allowed their hosts to claw themselves back into the game, whilst ruing missed opportunities to snatch both points. Four days later, four goals were again shared with the opposition, the visit of Tottenham Hotspur raising the curtain on the home fixture list. Despite the dropped point, it was an encounter that prompted the *Guardian* correspondent to comment that if the high standard of play is continued, then "United followers have a feast of thrills in store."

For those followers parting with their hard-earned cash at the turnstiles on the opening day of season 1955-56,[6] recent reconstruction work offered grandstand patrons some 3,000 extra seats, and had provided new refreshment bars below sections A and E. Around the ground, other work had been carried out during the summer break, giving rise to up-to-date offices, reconditioned dressing rooms and recreational facilities for the players. The latter came in for high praise when used for the first time on the opening day of the season for the match against Tottenham Hotspur.

The third game of the campaign, a home fixture against West Bromwich Albion, saw Old Trafford used as something of a guinea-pig by the BBC as they filmed the entire ninety minutes of the game and then rushed the film off to Ringway Airport to catch a flight for London, where it was then taken to their studios to be put through the processing labs. The recording, however, was never shown on television, as it had all been nothing more than a dummy run for a new Saturday night sports programme entitled *Sports Special*, which was due to begin on September 10th. Those with a television and a love of football were unfortunate to miss an absorbing encounter as United clicked into gear, overwhelming the Midlands side 3-1 in a match they controlled from kick-off, seldom giving the visitors time to catch their breath on a humid afternoon alongside the ship canal. As one correspondent penned: "United's lightweight boots and collarless jerseys were not the only pleasing innovations in the defeat of West Brom. They produced a Continental swift-moving, close-passing style to go with their new garb." But such attire mattered little to Duncan Edwards as he was once again receiving the plaudits for his performances, which hit new heights against Tottenham Hotspur at White Hart Lane as August drew to a close. Edwards scored twice as Spurs were swept

---

6 Admission to the ground was 2/- (10p), juniors 9d (4p). The covered terrace 3/6d (18p), juniors 2/- (10p). Unreserved seats in A and E blocks were 5/- (25p), while reserved seats in B and C were 6/5d (33p). A season ticket for Stand 'B' would have set you back the grand sum of £6.10/- (£6.50).

aside with a 2-1 defeat, a victory that kept United in touch with the four other leading clubs at the top of the table.

Goals were not an integral part of the boy-wonder's make up, although when the opportunity did arise he proved he was as capable, and deadly, as Tommy Taylor. The not-so-distant 23-0 defeat of Nantwich in the FA Youth Cup had seen him hammer five past a hapless goalkeeper, while on international duty with the England Under-23 side last season – in the inaugural meeting at this level with 'Auld Enemy' Scotland at Shawfield in Glasgow – he had reverted to a more forward role following a team-mate's injury, and had gone on to snatch a memorable hat-trick.

He was not on hand, however, to pull his team out of the mire at Maine Road, as City took the honours with a solitary goal victory, after Roger Byrne had got caught in possession, in the first of the season's local 'derby' fixtures.

Edwards was back on target as Everton were beaten 2-1 at Old Trafford, but again the result proved something of a false dawn as Sheffield United and Everton, in their own backyards, denied United victories. Following the surprise defeat in Sheffield, a match Edwards missed due to flu, Matt Busby confessed that this was probably his toughest job ever, trying to get through the heavy spate of extra midweek fixtures, more so when the likes of Taylor, Viollet and the boy from Dudley were missing.

Unfortunately, his team selection was also hampered by injuries to Central League regulars Pegg and Lewis.

A 3-2 win at Deepdale against Preston North End cast some light on the dismal start, although the 0-0 draw at Burnley seven days later failed to impress *Manchester Evening News* correspondent Tom Jackson, who considered their performance "too deadly dull for words". Throw into the mix a 5-0 defeat at Easter Road, Edinburgh against Scottish champions Hibernian, and these were becoming worrying times. Then suddenly, something seemed to click, the thick, smoke-filled foggy atmosphere around Trafford Park seemed to lift and, amid the fresh air, an unbeaten run of six games saw United leap from sixth to top spot, a point in front of Sunderland.

Strangely, the turnaround in fortunes was achieved with less than full-strength elevens. Geoff Bent made his his debut in place of Byrne against Luton Town (the United captain on international duty), and another local-born youngster, 17-year-old former England Boys captain Wilf McGuinness, stepped up from the Central League side to replace Goodwin the following Saturday against Wolves. McGuinness's debut proved to be a pulsating five-goal encounter.

Another former England schoolboy international had also recently broken into the first-team ranks, as his nine goals in nine Central League outings had not gone unnoticed. When another friendly fixture added to the ever-expanding fixture list, the trip to Gigg Lane, Bury saw seventeen-year-old Bobby Charlton given an opportunity to prove his worth. He didn't disappoint, scoring once in the 5-1 victory.

Against Luton, United had gone a goal behind before putting three past the newly promoted side. For the Wolves game – played in front of 48,638, the biggest crowd of the season to date at Old Trafford – Bent kept his place at left back while John Doherty stepped forward for a rare outing, on the back of his two goals in the friendly against Bury. It was a performance that gave United the belief that they needed – "a football heyday with a story book finish" was how one unnamed reporter saw it, while Peter Slingsby wrote:

> "Phew! Phew! Phew! That's just how I feel after easily the most thrilling, glittering spectacle I have ever seen in ten years of watching League football."

A goal behind at half-time, Wolves equalised on the hour, going 2-1 in front seven minutes later. Tommy Taylor pulled United level in the 72nd minute, only for the visitors to once again take the lead before the cheering had died down. Five minutes from time, Doherty snatched what many presumed to be the goal that would earn his team a deserved point, but as the final couple of minutes ticked away, a Byrne free kick floated into the area and Mark Jones claimed his first goal for the club.

Eight goals were shared with Aston Villa, three were put past Huddersfield without reply, while a single Tommy Taylor effort was enough to beat Cardiff City. The Yorkshireman's seventh in six games was then enough to save a point in the 1-1 home draw with Arsenal.

The £29,999 transfer fee was certainly being justified, as the former Barnsley player was on the mark again against Bolton, followed by a double against Chelsea, making it ten in eight games; but the Burnden Park fixture saw the home side bring to an end United's eight-match unbeaten run with a 3-1 reversal. The only plus point of the afternoon was the debut of the diminutive, Salford-born Eddie Colman. Unlike most of his contemporaries, Colman was to keep his place for the remainder of the season.

It was not just on the field of play that the club was laying its plans for the future, as on the evening of October 26th a posse of United officials headed over the Pennines to Sheffield Wednesday's Hillsborough stadium. They were not in the market for reinforcements, casting their eyes away from the on-field action to make mental notes regarding the Yorkshire side's £25,000 floodlight system which was considered the best in the country.

Floodlit football was still something of a novelty, but many clubs had invested in the venture as they believed it was the future. At Old Trafford, they were wary about sinking money into a project which could prove little more than a white elephant. But they had had already experienced playing under floodlights at home and abroad and did not want to be left behind should the Football League and the FA embrace floodlight fixtures for their League and Cup competitions.

Their failure to look earlier into the potential of floodlights was going to prove costly for United, not only in the future, but in a matter of weeks. Early in 1956 they were approached by the Argentinian side River Plate enquiring about availability for a friendly between the two clubs. With no lights and an afternoon fixture considered not viable financially, what would have been an attractive friendly had to be rejected.

If there was one thing that was going to prove advantageous to the quest for the First Division title in the weeks and months ahead, it was Busby's opportunity to field a settled starting eleven. Certainly, there would be injuries and international call-ups which would force a reshuffling of the pack – at this time, 'home internationals' were regularly played on Saturday afternoons during the season – but now even United's reserve side was reaping the benefits of many of its regular members having First Division experience.

At reserve team level, there had been a vast improvement, arguably greater than that in the senior side. Struggling in the bottom half of the Central League ever since the war, their results were poor with attendances to match. For years they had been considered one of the worst-supported sides at this level, but now things had changed with gates averaging around 3,200 compared with 1,965 last season – and the name of Manchester United sat at the top of the table.

Many of those involved at this level now had first-team experience and were under the on-field guidance of Jack Crompton. On the touchline was Jimmy Murphy, whose intentions were to build a second team that had in effect ready-made replacements for every position, presenting Matt Busby with a much stronger and healthier squad.

This upsurge in fortunes at reserve level was quickly acted upon by the club, with secretary Walter Crickmer saying:

> "We are all out to encourage young spectators as well as footballers. An adult can bring his son to a match and both can have a comfortable seat in the stand for a total of 2/6d – 1/9d for the adult and 9d for the juniors."

Although still in the fledgling period of their careers, those League debutants of recent seasons had endured the sometimes robust welcome to First Division football amid sly kicks and elbows, while there were still others in the all-conquering youth team who were champing at the bit for their induction into the side. The Central League players who had already tasted first-team football also yearned to be part of what had the makings of a formidable team.

The defeat at Bolton on November 12th (what was it about the likes of the Wanderers and Burnley when they played United?) was soon forgotten as little more than a blip along the way. The show was back on the road with a 2-0 victory over Chelsea at Old

Trafford, where Alf Clarke of the *Evening Chronicle* heaped praise on Colman, building on his reputation following his debut seven days earlier.

A draw at Bloomfield Road against current leaders Blackpool was considered satisfactory, as it was only goal average that separated the two at the top of the First Division table, although the Seasiders had a game in hand. Seven days later, a 2-1 win over Sunderland took them above their fellow challengers, but consistency was still not part of the game plan, as the long journey to Portsmouth ended with an even longer one back to Manchester having suffered a 3-2 defeat. Thankfully, that reversal was little more than a minor blip, as the next three fixtures produced not simply three straight wins, but eleven goals for and only three against – 3-1 v Birmingham City, 4-1 against West Bromwich and a 5-1 Boxing Day success against Charlton Athletic.

Christmas, however, didn't prove so very merry as the return fixture against Charlton at the Valley produced a complete turnaround, with the Londoners completely outplaying their visitors to snatch a 3-0 victory. But the curtain was to come down on the old year in emphatic fashion with a 2-1 victory over neighbours City, a victory that took United four points ahead of nearest rivals Blackpool at the top of the First Division, although still having played a game more.

Despite City being mid-table, the meeting between the red and blue factions of Manchester on that last day of 1955 saw the Old Trafford gates firmly locked prior to kick-off. An estimated 15,000 were still outside and there was chaos everywhere as masses of people, shoulder to shoulder, continued to try and get near to the already-packed stadium and closed turnstiles. The scene looking towards Warwick Road Railway Bridge was just as dramatic, the crowd so dense that it was almost impossible to get across. Extra police had to be called out, as streets around the ground were packed with a mass of bodies, resembling a sea of human heads bobbing up and down. Traffic had virtually ground to a halt as coaches trapped in the traffic jam nearer to the ground dropped off their passengers and attempted to turn back. Thousands of ticketless supporters hung around Warwick Road in the hope that the gates would re-open – which they eventually did, but only to let out people who could not see or who had found the crush inside too much to bear. Police and ground stewards did their best to prevent anyone from gaining wrongful admission. Inside, the crowd of 60,956 created a post-war record of which the majority went home happy, as goals from Taylor and Viollet overturned City's 1-0 half-time lead to earn the points.

There were even more incredible scenes to be witnessed seven days later at Eastville, the home of Bristol Rovers, when United, longing for a trip to Wembley, were found wanting as their Second Division opponents took a 2-0 half-time lead. Almost incredibly, they then doubled their advantage during the second forty-five minutes. The major Cup upset left the United management and the majority of supporters at a loss, unable to pinpoint the reasons behind this slump in form.

Some supporters, however, believed that despite the team's promise and the real prospect of future honours, a "team general" was required – someone to rally the side when things were going wrong. This was certainly no slight upon Roger Byrne's leadership, but letters into the *Manchester Evening News* spoke of a "dominant personality" being required, a player to "follow in the footsteps of Johnny Carey and by his demeanour and example on the field, urge this young side to meet the unexpected difficulties."

Busby, however, was unperturbed. Countering the criticism that came his way for fielding such a young side at Bristol, he replied:

> "Some people are saying it was wrong of United to play in this game so many youngsters, including Colman, Doherty and Jones, who were having their cup-tie baptism.
>
> "Wrong? Rubbish. United are a young team, and are good enough to be leading the race for the First Division championship.
>
> "United's present team is the result of our long-term policy. I have no regrets at all about playing such a youthful side at Bristol. Indeed, nothing else could be done as practically the entire playing staff at Old Trafford consists of youngsters.

"We may not be a strong side physically at the moment but we are a good footballing side, and I claim that our future is really bright. We will get over this and now we have the championship trophy at which to aim. There are difficulties to be faced in this struggle too, but they are less likely to throw United out of their stride than the tie at Eastville."

If excuses for the Cup defeat were required, then the absence of Duncan Edwards, due to a boil on his knee, was as good as any. When the man/boy from Dudley returned the following Saturday on an Old Trafford mudbath in the first league outing of 1956 – coupled with the re-introduction of Liam Whelan at inside-right – Sheffield United were soundly beaten 3-1. This, however, was only a ninety-minute return to normality, as the absence of Taylor and Berry at Preston brought yet another defeat, their third in five games.

With continued praise being heaped upon United's second string, one would have thought that no matter who was missing, their place could be automatically filled without loss of fluency or points. The inclusion of Webster and Scott was to cause minor disruption, although one recent observer of United's second string was quick to heap further accolades on these youngsters.

Manchester City's Don Revie, out of action with an injury, decided to see for himself what others were getting excited about and gave the recent United–City fixture a miss in order to watch the Central League fixture between the two sides, a game United won 3-0. The City forward confessed:

"What an eye opener this was. United's second team gave as fine an exhibition of football as I've seen all season.

"Just where Matt Busby finds all these starlets I wouldn't pretend to know. But if he isn't the happiest manager in Britain he ought to be.

"His first team (most in their twenties) top the First Division and are already being hailed as the team of the season. Yet his reserve team is so good that I wouldn't back the so-called first team to beat them. It's quite true. For twenty minutes I saw this reserve side roll the ball around with the slick precision passing which I thought was copyright of the Hungarians.

"I asked the United reserves team captain, goalkeeper Jack Crompton what he thought about these 'Busby Minnows' and he replied 'They are incredible. They play like this every week. We've lost only two games and I think these lads play as good as, if not better than, our great side of 1948 which won the Cup'.

"I don't think Jack was overstating the case."

It wasn't so much Busby finding the 'starlets', as Jimmy Murphy and Bert Whalley polishing them up to sparkle and shine. Of the twenty-four players called upon for First Division duty this season, twenty-one (twenty-two if you include Ray Wood, who arrived as a teenager) all came through the ranks. But as far as Busby being the happiest manager in Britain, the recent form had certainly removed the smile from his face. Nevertheless, the United manager kept a fatherly arm around his young charges, restoring their confidence with a few choice words, while others sought to discover the ingredients used in the creation of this football club, widely considered to be on the verge of greatness. In the *Guardian*, a 'Special Correspondent' put pen to paper with his thoughts on the matter, adding some additional spice to the already tasty platter.

"It is probably significant that Busby and Murphy were both international wing half-backs of constructive bent – players in the position which pre-eminently demands football, blending attack and defence, strength and control and flexibility in tactics. This helps to explain too, the balanced linking of defence with attack in teams they have produced.

"One of the most important features of their production of players is that, for all the emphasis upon mastery of the elementary skills, there has been no move – as might have been understandable if not commendable towards any form of stereotyped 'Manchester United' football. Each player has been encouraged to develop his particular gifts and urges to the advantage of the team, so that the dash of one, the shooting power of another, the speed of a third, the long passing of a fourth have been exploited in harness with the ranging of a fifth, the mobility of a sixth, the plodding steadiness of a seventh. Variety has been achieved without loss of balance, through mutual understanding of the game's problems, upon which the players are encouraged to think for themselves."

The writer went on to say that most of the successful post-war sides – Wolves, Newcastle, Tottenham and Arsenal – had all settled on a particular style of play, but with United,

"there is no characteristic style. Aiming to produce players of all-round ability, the club's planners have sought to place in the team the varied skills necessary to meet and defeat every type of play with which they may be faced. Thus, from match to match, defensive formation or attacking method may vary.

"It is remarkable too, that since Morris and Mitten were transferred, no player – more important, no reserve player of appreciable gifts unable to win a place in the first team – has appeared to wish to leave the club. Such a state of contentment among the players is a basic factor in maintenance of adequate reserve power.

"Sober assessment of the present play, playing strength, organisation, and their reasonable potential, suggest that Manchester United may be no more than part-way towards the establishment of a period of remarkable supremacy in English football."

But had the dismal results of late dented the club's immediate ambitions, and sown seeds of doubt into the minds of United's aspiring, hitherto positive-minded professionals? Could they shake off the clawing fingers of Blackpool as they attempted to snatch the championship crown from United's grasp? Two points still separated the sides, although the Seasiders continued to have that haunting game in hand along with a superior goal average. Certainly, there was still much to play for. Fourteen fixtures, spread over three months, were still pencilled into United's First Division agenda.

Army duty robbed Foulkes of his place not just for the visit of Burnley, but for the remainder of the season – this due to the form of his replacement Ian Greaves. Meanwhile, the rest of the side more or less selected itself, although Doherty was to regain his place at the expense of Whelan as the campaign moved towards its final handful of fixtures.

Tommy Taylor celebrated his 100th appearance with the crucial opening goal against Burnley, Viollet adding a second; then on a snow-covered Kenilworth Road, Luton Town were no match for the fleet-footed United, as Viollet again, and Whelan, scored the goals that ensured victory. It was a game that could easily have ended in defeat through no fault of Matt Busby or his players.

The clash of international fixtures with normal Football League matches was a great enough hindrance to Busby and his fellow managers. But then a new obstacle was thrown in front of United's drive for the championship, when the army demanded the services of Foulkes, Colman and Edwards for a match in Brussels, scheduled for the day after the trip to Luton. Busby could, in all honesty, have little complaint as the army was always sympathetic to his cause when he requested leave for his players.

A Taylor double ensured two points from the visit to Molineux, as United stretched their lead to six points over Blackpool, although still having played that game more, while a solitary Liam Whelan goal against Aston Villa was enough to make it four wins out of four and without a goal conceded.

Despite the points difference, Blackpool were certainly not going to give up on their title challenge, determined to match United result by result. Pegg, Taylor and a Viollet double ensured a 4-2 victory at Stamford Bridge, but that same afternoon, Blackpool hit five against fourth-placed West Bromwich Albion. A surprised dropped point against Cardiff City at Old Trafford could have given their title rivals an unexpected boost, but again they matched United's result, drawing 3-3 at near neighbours Preston.

The race was suddenly flung wide open when a Roger Byrne penalty miss proved fatal at Highbury. Viollet did give United the lead, but Arsenal managed to claw themselves back into the game and claim a point. Blackpool, on this particular afternoon, brushed Newcastle aside with a 5-1 win, narrowing the gap to five points.

If United needed a wake-up call, a quick jolt to remind them of what was at stake, it came on Saturday March 24th, not at any football ground, but at a sporting venue little more than half an hour from Manchester. With the crowds at Aintree watching the Grand National mentally calculating their winnings as the afternoon's favourite horse – the Queen Mother's Devon Loch – galloped towards the finishing line some fifty yards clear of the chasing pack, a famous sporting shock occurred. Racegoers were left open-mouthed as the horse suddenly shied and slipped, allowing 100-7 outsider E.S.B. to gallop past and cross the finishing line in first place. It was an ominous warning for all at Old Trafford – or if you wish to quote Shakespeare, "Beware the ides of March."

Bolton, certainly not one of United's favourite opponents, failed for once to get the better of their opponents' defence, and Tommy Taylor repaid another chunk of his transfer fee with the only goal of the game in the twenty-ninth minute. His goals of late had been infrequent, only two in five games, but his latest strike was enough to earn the first win in three. This at a time when all of United's previously free-scoring forwards were suddenly struggling to find the net.

Easter had long been considered a telling period on the football calendar, a time when championships, promotions and relegations were often decided. For United, it was Newcastle at home on Good Friday, followed twenty-four hours later by a short trip over the Pennines to Leeds Road, Huddersfield and a longer journey to Tyneside for the return fixture against the Geordies on Easter Monday. Three fixtures that could perhaps secure the First Division title for the first time since 1952 – or else bring dreams and expectations crashing down. United form aside, so much depended on how second-placed Blackpool fared, five points behind with a game in hand.

In his report in the *Daily Mirror* on Newcastle's visit to Old Trafford, Derek Wallis wrote:

> "I cannot fathom Manchester United. They raise you to the heights with blinding power, then leave you stranded high and dry just as you are about to acclaim them as a wonder team. Yet here they are striding towards the League championship.
>
> "I cannot put my finger on the mysterious 'something' that this team possess.
>
> "Against Newcastle, yesterday, they thrilled – and then, stifled the cheers in the next minute. At half-time, the match could have gone either way."

For the throbbing 58,994 crowd packed into Old Trafford, the third best attendance of the season, the result thankfully went United's way with an emphatic 5-2 win. It took United a mere six minutes to open the scoring, the ball catching the Newcastle defence on the wrong foot as it rebounded from a corner flag, allowing Berry to direct one of his pinpoint crosses into the area where Pegg, with little hesitation, brought the ball under control and slipped it into the net.

Pegg had already come close to scoring, while goalkeeper Wood had brought cries of anguish from the home support when he took a wild swing at the ball and missed completely; but, to their relief, Mitchell's lob towards the open goal was charged down. With half an hour gone, the match had suddenly swung on its axis and Newcastle twice had the ball in the United net. First, Hannah was dismayed to have his effort struck off for offside, but an exchange of passes between Hannah and Keeble saw the latter beat Wood to level the scores.

As Derek Wallis had written, the match was perfectly poised. As the second half got underway, Hannah once again came close, his shot rolling narrowly past the post. Recovery was quick and a Colman–Doherty–Pegg move ended with Taylor beating Simpson with ease to give United the advantage. But still their defence continued to stutter along, Davies and Milburn uncharacteristically wasting golden opportunities.

Possibly upset by recent comments that a commanding on-field figure was required, Roger Byrne was to turn in a second-half performance that Don Davies of the *Guardian* considered his "finest for two seasons" as "he rose to his full stature", and it was no coincidence that his team-mates quickly took the game by the scruff of the neck. A Pegg–Taylor move produced the third, Viollet back-heeled a fourth, while Doherty scored a well-deserved fifth. Two minutes from time, with victory assured, Newcastle grabbed a second through Stokoe.

Along the 'Golden Mile' on the Lancashire coast, Blackpool supporters were stunned not only by United's emphatic victory following their somewhat indifferent form, but their own team's failure to beat Bolton in a dismal 0-0 draw. All, however, was not lost, as a handful of games still remained, including a meeting between the top two at Old Trafford.

Twenty-four hours later, the Seasiders dropped another vital point in a 1-1 draw with relegation-haunted Sheffield United at Bloomfield Road, while a Tommy Taylor double ensured both points from the visit to Huddersfield. The title was now within United's grasp and could be secured on Easter Monday if the visit to St James' Park yielded a victory and Blackpool continued their run of poor form in their return match against Bolton.

Like a rabbit caught in car headlights, United hesitated, stage fright got the better of them and the champagne that the Newcastle directors had laid on had to remain unopened and sent to Manchester for future use following the goalless encounter. Blackpool, determined at least to go out with a bang, defeated Bolton 3-1.

If United were to clinch the title in front of their own support, then they were going to have to do so without their manager, as a family bereavement meant a journey north, leaving Jimmy Murphy to rally the troops, all but two of whom had passed through his hands in the junior ranks. With the Welshman in charge of such an important fixture, there was only ever going to be one outcome.

Rather surprisingly, United had not made the fixture 'all-ticket' and, for many, it was an early-morning journey to the ground to ensure a place on the terracing. Nine-year-old Roy Cavanagh was more than aware of the important fixture due to be played out a short walk from his family home in Ordsall Lane. He had planned to kick his ball about in the street, straining his ears for the muffled cries of the crowd which would signal a United goal. But that was before his Uncle Tom arrived and casually asked if fancied going to the match. Roy recalled:

"I did not need to be asked twice and was soon dragging my uncle down Ordsall Lane, past the green buses lined up having dropped off their fares and were awaiting their return, heading towards the large swing bridge on Trafford Road, hoping that our progress would not be delayed by anything on the canal.

"A copy of the *United Review* was a must and as the crowds thickened I got caught up in the atmosphere. Although it was pay at the gate, it never really concerned me that we wouldn't get in, even with the huge queues building up at the turnstiles as we walked round the ground looking for one that was quieter than the rest. Finding one at the Stretford End, we were in and up the steps to be engulfed in a sprawling mass of bodies. Much to my disappointment, there was no way that I was going to see much of the action, or indeed anything at all, but I was still part of it all.

"My uncle happily gave me a running commentary, as I turned my back on the title decider to watch the Glovers Cables works side on their makeshift pitch adjacent to their factory."

In the United dressing room, as kick-off time drew closer, the atmosphere was more subdued than normal, according to Roger Byrne:

"Normally before a League game just prior to the team leaving for the field everybody is bustling around requiring all the little essentials such as petroleum jelly, new laces. On Saturday, everybody was ready at least 10 minutes before the kick-off time, I have never known the dressing room so quiet. Everybody was trying to create a feeling of complete relaxation when in actual fact they were all keyed up to fever pitch. In fact one wit said, 'Somebody has dropped a pin,' so quiet was the room."

Young Master Cavanagh was fortunate to gain admission, as the gates were locked fifteen minutes before kick-off with 62,377 inside. Outside, squads of policemen, some mounted, attempted to bring order to the vast number of supporters locked outside, many still debating whether to make their way back home, to go to the nearest public house, or simply remain at the ground and listen to the noise emancipating from behind the red brick walls. The sound of the crowd would tell its own story as the afternoon's drama began to unfold.

A call over the loudspeakers for a doctor to return to the General Hospital might have reduced that total by one – or perhaps a patient had to endure an hour and a half's pain while the doctor suffered turmoil on the terracing as Blackpool stormed into the lead in the second minute. Durie rose above Colman to head firmly past Wood. Blackpool's live duck mascot, accompanied by his 'eastern prince', had certainly brought good fortune with them from the Lancashire resort. At the back of the Stretford End, young master Cavanagh didn't need his uncle to tell him what had happened.

Undeterred, United pushed forward, and Viollet almost equalised minutes later despite the close attention of Gratrix and Wright. Doherty hit the upright with a header after Colman's shot had been blocked before play swung back towards the United goal. Matthews beat Wood with a tantalising centre, only to see Byrne heading clear at the expense of a corner, then Wood took two attempts to gather a drive from Mudie.

Byrne set up Viollet, but the United forward, for once, failed in front of goal as the game continued to flow from end to end. Wood cut out a Durie centre, Farm saved at full length from Viollet, then Berry mesmerised the Blackpool defence before lobbing the ball forward towards Doherty. The United inside-forward headed goalwards, but with the crowd about to scream 'goal', Frith headed off the line.

Former Manchester City keeper Frank Swift, now a reporter for the *News of the World*, described the match as "an epic of never-say-die spirit from that explosive first minute", going on to add "seldom have I seen a goal so charmed. Though the ball rained in on Farm, United could not put it in the net" – a blight that continued when Tommy Taylor's body got in the way of a goalbound Viollet shot to ensure that the visitors went in at half-time still holding on to their one-goal advantage. During those ten minutes under the stand, Murphy rallied his troops, his Welsh brogue installing renewed confidence.

Within minutes of the second half getting underway, it looked as though Pegg was finally going to make the breakthrough, but the winger fired over with an open goal gaping in front of him. Ten minutes later, both sides were temporarily reduced to ten men, as Taylor and Wright went off with cut heads. It was during the four minutes of ten-a-side that United finally secured the vital equaliser. Doherty lost possession in front of goal but, in a panic, Farm came out of his goal and lunged at the United player, catching him on the hip. The referee was left with no option other than to point to the spot. "It was never a penalty," declared Farm, "I bumped into him accidently." Berry, unnerved by neither the occasion nor the protests, calmly fired the ball past the aggrieved keeper.

It was now game on, but it wasn't until ten minutes from time that the outcome was settled. Having outshone Matthews all afternoon, Berry danced down the right before swinging a cross into the Blackpool area. Farm failed to hold the ball and it slipped towards Taylor who managed to prod it towards the line as he fell. Frith, on the goal line, tried to scoop the ball away with his hand but only succeeded in helping it over the line. For a second the crowd held its breath, wondering if the referee would award a penalty or a goal. Much to their relief, it was the latter. Berry, who had enjoyed one of his best games for the club, was gratified that the referee had decided to award the goal, as he later said: "I hadn't the strength to take another penalty by that time."

Despite the victory, many were left disappointed that there was to be no trophy presentation to round off a memorable Saturday afternoon, their excitement dampened by the placid tones of United secretary Walter Crickmer coming over the loudspeaker system to inform them, "No presentation today chaps, so don't swarm across the pitch if you please. Out in the normal way through the exits."

As the final whistle blew and the celebrations began, Busby was still en route from Glasgow to Manchester, having stopped at Abbington to phone Old Trafford, only to be told that his team was a goal behind. A second call from Lockerbie brought better news: United were 2-1 in front, but from south-west Scotland to Manchester there were no further calls, and it wasn't until he pulled up outside the ground that he was given news of a double celebration, as the Central League side had also been crowned champions.

"It has been a wonderful season for us," Busby was later to say. "I am delighted we have won the championship. I congratulate all the players and pay tribute to Roger Byrne's captaincy."

Looking back over the ninety minutes, Roger Byrne noted a change in his team-mates once the first whistle blew.

> "On the field, everything was forgotten except the job in hand. The early goal certainly shocked us, but it was probably the worst thing that Blackpool could have done. It made us realise how hard the game was going to be, and only a superb effort was going to achieve victory.
>
> "The whole eleven players played harder than ever before. I heard at half-time one person say, 'United will never last the pace.' How wrong he was!
>
> "The longer the game went on the stronger we became and the more demoralised became Blackpool.
>
> "I don't think I can remember the Old Trafford crowd being behind us more. On Saturday there was no doubt that the roar spurred United on more than Blackpool. The pleasing thing was the way the stand rose to us at half-time even though we were one down at the time.

"Many people have asked me why I did not take the penalty. That job had already been allocated to Johnny Berry two weeks prior to the game. After the ball went in, I knew we would never lose, yet only two magnificent interceptions by Mark Jones saved the game in the later stages.

"Team spirit plus ability has definitely pulled us through and had it not been for this companionship we would have wilted long before now under the strain."

Two days later, the champions were brought back down to earth, as even though the destination of the First Division title had been balanced on a knife edge, a friendly had been agreed with Dundee. Certainly a case of bad planning by the United management, though fortunately things had worked out in their favour. Still, it was a makeshift eleven that travelled north to Dens Park, five changes being made to the team that had beaten Blackpool, including the untried Paddy Kennedy and Bobby Charlton. Those changes were perhaps reflected in the scoreline, a 5-1 defeat, although Ray Wood had gone off with an ankle injury when the score stood at 2-0, his place taken by reserve full-back Kennedy. The reversal was of little concern to anyone at Old Trafford, soon confined to the record books where it would disappear into obscurity.

Despite the celebrations, there were still two more League fixtures to fulfil, plus another friendly north of the border at Parkhead against Celtic (which ended as a 2-2 draw). But now the pressure was off, no-one cared if England wanted Roger Byrne, Duncan Edwards and Tommy Taylor for their team to face Scotland at Hampden on the same afternoon as United played their penultimate game at Sunderland. Had the title not been clinched seven days previously, then the telephone lines between Old Trafford and the Football Association would have been red-hot. Even without the talented trio, United secured a point with a 2-2 draw, rounding off their campaign with a 1-0 home victory over Portsmouth. It was an uninspiring ninety minutes, with many of the United support creating their own excitement with a pitch invasion a couple of minutes before the end. But they were back on again, in greater numbers, as the referee's whistle finally signalled full time, heading to the mouth of the tunnel in front of the main stand in order to get a close-up view of the championship trophy being presented to captain Roger Byrne.

"We have a great young team – and I mean great, because they are only starting," Matt Busby told a crowd of over three thousand packed into Albert Square, speaking from the steps of the Town Hall prior to a civic reception. "The future of United in my opinion is wonderful."

Strangely enough, if Busby had listened to some of his army colleagues then things could have been so much different, as Joe Mercer confirmed.

> "When we left the army after the war some of us, people like Stan Cullis and myself who fancied our chances as coaches, were cynical about the young players who had come into the game. 'Can't play,' we used to say. We knew Matt was preparing to put his faith in kids.
>
> "We told him he was wrong, but he stuck implicitly to his ideas and proved us wrong."

Chapter Six

Jousting With Giants

Season 1956-57

S O, the First Division championship trophy once again stood proudly in the Old Trafford directors' room. Although United hadn't exactly dominated the First Division from start to finish during that 1955-56 campaign, they had eventually stormed ahead, ending the season eleven points ahead of second-placed Blackpool. It was a title well deserved, going hand in hand with the plaudits that had been thrown in United's direction over the past couple of seasons. They had been there before, of course, in 1952 with an ageing team, but now there was the elixir of youth, new foundations had been laid, and continuing this initial success with arguably the youngest first and second teams in the country was paramount.

The future of Manchester United was certainly bright, the championship success sounding out a warning to the rest of the Division that despite the injuries, the lack of form and the introduction of youngsters, they were a force to be reckoned with – the team to beat, if others wanted to claim their crown. For those would-be contenders, there was also the frightening prospect that the Old Trafford club could only get better. A daunting prospect, indeed!

There was of course the FA Cup to recapture, but it was not only on the domestic front that Busby looked to excel. He was aiming much higher.

Past close-season tours of America and Canada, and more recent trips to Scandinavia, had not simply been relaxing breaks with a handful of fixtures thrown in to amuse the locals and to keep the United players in shape; nor were they money-making ventures. They were all part of a development programme, a learning curve for both manager and players alike. Such tests against opponents from different countries and continents meant United had to adapt to compete. Friendlies at home and abroad often involved a mixture of personnel and although a competitive streak could often be found within each ninety minutes, results mattered little.

With the dark shadow cast by the Second World War all but past, everyday life was changing for the better, while football as a game was progressing in a positive direction. Floodlighting was one such area of development, with Wolves – First Division champions in 1953-54 and runners-up the following year – using their pedigree to organise midweek friendlies against the likes of Racing Club of Argentina, Spartak Moscow and Honved. Such encounters did not go unnoticed, and when a journalist for the French sports paper *L'Equipe* reported back to his editor about the success of the South American inter-club championship, Gabriel Hanot, amused by the Molineux club's claim to be 'Champions of the World', began to put into place a concept for a similar tournament in Europe, eventually presenting his ideas to UEFA. His ideas were duly accepted and in the summer of 1955 invitations were sent out to sixteen clubs, not necessarily the champions of their respective countries, to take part in the inaugural competition. One such invitation went to English First Division champions Chelsea, but when they approached the Football League for permission to enter, they were informed in no uncertain terms that they could not take part.

Matt Busby, however, was delighted when a letter, dated 23 April, from the general secretary of UEFA, Pierre Delaunay, dropped through the Old Trafford letter box requesting United to take part in the 1956-57 'Coupe des Clubs Champions Européens'. Busby was no pushover, and he had no intention of bowing to the conservative demands of football's domestic administrators.

As expected, the Football League quickly stepped in and informed United that they should not enter the competition.

League secretary Alan Hardaker, who had played his part in bullying Chelsea into submission the previous year, was quoted as saying, "I don't like dealing with Europe. Too many wops and dagoes." Back in February 1956 the single-minded organisation had sent a circular round all the clubs as they were concerned about the drop in attendances, part of its contents stating that the Football League was not primarily concerned with football as a world game, nor as a British or an English game as a whole, but with the League competition alone. No mention was made of the players.

United did, however, receive the backing of the Football Association, its secretary, Sir Stanley Rous, writing to Walter Crickmer on May 14th:

> "You will no doubt have heard of the European Champion Clubs Cup competition in which last season Hibernians took part and Chelsea FC withdrew. The final of this competition will be played on June 13th in Paris between Real Madrid and Reims.
>
> "The Committee of the competition is most anxious that for this coming season all the champions of the various countries in Europe should take part and they ask whether your Club would consider entering the competition.
>
> "The financial advantages are many and the competition is run on the usual Cup system. Each team will meet the same opponents twice, on a home and away basis. The Clubs are paired by drawing lots.
>
> "I enclose herewith the Regulations of the Competition and I should be grateful if you would study them and let me know whether your Club intends to take part. I should be grateful for an early reply, as the European Union should be notified before May 20th.
>
> "All the matches in the competition are mutually arranged between the clubs concerned on dates which are convenient to both. Last year Hibernians were called upon to play six matches and were knocked out in the semi-final tie by Reims: their matches were all played on midweek

dates, which fitted in quite conveniently with their league programme.

"I think this could be an excellent opportunity for your club and should show good financial return."

With the FA's backing, United were even more determined to ignore the Football League, although Busby did have to convince his board that despite venturing into unfamiliar territory, it was an enterprise which would benefit the club in the long run, and not just financially. Somewhat apprehensively, chairman Harold Hardman shrugged his shoulders and said to his manager, "if that's what you really feel". The decision had been made.

United confirmed their acceptance of the invitation and in the late June draw found themselves installed in Group Two along with Nice, Aarhus and their opponents in the preliminary round, Belgian champions Anderlecht. Also in this group were Glasgow Rangers, Norrkoping of Sweden, Real Madrid and the yet undecided champions of Holland. The latter four clubs were exempt from the draw.

The immediate minor problems, fixing travel arrangements and the like, would take care of themselves, but the difficulty looming centred around the preliminary-round home leg match. Floodlight installation at Old Trafford was now well past the planning stage, but the second-leg home tie would still have to be played in the afternoon to ensure that the game would be completed in daylight. This would undoubtedly have an effect on the attendance, with the club also coming in for criticism from local businesses due to the rate of absenteeism that would materialise. There was, however, one other option: to go cap in hand to neighbours City and ask if they would be prepared to hire out Maine Road for this and hopefully subsequent fixtures in the competition.

The request was made and on August 13th came the awaited reply from the City secretary:

"Dear Mr. Busby, Further to Mr. McDowall's (the City manager) conversation with you, I wish to confirm that my Board will be pleased to loan you Maine Road Ground

on 26th September for your European Cup-tie on terms
of £300 or 15% of the Nett Gate whichever is the greater."

The ball was rolling.

Even so, the matter could hardly be considered cut and dried. A
letter dated 21st August arrived at Old Trafford from the Football
League which read:

"The Management committee have considered your letters
with regard to your entry into this competition and they
quite understand that you entered the Competition in good
faith. Nevertheless, I am instructed to write you as follows:-

"The Management Committee consider that
participation in such a Competition is not in the best
interests of the League as a whole, clashing as it does with the
League Competition. They therefore ask you to reconsider
your decision to participate in the light of its possible effect
on attendances at League matches, when you are playing
at home."

A two-worded reply might have been forthcoming, but the United
board and manager had a little more diplomatic tact. Dated 24th
August, their response read:

"Your letter of the 21st instant was submitted to my
Directors at their meeting last evening.

"My Board very much regret that at this late date
it is impossible to withdraw from the Competition. All
arrangements have been made for the home and away games
v Anderlecht, tickets have been printed and the applications
are now being dealt with.

"My Directors are pleased to note that the management
Committee realise that we entered the Competition in good
faith, and, notwithstanding that the existing rule does not
call for any payment to the Football League from the receipts
of matches in the Competition, my Board instruct me to say
that they will in any event make the usual payment of 4%

to the League, so long as our interest in the Competition continues."

Bribery? No just a little softener, and United's way of showing that they were happy to pay their way if the Football League felt they were losing out. It was a generous gesture by United, considering the Football League had been set against their entry in the first place, and that they were already forced into sharing match takings with neighbours City.

The lack of floodlights at Old Trafford was now becoming a real priority, though the system that had been selected for installation cost £40,000, bringing the total outlay on ground improvements and war damage repairs to over £220,000. The need to rent Maine Road could have been avoided had initial plans for floodlighting been put into place last season, but they were not considered as important as repairing the stand. At that time, midweek European competitions had never been considered, and must have seemed a long way off.

The 1956-57 season got off to a stuttering start: a goal in front at home against an invigorated Birmingham City side, they were soon to find themselves 2-1 down before Dennis Viollet rescued a point with his second of the afternoon, preventing an opening day embarrassment. Five straight victories, however, (3-1 at Preston, 3-2 at the Hawthorns against West Bromwich, 3-2 and 3-0 home wins against Preston and Portsmouth respectively and a 2-1 victory against Chelsea at Stamford Bridge) saw the now familiar move to the top of the First Division table.

Despite this favourable start, there was only one thing on the minds of everyone associated with the club and that was the European Cup, with the preliminary round first leg taking place on September 12th in Brussels. A 1-1 draw at Newcastle served as a warm-up for the tie against Anderlecht, ideal opposition for this ground-breaking fixture as the Belgians had enjoyed trophy success on their home soil and had already experienced the thrill of European football, having appeared in the inaugural competition the previous year. Their mixture of amateurs and part-time professionals had proved no major drawback.

United treated that first-leg tie at the compact Astrid Park with obvious caution, international honours having introduced only Roger Byrne, Duncan Edwards, Tommy Taylor and Liam Whelan (who had only one solitary Republic of Ireland cap to his credit) to a stiffer opponent than their familiar First Division foe. But international experience mattered little as the novice Reds were far from out of place.

Still, it was with some relief that they took the lead in the 25th minute. Jones cleared a threatening Anderlecht attack, the ball finding its way to Colman who in turn pushed it towards Viollet positioned just over the halfway line. Outpacing centre-half de Koster, he hit the ball wide of the Anderlecht keeper from six yards out.

Although shaken, the home side, to their credit, showed considerable resilience, putting up a commendable fight, as could be expected from a country strewn with numerous historic battlefields. Had they equalised from the penalty given just after the interval when Jones handled, the scoreline might have told a different story; but Wood did well to save from de Wael after Lippens's spot-kick had hit the post.

The plucky Belgians kept the visitors' advantage down to that solitary goal until fifteen minutes from time, when Pegg crossed the ball towards Taylor who headed home with accustomed ease, the United centre-forward having seen an earlier attempt disallowed for offside.

There was no post-Anderlecht hangover, no travel tiredness, as Sheffield Wednesday were made to look second rate in a 4-1 defeat at Old Trafford. And four days before the Belgians' arrival in Manchester, United warmed up in style at Maine Road, defeating neighbours City 2-0. The scoreline once again flattered the opposition, as the United forwards squandered numerous scoring opportunities.

Those missed chances would be considered as little more than shooting practice following the European Cup second-leg tie at Maine Road, which was certainly no mirror image of the first. Instead, it sent out a warning to the other sides in the competition, a bold statement of intent that Manchester United were no novices and had an eye on ultimate victory. The 10-0 scoreline may have surprised many, but it proved that Busby's team were not out of their depth when stepping on to this new stage. Future opposition would certainly be tougher, but on this result, the future held little fear. "Manchester United Superb" declared the *Guardian*, while Frank Taylor in the *Daily Dispatch* penned: "Hail the Busby Babes, the new soccer supremos, for a display of clockwork football which ground Anderlecht out of the European Cup. It was a savage soccer slaughter as Manchester United strode majestically on into the next round."

Pools of water from the heavy pre-match rain studded the surface of the pitch, but it was the Belgians who floundered, struggling against a tidal wave of red-shirted attacks – though, to be fair, they were unfortunate not to take an early lead when Mermans, their most dangerous player, prodded the ball through to de Wael in the opening minute, only to see it come to a sudden halt on the sodden turf, the opportunity going amiss.

In no way did David Pegg find the conditions underfoot to be a disadvantage, leading the Belgians a merry dance. His crosses from the left in the eighth and 21st minutes provided scoring opportunities for Taylor to score his eighth and ninth goals of the season.

By half-time, the outcome was clear. A Viollet hat-trick from goals in the 27th, 34th and 40th minutes saw the dejected visitors leaving the pitch with heads bowed, surrendered to their fate. They had, however, further punishment to come.

Particularly under the conditions, United could have been forgiven for easing up in the second half, but they simply picked up where they had left off, increasing their lead three minutes after the restart through Taylor, going on to match their first-half haul with a further four goals through Whelan in the 64th and 87th minutes, Viollet with his fourth in the 75th minute and Berry ten minutes later.

Try as they might, the goalscoring United forwards failed to conjure up a goal for the only member of the front five not to find the back of the net – David Pegg – but the Doncaster boy cared little as he had taken central stage on a memorable night for both

Manchester and British football. "I can never hope in the rest of a lifetime to see anything better than this," proclaimed Busby, but even the master was to be proved wrong.

Despite their humiliation, the Belgians applauded their victors from the field. "Better than Honved, better than the Russians," they later proclaimed, while Frank Taylor wondered what the reaction of the Football League officials would be, having been keen to exclude United from participating in the competition. There was none. But no-one needed their approval, as the newspapers of the following day told the story.

Many more than the 43,365 on the Maine Road terraces were witness to the incredible display, as the game was beamed live to the continent. Sadly, a larger British audience was not privy to the events as they unfolded in Moss Side, as Football League clubs called for the broadcast to be banned, worried about its potential effect on attendances at the three Third Division North and four Third Division South fixtures being played that night. Players' Union chairman Jimmy Guthrie was far from happy, voicing his opinion:

> "Fancy stopping the British public from seeing this match because it might affect the gate at the Reading–Southend Third Division match under lights at Reading. I ask you!
>
> "They'll be stopping Manchester United playing any matches in London on Saturdays in case their appearance affects the gates at the other grounds that day. Why not do the job properly? Stop United playing at all, except where there isn't another match within 100 miles."

To the surprise of many, there was no fall-out from the demoralisation of the Belgians, no hangover or drop in momentum, as three days later Arsenal were beaten 2-1 at Highbury, making it twenty-four League games without defeat. According to one report, United merely ambled through the ninety minutes, their performance leaving no doubt as to their tremendous potential.

A week later the twenty-four match run became twenty-five with the 4-2 defeat of Charlton Athletic at Old Trafford, making it a record-breaking[7] thirty-one games undefeated, if one counted in the two European Cup ties and four friendlies.

However, it wasn't the record that captured the headlines, but the performance of yet another Central League prodigy making the step-up on to the big stage. Ashington-born youngster Bobby Charlton, just 18 years old, had marked his First Division debut with two goals.

Replacing Tommy Taylor, who was on international duty alongside team-mates Roger Byrne and Duncan Edwards, Charlton, along with McGuinness and Bent, gave the United line-up an even more youthful look, but it made little difference to the overall performance. The debutant's performance, however (where in reality he should have claimed a hat-trick), was simply something for the record books. The following Saturday Charlton was back to the second eleven as the seniors not only extended that unbeaten run, but maintained their three-point advantage at the top of the First Division.

It had been obvious from the outset that, unlike the domestic cup competition, where clubs from a lower division could progress well beyond the early rounds, the European Cup would create a completely different scenario, each round undoubtedly pairing United with a team of greater experience and of a much higher quality. The Germans of Borussia Dortmund would therefore present United with a far sterner challenge than the Belgians of the previous round.

There was also the new experience of having to play the first leg on home soil – again hired for the night over the city at Maine Road.

Frank Taylor, who had praised United following their overpowering display against Anderlecht, offered a completely different view to the ninety minutes against the Germans, a game that saw United secure victory by the odd goal in five. As the *News Chronicle* reporter wrote:

---

7 Beating Burnley's 1920-21 record of 30 undefeated matches, all of which were League games.

"The Busby Babes, pride of British football, were altogether too cocky at Maine Road last night, and almost got kicked out of the European Cup in the process. Make no mistake, the shimmering gold shirts of the German champions blinded the United by their brilliance in the second half.

"Let this be a lesson to Manchester United. I'm sure it will. Manager Matt Busby is not the man to go storming into his players, but I am sure he will impress on them that you just can't afford to take chances in football.

"A single goal lead is not likely to be enough when the second leg is played, not on this showing anyway. The facts speak for themselves."

Taylor pointed his finger at Roger Byrne, blaming him for a slip which started a wave of Dortmund attacks. Instead of clearing the ball, he attempted to chest it back to Ray Wood, and could only stand in horror as Kapitulski nipped in to score. The *Daily Dispatch* man also blamed the United defence for Dortmund's second goal, Colman and Edwards for failing to get a grip of the game and Taylor and Whelan for not bringing their wingers more into play. One wonders what the scribe would have written had United actually lost!

Watched by a crowd of over 75,000 – an increase of some 32,000 on the Anderlecht fixture in the previous round – United had taken the lead in the 11th minute when an error by Sandmann allowed Berry to find Viollet who smashed the ball home. This was increased to 2-0 in the 26th minute when Foulkes intercepted a Bracht pass before pushing the ball through to Viollet to score with relative ease. It became 3-0 ten minutes before the interval when a shot by Pegg was deflected into his own net by Burgsmueller.

United were strolling, the pre-match assumption by many fans that age would be the telling factor in the eventual outcome looking to be proving correct. The 'Babes' ran their older opponents ragged, keeping Kwiatkowski, wearing a jersey borrowed from his fellow countryman and Manchester City keeper Bert Trautmann, on his toes. Age, however, was soon to be struggling in the face of experience, as with twenty minutes remaining, the Germans fought back. First was that slip from Byrne that allowed them back into the game, then there was a lack of concentration in the defence which allowed Preissler to pounce on a loose ball after Wood failed to hold a cross from the left, giving the visitors a lifeline for the return in Germany.

Busby had looked to the European Cup as a source of further education in football, and would have picked up much from this encounter. The rather dismal and out-of-character second-half display lingered on as the action switched across Manchester to Old Trafford three days later, when Everton, fourteen points adrift of United swept them aside in a dramatic 5-2 win.

Some saw it as a blessing in disguise, a defeat that would banish all talk of records and of the team that was going to rewrite football history. Even Matt Busby breathed a sigh of relief, saying: "I am glad this record business is over. Now we can settle down to playing normal football again." But there was little 'normal' about his talented team. The setback would only be momentary, soon shrugged off and the momentum once again taken up with further invigorating displays.

October 24th brought a rest from the gruelling domestic and European fixtures with the FA Charity Shield fixture against Manchester City at Maine Road. Although a local 'derby' and with a trophy at stake, only pride would be damaged by defeat. It would also have been an ideal fixture for Busby to rest one or two of the regular faces, but the same eleven who had faced Everton were given the opportunity to rectify that unexpected defeat. However, that rather incompetent forty-five minutes against Dortmund, coupled with the Everton defeat, appeared to have an ongoing effect on Busby's team. In the *News Chronicle*, Ian Wooldridge wrote:

> "Take heart, you First Division clubs. That so-called soccer machine named Manchester United IS quite human after all. True, they put yet another trophy – the FA Charity Shield – in their strong room last night. But don't be kidded. Their long and glorious reign is tottering.
>
> "Everton hinted at it on Saturday. Manchester City, down-at-heel basement boys until a few days ago, proved it last night. United, the men who murdered Belgium's

champions on this very Maine Road ground just two weeks back, are panicking."

It was perhaps an uncompromising display, but for one individual, sixteen-year-old David Gaskell who had been watching the game unfold from the touchline, it threw him into the spotlight, if only for an hour. David recalled:

"The real story was never told about my so called 'debut', I was never asked to go to Maine Road. I had travelled across Manchester by bus, after having finished work on the Old Trafford ground staff intending to be nothing more than one of the crowd. After Ray Wood got injured and left the field, a member of the coaching staff remembered seeing me going into the ground and I was located and taken to the dressing room where I had to borrow Colin Webster's boots to play in.

"I travelled back to my digs on the bus, with fellow passengers discussing the game, completely unaware that I had actually been part of it all.

"When I got back to my digs, they wouldn't believe that I had been playing, because on TV, they said it was Ray Wood. It wasn't until I produced the Charity Shield plaque that they finally realised I was telling the truth."

Following Wood's hip injury in the thirty-seventh minute, Duncan Edwards took over in goal until the sixteen-year-old was found and kitted out in a game that United should have had sewn up after twelve minutes; but five misses by Taylor and almost as many again by Viollet kept the scoreline blank until eighteen minutes from time when the latter of the guilty pair secured victory.

Gaskell, perhaps surprisingly, turned in a competent display for one so young, most probably due to having no time to get nervous, and was to prove United's saviour, making a superb save from Dyson four minutes from time.

Tommy Taylor made amends for his glaring misses against City by scoring both goals in a 2-2 draw at Bloomfield Road, Blackpool, his second coming a mere thirty seconds from time to prevent a second successive defeat.

And if anyone thought that the bubble had finally burst, they were made to rethink as Wolves were brushed aside in a 3-0 defeat at Old Trafford.

> "The carping critics who said that Manchester United were suffering from too much football will have to go into hiding after this match," proclaimed Frank Swift in his *News of the World* match report.
>
> "The League champions gave them the 64-dollar answer by avalanching the Wolves with a display of champagne soccer surpassing anything seen from them in the League competition this season.
>
> "This was United's Anderlecht form all over again."

It may well have been "Anderlecht form", but it disappeared as quickly as it had re-appeared, as the newspapers of seven days later reported very different form – or lack of it. United disappointed their travelling support with a hugely unimpressive performance at Burnden Park, losing 2-0 to Bolton Wanderers.

According to 'The Tramp', pen-name for the Wanderers correspondent in the *Bolton Buff*,

> "There was early evidence of the season's biggest crowd for the visit of the League champions. Scores of coaches supplemented the Manchester and Salford contingent who arrived by rail and that was estimated to be in the region of 10,000 followers all told."

A considerable number, despite the relatively short distance between the two clubs – and it could have been more if not for the indifferent weather.

The proud record of being the only unbeaten team in the country was shattered. According to 'The Tramp', United were "humbled" and given a "stiff hiding" over the course of the ninety minutes, as,

"Banks disproved that Roger Byrne is the best left-back in England and as to the international wing-halves of the champions, they had nothing on their Bolton opposite numbers today."

Despite the hint of local bias, the visitors were indeed poor; but the true mark of champions is the ability to bounce back from adversity. It was to take a rather uninspired opening period against Leeds United at Old Trafford before the machine clicked and a 1-1 half-time stalemate was converted into a 3-1 lead just after the hour. The game and points were United's. Not even a Charles penalty three minutes after Whelan put his side 3-1 in front could prevent victory, the ideal preparation for the daunting trip to Germany four days later.

In reality, nothing could have prepared Busby or his players for their trip. They realised the ninety minutes ahead would be gruelling toil, arguably against the odds, as only two weeks previously, the Germans had once again crossed the Channel to face English opposition, taking on Birmingham City at St Andrew's in a friendly. Again, as at Maine Road, they found themselves behind, 3-1 down, but gave a watching Matt Busby plenty to think about, pulling back to draw 3-3 with a highly creditable performance.

"If we can strike form, and keep punching away at goal, I am confident we will win our way into the quarter-finals," proclaimed Busby. "I don't suppose for one minute we can make it an 'Anderlecht' night, but I think we can add a goal margin to the one we already have on the credit side.

"We'll certainly have the right sort of encouragement, for apart from a sprinkling of fans making the trip, there'll be a host of British servicemen stationed in Germany rooting for us."

The encouragement was certainly there, but the predicted goals failed to materialise.

Having travelled to Germany on the Tuesday afternoon, making their headquarters in Dusseldorf, some sixty miles from Dortmund, and enjoying a light training session at British Forces Rhine Centre on the morning of the match, United arrived at Dortmund's ground to find the playing surface akin to a skating rink, a problem that they had certainly not prepared for or ever envisaged.

Rubber studs were not an inclusion in trainer Tom Curry's kit hamper, leaving the only option a shorter stud which was hastily fitted to each boot. These, however, were leather which gave the United players only a limited grip on the treacherous underfoot surface, giving the better-prepared Germans a distinct early advantage.

The match, played under the newly erected floodlights, never rose to the heights of the first-leg encounter and, had the home side shown a little more composure in front of goal, then the 1,000 British troops would have returned to their barracks disappointed. As it was, many of the servicemen paraded around the ground prior to kick-off with a red and white banner showing a baby in nappies alongside the slogan, 'Play Up the Busby Babes'. Ultimately, they obtained satisfaction in the fact that they were able to see in the flesh, a team and players they had heard so much about and offer their encouragement in the march to further European glory.

If he had misplaced the mantle of England's finest full-back, Roger Byrne once again had it placed around his shoulders, leading by example and cajoling his team-mates to success. He was ably assisted by Mark Jones and Ray Wood, the latter cutting a strange figure with his red tracksuit bottoms tucked into his socks. The defensive trio held firm, denying the Germans a goal, although unable to inspire their forward colleagues to increase United's advantage. The 0-0 scoreline, however, was enough to take them into the quarter-finals.

United were in no hurry to return to Manchester, having planned to spend the morning after the match sightseeing, before flying back to London on the Thursday evening. Enough time, considered Busby, to prepare for the match against second-placed Tottenham Hotspur at White Hart Lane.

Fitness tests for United's undoubted midweek heroes, Byrne and Jones, at Chelsea's Stamford Bridge ground, saw the latter reduced to a spot on the sidelines. The big defender was sadly missed as the home side set out from the start to reduce the two-point gap at the top of the table, giving those who had paid £3 for their 10s 6d ticket value for money.

They only had to wait until the fifth minute for that opening goal, Harmer scoring from the spot after Foulkes and Blanchflower had sandwiched Smith. Two minutes later it was 2-0, Robb racing between the same two United defenders, before driving the ball past a helpless Wood. Brookes should have made it three, but he was denied by a superb save from Wood, the keeper stretching full length to touch the ball round the post for a corner.

Despite Byrne hitting the crossbar and Edwards the foot of the post, it appeared at times that the opening forty-five minutes had simply been used for a limbering-up session, loosening those tired muscles from the midweek exertions. But once the second half got underway the United players looked revitalised and hungrier, and were suddenly back in the game within four minutes of the restart, a corner kick from Pegg finding Whelan whose low cross was turned in by Berry.

Tottenham were now pushed on to the back foot, but as the minutes ticked away it seemed they would still earn both points as everything United tried failed to materialise into a goal. That was, however, until two minutes from time when, amid a goalmouth scramble, the diminutive figure of Colman latched on to an Edwards pass to snatch a dramatic equaliser.

Europe, for the time being, was put on hold as the quarter-final ties were not scheduled to be played until the following January and February, though the cup draw gave United plenty to consider. In the last eight, United were paired with either the Spanish side Bilbao or the Hungarians of Honved. If it were to be the latter, then all the potential European Cup problems that United had hoped to avoid would rise to the surface.

Hungary at this time was beset with political unrest and a trip to Budapest might have seen visas not being granted to United for a trip behind the Iron Curtain. Honved and fellow Hungarians Red Banner, both currently on tour, had been ordered by their governing body to cancel all their outstanding games and to return home immediately; but if the players decided against such a move, there was still the possibility that they could be banned, with Honved having to field a completely 'new' team against United. Would this be something that the European Cup committee would allow? There was also the possibility of the competition being abandoned, or if it did proceed, United's next fixture being played in a neutral country. Matt Busby hinted at Paris, but also suggested there was a possibility that it could take place even nearer to home, at Wembley. In the end, the ifs and buts mattered little as Bilbao went through on aggregate. With a sigh of relief, United were bound for Spain.

For regular observers, the changes in United over the past year would have been quite noticeable. They would have enjoyed watching the progress of the players first seen as little more than schoolboys, who were now blending into an experienced and formidable team. They were maturing like golden apples on a tree, waiting to be picked. Performances had undoubtedly improved. Yes, there would still be the odd upset and disappointing defeat, but such reversals were soon shrugged off, with winning ways hastily resumed.

There was also an all-round strength to the side, with no weak links, the Central League side being more than capable of giving the first-choice eleven a run for their money. So much so that other clubs were beating a path to Old Trafford and enquiring about the possibility of signing players locally regarded as second choice. Busby was also forced to admit that players themselves had paid him a visit in regards to their lack of first-team football:

> "It was inevitable that sooner or later, Manchester United would have to face up to the question of one or two players at present in the second eleven asking to be put on the transfer list.
>
> "That time has now arrived and, without personalities in any way affecting my decision, my answer, dictated by the needs of the club, has had to be a firm 'no' to these requests for a move.
>
> "There is a general impression around that United have a big staff of professionals on their books. That is far from being the case. The idea, I imagine, has grown because so

many of our youngsters have done so well and received such
a good Press.

"Actually, United carry one of the smallest professional
staffs in the First Division."

Although not naming the players himself, the photographs of John
Doherty and Geoff Bent accompanied the article, with the caption,
"they both asked for a transfer." Busby added:

"We make no distinction between League eleven players and
Central League men at Old Trafford: they are all classed
as first team standard – and treated as such. My boys don't
play for the first, second or even the third team – they play
for Manchester United.

"In that lies our strength. We have double man power
for the job that lies ahead. It was only in the knowledge
of this that I was able to take on the extra European Cup
commitment at the start of the season."

With the strength in depth and the quality available to Busby, there
was never a hint that Manchester United were a one-man team,
reliant on any single individual to haul them out of the mire should
the need arise, to score those necessary goals to take them to victory.
There was no one-upmanship, no star individual, no-one felt they
were more important than the others. They were a team on and
off the pitch. What helped tremendously was the similarity in age
between the majority of the players. The likes of Berry, Byrne and
Foulkes could be considered older, perhaps more mature or more
refined in their ways and were happy to distance themselves from
their more youthful, modern team-mates once training was over
or when the final whistle had blown on a Saturday afternoon. For
the younger element, it might have been considered akin to a youth
club scenario with their music, the latest fashions and nights on the
town, either at one of the numerous cinemas or dance halls in the
city centre. Some had an eye for more than goals. But no matter
what, there was a strong camaraderie and friendship between them
all, enjoying a joke during training laps of the Old Trafford pitch,

on the runs up and down the terraces, and in odd bouts of exercise in the gymnasium beneath the main stand. There was also the 'highlight' of five-a-sides on the hard, uncompromising surface behind the Stretford End, where confrontations were at times much more physical than the ninety minutes of a Saturday afternoon. But kicking lumps out of each other in those impromptu us-versus-them kickabouts only served to strengthen the bonds that held the team together.

Whilst saying that no player stood out or was looked to for that extra yard or to hoist United from the jaws of defeat, the importance of Duncan Edwards and his diminutive sidekick Eddie Colman could not be overlooked. To say that they were United's Laurel and Hardy would be wrong as there was nothing comic about them. The more physical Edwards added the muscle, taking a game by the scruff of the neck, while the smaller Colman would weave merlinic magic across the pitch, the crowd swaying in unison as he waltzed past opponents. The Lone Ranger and Tonto would perhaps be more apt.

Jimmy Murphy loved Duncan like a son, and he could do no wrong. The Welshman called him "the Kohinoor diamond amongst our crown jewels", and the boy from the Black Country was always being used as an example when any raw recruit arrived at the club. Meanwhile Matt Busby, writing in the *World Sports* magazine of December 1956, said of the player:

> "Few managers have had such extensive dealings with young footballers as I. It has not been an easy task, but the results have proved even more gratifying than I would have cared to predict.
>
> "I have often asked him to play at centre-forward or inside-left, and he has consented willingly. Tell him to do a particular job, and he does it without question. Part of his natural ability to solve problems on the field comes through the uncanny sense of anticipation; an intuition that sends him confidently upfield on the attack one moment and roaring back to defend his own goalmouth the next. Never ruffled, and anything but temperamental,

he is the greatest young player I have ever seen, either as a player or manager.

"Always willing to learn, he often asks me, 'Did I do anything wrong boss?' and listens intently to any advice. Still a schoolboy at heart, he remains a big, unspoilt youngster."

To say that Edwards could play anywhere, acquitting himself exceptionally in any position, was confirmed at Portsmouth when he found himself given the number nine shirt in the absence of Tommy Taylor – and he turned in yet another virtuoso display.

"He may have lacked Taylor's easy adaptability, especially under the conditions, but a hint of danger lurked behind all he did.

"And he scored the goal which put United in the lead after being a goal down at the interval. Indeed all the time he was operating, he showed unshakable confidence. And it wasn't cockiness," wrote one correspondent.

While a couple of seats along in the press box another was to pen:

"It is, of course, comparatively easy for any centre-forward to fit into this brilliant United attack. The fact that the easy grace with which the United attack invariably functions was in no way disturbed."

Eddie Colman was the perfect sidekick for Edwards in the United midfield double act, and perhaps Don Davies, who wrote under the pen name of 'An Old International' for the *Guardian*, caught the essence of the local-boy-made-good better than anyone. In a summary of a match against Newcastle, Davies wrote:

"The feature of the first half was a brilliant display by Colman. Never has this gifted young half-back intervened more cleverly, used the ball more wisely, or sold his dummies more slyly than in this instance. He had on the other side a formidable rival by the name of Scoular; himself a strong tackler, a wise distributor and a subtle tactician in the Newcastle interest. Colman might have been the 'premier danseur' in a Footballers' Ballet and Scoular the dogged leader of a Chain Gang.

"One of these days, perhaps, when Colman is in the mood, we shall see the Beswick Prize Band accompanying him with snatches of reasonably tuneful ballet music, say, from Swan Lake. Then we shall see the little fellow at his best."

His inclusion in the United line-up, however, was not always a formality. This was neither down to his playing ability – of which there could be no doubt – nor his fitness. It was, in fact, dependent on his availability due to national service. Even for the likes of the European Cup tie against Anderlecht in Brussels, Matt Busby faced red tape, having to write to Colman's commanding officer, Major Pounds.

"Dear Major, My club are very honoured, as Champions of the Football League, to be invited to play in the European Cup Competition, which is only open to the champion clubs of their respective countries.

"We are drawn to play against Anderlecht F. C. in Brussels on 12th September, and it is naturally my earnest wish to field the strongest possible team with a view to uphold the prestige of our English clubs

"With this idea in mind, I respectfully seek your permission for special leave to be granted to 23149671 Sig. E. Colman, from twelve hours on Monday, 10th September to twelve hours on Friday 14th September.

"For your information, our travelling arrangements are as follows: Depart Ringway Airport Tuesday, 11th September 10-45 hrs. Arriving back at Ringway Airport on Thursday, 13th September 22-15 hrs."

Colman was given his leave.

The versatility of Edwards had seen the dynamic duo split up against Tottenham and again against Luton Town, when he was to find himself playing in the not unfamiliar position of inside-left, scoring the opening goal in a 3-1 win. It was a game that saw fingers pointed in United's direction, accusing them of being 'cocky' and 'taking it easy', but despite those accusations, the praise was still there. "Call them cocky, big headed or just plain over-confident. But this superbly fit, well drilled Manchester United outfit is still the finest advertisement for English football," wrote Peter Slingsby in the *Sunday People*, while an unnamed journalist told of how "Luton's defence was breathless, chasing these bewildering United men."

Three seemed to have materialised into United's favourite number, with 3-1 victories continuing against Aston Villa, Cardiff City and Portsmouth. Chelsea were beaten 3-0 on New Year's Day, but the five-game sequence was not consecutive, as sandwiched in between the victories over Villa and Cardiff came a shock defeat at the hands of Birmingham City – surprisingly enough by a 3-1 scoreline. How did Birmingham City manage what others had failed to do? Simply by blunting the effectiveness of Taylor, Viollet and Whelan whilst harnessing the attacking threat of Colman and Edwards. A supreme display in defensive football.

On December 22nd 1956, United were scheduled to play West Bromwich Albion at Old Trafford and on the terraces, despite many being dragged off to go Christmas shopping, a large number of supporters were all ready and raring to go. So too were the United team, the referee and his linesmen. However, there was no West Bromwich Albion, or Matt Busby for that matter. The United manager had travelled to Brussels to watch forthcoming European Cup opponents Bilbao play Honved, but his return train from London to Manchester was held up in the Midlands due to fog. He telephoned his son, Sandy, asking him to come to Crewe to pick him up, so that he could make the game, but events at Old Trafford were not developing as expected. Kick-off had been put back from 2.15 to 2.30, but there was still no sign of the West Bromwich Albion team and officials. It was 4pm before they eventually arrived in Manchester, though by that time, the game had long since been postponed, the ground was in darkness and everyone had gone home.

That 3-0 New Year's Day victory over Chelsea gave United a four-point advantage over Tottenham at the top of the First

Division; Arsenal were third, six points behind, but having played two games more. The bookmakers had Busby's team down as favourites, Tottenham's only hope being their slightly superior goal average should they manage to claw back the necessary points. And with the FA Cup kicking off in earnest, United were again the bookmakers' favourites at 8-1 to lift the trophy at Wembley in May. The elusive Double?

United's FA Cup form in the 1950s was far from impressive, with every opponent, irrespective of status, relishing the opportunity to catch the Old Trafford outfit on an off day, playing them in their own backyard and using the magic of the Cup to their advantage. Hartlepools United were no exception, heading into a dream world following the draw for the third round which sent the League leaders on a journey into the unknown in the north-east. Cup fever grabbed the town the minute the draw was made, all focused on the biggest ever game in the forty-nine year history of the club now plying its trade in the Third Division North.

In the second round of the competition, Hartlepools had struggled to defeat Blyth Spartans 1-0, but their current league form was creditable, sitting level on points with Bradford City at the top, having won fifteen of their twenty-seven games, the other twelve split evenly between draws and defeats. Current form would matter little for either side and despite United fielding a team consisting of nine full internationals, the 'all-local' north-east side, in their spartan home arena, were more than up for the challenge.

The run-up to the game was tinged with controversy, certainly amongst the locals, as Hartlepools decided to double their normal admission prices, charging 4/- for adults and 2/- for children for a place on the terracing and 8/- for a seat in the stand. Letters of protest flooded the local newspaper, one correspondent stating that the regular supporters should have been charged normal prices due to the 'recent exhibitions of football we have had to endure'. Compensation did come to some in a roundabout sort of way, just as long as you weren't teetotal, as the local pubs and clubs were granted an extension of their opening hours, being allowed to open at 11.00am instead of 11.45am and then to re-open at 3.45pm instead of 5.00pm. Closing time remained the same – 10.30pm.

On a wet Saturday morning in the north-east, there were queues outside the Victoria Ground from 9.00am for the 2.15pm kick-off, with three 'special' trains arriving from Manchester – this despite United having returned a considerable number of their 900 allocated tickets. By kick-off, 17,264 were inside, generating receipts of £3,470. Many more were outside, wishing they were on the opposite side of the wall, or were brave enough to join a cameraman perched precariously on the roof of the Mill House Stand. Ever more so as the ninety minutes unfolded...

Reporting for the *Northern Daily Mail*, 'Sentinel' called it,

> "the most remarkable soccer match I have ever seen – including FA Cup finals and internationals. The first half craftsmanship of Manchester United against a 'Pools United overawed by the reputations of their rivals, promised goals by the cart load. The Babes made it look easy, with Berry and Pegg running amok on the wings and smacking in tremendous drives, the match looked to be as good as over after half an hour."

Those opening thirty-two minutes saw United take a three-goal lead. Whelan opened the scoring in the seventhth minute, with Berry and Taylor giving the Cup favourites a seemingly comfortable advantage on a heavily mudded pitch. Ten minutes before half-time Stamper clawed a goal back following a mis-kick by Byrne, much to the home supports delight, but the outcome still looked a foregone conclusion – especially when the injured Johnson began the second half hobbling on the right wing.

As expected, the second majority of the action continued to be around the Hartlepools penalty area, goalkeeper Guthrie saving well from Colman and Berry, with any breakaways easily subdued by the commanding Edwards. But it was to prove a false dawn, as the eight minutes of constant pressure was suddenly subdued, and the action moved to the opposite end of the pitch.

Anderson gained possession, pushing the ball into the path of Luke on the left. Quickly, the ball was centred, curving away from the United defence, but suddenly, as if out of nowhere, the limping

Johnson flung himself towards the ball, heading it decisively past a helpless Wood. It was a goal that swung the game on its axis. Suddenly it was the blue and white halved shirts who were in command, given a new lease of life as a sliver of light appeared through cracks in the United defence, where even the usually calm Byrne began indiscriminately booting the ball clear.

Twelve minutes later, all hell broke loose. Newton, with the road to goal seemingly blocked by a mass of bodies, decided there was little to lose with a long-range shot. Surprisingly, the ball flew past everyone, including an unsighted Ray Wood, and the crowd rose as one with a deafening roar. The impossible had happened. But could they go on and grasp a winner?

Those Hartlepools players were, on the whole, ageing professionals, and with only ten of them fully fit and twenty-five minutes still remaining, it was perhaps too much to expect a victory to be achieved. The minds were willing, but the legs were feeling the strain. As even the staunchest home supporter might have suspected, United drew upon all their youth and experience and snatched victory from the jaws of defeat: Whelan joyously latched on to the ball as it skidded across the muddy surface after Guthrie could only parry a shot from Berry. As the Hartlepools 'ten minute' flag was slowly lowered, the home support realised their dreams would not be fulfilled, but the relief on the faces of the United players at full time was clearly evident. There was little need for the 1,000 replay tickets they had brought with them.

If the Hartlepools cup-tie was a warning to Manchester United, then the 6-1 victory over Newcastle United at Old Trafford was a clear sign of intention to the Spaniards of Bilbao. There was no hangover from the trip to the north-east, the events of the ninety minutes had clearly been noted, and a repeat performance was unlikely, at least in the immediate future.

The six-goal rout of Newcastle was also a clear indication to Tottenham, Arsenal and anyone else who were contemplating laying a claim to the First Division title that they did not have a hope in hell of knocking United off top spot. Each report mirrored another, seducing its readership with tales of United's "pace, power, poise and positional play". How they should have "scored ten or twelve, not six in what was a glorious exhibition of football on a sticky ground that made little difference to how United moved the ball around with draughtsman's accuracy."

And so Bilbao beckoned. A team who had lost only one match on their home turf over the course of the past three years. The United players were going to have to pull out all the stops if they were to earn their £2 win bonus – although they would probably have been content with £1 for a draw, which would have to be considered a favourable result at a difficult venue. They might also have hoped for the need of floodlights, which would have added an extra £3 to the pay packet; but one thing they did not expect was snow.

"Conditions were vile," reported W.R. Taylor for the *Guardian*,

> "It was more like playing in a swamp than a football pitch, for rain and snow had fallen for 48 hours and Byrne, the United captain, said they were the worst he had ever played in."

Those conditions were far from ideal, in truth, more akin to Manchester than Spain.

> "The pitch, lightly covered in snow, was very green at the start, but turned into a sea of mud and slush, and after play had started the water came to the surface as though a heavy roller had been put on it, particularly on the wings, where the players, at times, seemed to be paddling."

Prior to kick-off, the terraces were a sea of black umbrellas, which slowly came to resemble a huge spread of dominoes as the snow continued to fall. But those brollies were soon to disappear at kick-off, leaving their owners to the mercy of the inclement weather. Now the air took on a greyish hue as a low-lying cloud of cigarette smoke, like rising steam, enveloped large areas of the ground.

The rain, sleet and snow were soon to be forgotten, but not before United, playing in unfamiliar blue jerseys, almost stormed into the lead. Viollet forced himself through the middle, sending a forceful drive towards the Bilbao goal, only to see it come to a sudden halt on the goal line. The frantic up-field clearance would, under normal circumstances, have been cleared by Jones, but the centre-half slipped, presenting Uribe with the opportunity to open the scoring.

Pegg tormented the Spanish defence and saw a shot bounce back off the post, but on the half-hour – and against the run of play – Uribe made it 2-0 following a goalmouth scramble that saw the ball yo-yoing in and out of the goalmouth three times. With the interval looming, Bilbao scored a third from a Marcadia header following a corner, leaving United with a mountain to climb in the second period.

Carmelo, who had made three outstanding saves during the opening half, was to find himself under immediate pressure as the second forty-five got underway and with only nine minutes gone had picked the ball out of the net twice. Whelan forced a corner and from the resulting kick Taylor scored from a Viollet pass to make it 3-1. Then Viollet himself scored from close range following a goalmouth melee. United were back in the game.

Despite continuing to push forward, United could not force the equaliser and were soon to find themselves back two behind following goals from Merodio and Artiche. At that point, many sides would have decided to shut up shop and hold on for full time, but not United. Determined to keep the tie alive in Manchester, they continued to push forward and were rewarded with a third goal from Whelan, the Irishman scoring with a powerful drive after beating three opponents.

Reducing the deficit back in Manchester was now the main focus of the travelling party, but upon arrival at Bilbao airport, they were informed that their stay in snowy Spain could well be lengthened, the flight captain insisting that his plane would not take off until the ice and snow was removed from the wings. Having no inclination to remain in Spain for any longer than necessary, a number of the United players grabbed brushes and shovels to get the plane to an approved standard and ready for take-off. Almost four hours later they were strapped in their seats awaiting the surge of the engines.

Perhaps it was the shock of conceding five goals, a delayed thawing out from the freezing cold of Spain or simply an off-day.

No matter, United were well below par at Hillsborough three days later where Sheffield Wednesday made the most of their opponents' lack of endeavour to snatch a 2-1 victory. Perhaps Busby should have reshuffled his side, throwing in some Central League regulars who were eager for some first-team action. In hindsight, it was probably something that he regretted not trying.

An injury to Berry brought a forced change for the trip to Wrexham in the fifth round of the FA Cup with Colin Webster getting a rare run out in the first team. But if the Welshmen though they could emulate Hartlepools or snatch an odd-goal victory like Sheffield Wednesday then they were misguided. Perhaps they had read Derek Wallis in the *Daily Mirror* who speculated:

> "This game may be one for soccer's history books.
>
> "I believe Wrexham will not merely hold the champions. THEY WILL BEAT THEM.
>
> "Remember how they fought back from 2-1 down five minutes from time in a second replay against Scunthorpe and won 6-2 in extra-time? I couple this with United's momentary loss of the poise of champions. It may return today. If it doesn't the 35,000 crowd will see the biggest sensation since Walsall beat Arsenal."

The playing conditions at the Racecourse Ground were another minus point as far as Wallis was concerned – "Manchester United are not at all happy on a mudded pitch either," he added to his pre-match predictions – and the atmosphere promised to be hostile as the 35,000 tickets had been snapped up well in advance, with 2s 6d tickets changing hands for 25s at least on the black market. There was no giant-killing, or even a hint of a cup shock, and Wallis was left wriggling with embarrassment as United trounced the Welsh side 5-0, a scoreline that in all honesty flattered Wrexham as the visitors failed to make the most of the opportunities that they created. As one report began: "This was no match – it was a massacre."

Despite the Welsh players being stirred by 'Men of Harlech' and 'Abide with Me', there was no blood to be seen, other than the normal matchday scratches. From the first blast of the referee's whistle, Wrexham were on the back foot, United taking the lead as early as the eighth minute through Whelan. Byrne made it 2-0 from the penalty spot eight minutes later, Taylor adding a third ten minutes before the interval.

Hoping for a reprieve in the second half, Wrexham were totally out of luck, as Whelan made it 4-0 within a minute of the restart, and Taylor added a fifth with a cheeky back-heel just before the hour mark. Many in the crowd had now endured enough and were soon heading for the exits, cursing those who had instilled them with confidence, perhaps even motivating United to give lie to the assertion that they were on the slide.

A short journey across Manchester four days before the eagerly awaited return against Bilbao again offered a full dress rehearsal on the Maine Road pitch which was already something of a home from home for United. Their opponents, City, provided a testing ninety minutes, offering the opportunity to flex the muscles and grab a confidence boosting victory. Both were achieved.

The physical aspect of the ninety minutes could be attributed to Roger Byrne, the United captain ruffling the feathers of the home support with some uncompromising challenges, but the louder the boos the more determined he became in his search for victory.

City were to rue their opening-minute miss, as they were a goal behind three minutes later. They did manage to draw level, but by the interval they were 3-1 behind. When they grabbed a second a quarter of an hour from the end, a draw looked probable, but it was then that Byrne came to the fore, cajoling his troops, squeezing that extra something from the tiring legs. The boos continued, but were ultimately silenced with ten minutes remaining when Edwards clinched victory with a superb strike. Bring on Bilbao.

The defeat against Sheffield Wednesday had been shrugged off quicker than it took for the mud and grime from the afternoon's endeavours to be washed away. Yes, it was two points lost, but a four-point advantage over Tottenham at the top of the First Division was not to be shunned, especially as the Londoners still had to to visit Old Trafford. Even the satisfaction of victory over neighbours City was a distant memory by the Sunday morning, as the thoughts of players and supporters alike were occupied by the ninety minutes looming on the horizon against the Spaniards.

Prior to flying to Manchester, Bilbao had sent out nine reserves against Barcelona and lost 2-0, a result that dented their title hopes, but clearly emphasised the importance of getting a result against United. Victory on the night was a minor concern due to their two-goal advantage, as they would be content to keep United at bay and go through on aggregate. "If they want to play defensively, we'll have to find the way through," declared Matt Busby, "and the way through is push the ball through quickly. We can do that if we are on form."

"If United can score an early goal, as Bilbao did in the first match, then success could be within their grasp," was the opinion of a *Guardian* reporter.

Workplaces were abandoned early, while countless housewives had been informed that morning "don't make any tea for me tonight, luv". Schoolboys dashed home, some to get the homework done quickly, others preferring some form of punishment the following morning to wasting time with such trivialities. Moss Side was the only place to be on the night of February 6th 1957.

To call the 65,000 who were squeezed into City's ground that night 'partisan' is an understatement. The normal good sportsmanship and appreciative applause for the opposition was forgotten. Tonight was all about a United victory and by a goal margin that would ensure passage into the European Cup semi-finals.

The voracious assembly was intent on their vocal encouragement outdoing even the 'Hampden Roar', acting as twelfth man, the inspiration behind a memorable success.

What unfolded was arguably the greatest night in Manchester footballing history. In the *News Chronicle*, Ian Wooldridge wrote:

> "It was the game of the century. Thousands of rattle-clacking fans were still roaming Manchester late last night. They couldn't go to bed. For their heroes – the eleven modest men of Manchester United – had won from Europe's top

critics the title of the 'Greatest Soccer Team of All Time'. It was an accolade deservingly given by a vanquished foe, a team who had victory within their grasp courtesy of a two-goal first-leg advantage, but one who had succumbed to a team of immense talent, a team still on something of a learning curve when it came to European competition, but one who were surely destined to wear the crown of the continent's best."

After the thunderous reception the red-shirted eleven were given as they emerged from the tunnel, the packed ground was cruelly kept on tenterhooks, as the early goal everyone hoped for failed to materialise. The opening minutes were frantic, perhaps too hasty, as United pushed forward, stretching the Bilbao defence to its limits; but the Spaniards stood firm, and the longer the game remained goalless, the greater the anxiety and tension grew. On the touchline Busby was more than aware that with each passing minute the game was slowly slipping from United's grasp. Urgency prevailed with only three minutes remaining until half-time, and a call to the talisman saw Duncan Edwards move further upfield. With the ball at his feet and the goal in his vision he unleashed a shot, but the out-thrust foot of Garay blocked its route to goal. As the ball rebounded into play, Viollet pounced and quickly fired past Carmelo. One goal behind and forty-five minutes remaining.

Into the second half and Viollet once again pushed the ball past Carmelo only to see his effort disallowed for offside. A minute later Whelan prodded the ball home, but once against the German official denied United their second. David Pegg hit a shot on the turn from six yards out, but the ball went wide. Taylor hit the post. Agony prevailed.

With eighteen minutes remaining, Colman slipped a quick free kick towards Taylor, a dip of the shoulder then a turn in the opposite direction wrong-footed Garay, creating the opportunity for the United number nine to drive home with his left foot. United were level and a third game in Paris loomed. Slowly, the minutes ticked away and with five remaining it was Taylor again in the thick of the action, leaving Garay in his wake as he stormed down the right touchline. Looking inside, the diminutive form of Berry caught his eye and he quickly rolled the ball into his path. The United number seven right-footed the ball past Carmelo to ignite the blue touch paper, and Maine Road exploded.

But even in the dying seconds there was still drama. A poor clearance presented Gainza with a half chance, but Wood slithered across the muddy goalmouth to clear. Then Bilbao forced a corner, but it was to little avail as a shrill whistle signalled the end of the game. United had done it.

On the touchline, as Berry's shot went in, Busby leaped from his seat, grabbing Jimmy Murphy before performing an impromptu celebration dance. Murphy himself was to confess, "I cried when we scored that third goal. I don't mind admitting. Silly isn't it? After all these years in the game as a player and club official. But this is the greatest night of my life in soccer." Manchester United had done what many thought was impossible.

Minutes later, as the euphoric crowd celebrated on what were for many the unfamiliar streets of Moss Side, the hero of the hour sat drinking beer out of a chipped mug. "I couldn't see a gap," admitted Berry, "but I just knew this was it. So I let fly… then I ducked as I thought the sky was falling in."

For anyone to select a man of the match from the victorious side was nigh impossible. Colman had pulled the strings in midfield, Byrne had led by example, while Edwards, instigator behind the opening goal was simply his usual effective self; but, if pushed, the majority of the hoarse and intoxicated crowd would have most probably opted for Tommy Taylor.

Even Henry Rose, another of the press corps who travelled up and down the country in the wake of Busby's team penning his opinions and the true hard facts for the readers of the *Daily Express*. Rose had not endeared himself to the United faithful a few weeks previous, having criticised Taylor despite the burly number nine having scored a hat-trick for England against Denmark, the man from the *Express* declaring that if "Taylor was England's best centre forward, then he was Santa Claus." From the Maine Road press box, however, his match report read:

"My hands are still trembling as I write. My heart still pounds. And a few hours have passed since, with 65,000 other people, I saw the greatest soccer victory in history, 90 minutes of tremendous thrill and excitement that will live for ever in the memory.

"Hammering in my brain almost shattering my senses is the still-fresh memory of the spectacle of 11 brave, gallant footballers battering, pounding until they had them on their knees almost crying for mercy, a team of Spaniards ranked as one of the best teams in the world." But he was to add something of a postscript, saluting United, apologising for doubting them and giving praise to the performance of Tommy Taylor – "Santa Claus salutes you, beard and all."

"I'm going on record that this is the finest Manchester United side I've seen," wrote Edgar Turner in the *Sunday Pictorial*. "The greybeards who can remember 'em can have their Duckworth, Roberts and Bell. But I would say the present dynamic dazzlers could give a goal and a beating to them. And to those 1948 'greats' of Rowley, Pearson and Co. This side now possess something that Matt Busby has been waiting for – bite and unrelenting determination." A few feet along in the press box, colleague Frank Hallam was busy scribbling: "Barnum and Bailey (an American circus company billed as The Greatest Show on Earth) should have been here. They would have been green with envy. Because Manchester United are THE Greatest Show on Earth. They completed, as Barnum would have agreed, the most fabulous, stupendous, fantastic, gigantic eight days' football show of this year or any year," while Derek Wallis considered it "the nearest thing I have seen to torture on a soccer ground."

"That magic moment, five minutes from time, when Maine Road went mad and United were – All Berry And Bright!" proclaimed the *Daily Mirror* above Archie Ledbrooke's report. "Call this the match of the century? Don't know, I haven't lived that long. But I do know that this was one of the matches I'll never forget, one of the best half dozen I've seen in nearly 2,000. The crowd of 65,000 will say this morning that they've never seen anything like it. They are probably right."

Frank Taylor, another regular United watcher wrote; "Hail the Busby Braves! For 90 thrill packed minutes under the Maine Road floodlights last night, the champions of England pounded the Spanish champions until they were sunk by a three-goal salvo. What a triumph for Matt Busby! What a triumph for British football." He went on, "It was the most nerve wracking game I have ever sat through. I thrilled as United pulled back one goal; then two; then shot into the lead and into the last four of the European Cup. At the finish 65,000 fans sang and cheered the triumph of these young soccer stars from Old Trafford. But when I saw the team in the dressing room they could hardly raise a smile. They had run themselves into the ground. They were too tired to even sing."

For many footballers, a performance such as United's against Bilbao would have drained them both physically and emotionally, producing a hangover that would take days to get over, despite the high the result would have undoubtedly produced. But it was becoming obvious, even to the most biased observer, that Manchester United were no ordinary team. They could scale heights that others could only dream of and achieve results that few would expect, thanks to players that every manager would have loved to have been able to select. Three days after trouncing the Spaniards, United bordered on immortality by not simply defeating championship challengers Arsenal, but trouncing them 6-2 – and that was after Arsenal had taken a sixth-minute lead!

The words of Don Davies, the *Guardian*'s 'Old International' can be found throughout this book as few could match his writing skills, or paint a better picture with a few strokes of a pen rather than a brush. Of that victory over the Gunners he was to write:

"For Manchester United scored six goals to Arsenal's two, in a display which was fallible enough at times to keep it human, but which had moments of enchantment, which the 60,384 spectators will not soon forget. The wonder was not the blend and balance and tactical resource of this remarkable club side – to these we are accustomed – but the freshness of approach, the gaiety of mind, and the physical resilience so soon discernable after the Bilbao ordeal."

None could seemingly match United as now they flitted from good to sublime with comparative ease, although some individuals seemed to view a match against the probable champions – or could that be triple champions, throwing the European Cup and FA Cup into the mix? – as an opportunity to establish a one-man crusade against the powers of the infidel red shirts. Such an individual was Albert Dunlop, the Everton goalkeeper in the fifth round FA Cup tie at Old Trafford on February 16th.

Everton took the game to United in the opening half hour or so, buoyant on the back of their 5-2 success at Old Trafford earlier in the season. With their approach perhaps overly physical, Ray Wood received a head injury following a collision with Harris and played out a considerable part of the first half in a daze. But the action quickly swung to the visitors' goalmouth with a dozen near misses over the course of the following half hour, not to mention some excellent saves from Dunlop. Everton were riding their luck; but it was soon to run out.

Not for the first time, it was down to Duncan Edwards to turn the tide for United, scoring in the 67th minute what was to be the only goal of the game with a twenty-yard drive that barely left the ground as it flew past Dunlop, for once helpless.

Few were now surprised by the contributions of the Black Country boy. It was difficult to remember that he was little else, but for many he was already the complete footballer. Matt Busby was firm in his opinion of the secret of Edwards's successes:

"Power, ability, enthusiasm and character. He is the most complete footballer I have ever seen. He was due to play for his unit in an Army Cup semi-final. He chose this as the psychological moment to ask his CO for leave to play for United against Everton in the fifth round tie some days later.

"'You can have your leave if we get to the final,' said the CO. In spite of this incentive, Edwards's unit was losing 4-2 in the second half. Thinking of the FA Cup tie, this determined young man strayed to the touchline, asked permission to switch from left-half to inside-left. Fifteen minutes later his side were winning 7-4. Edwards had scored five goals. He got that leave!"

If he had a chink in his armour, an Achilles heel, then it certainly was not visible on the field of play; but there was something that proved he was a normal human being and that was his dislike of travelling overseas, either by plane or boat. The trip to Bilbao, not the smoothest of flights, saw him suffer, while a boat trip across the English Channel on army duty found him lying flat out on the deck with a severe bout of seasickness, rolling across the floor in time to the heaving ship.

Edwards, however, was missing for the trip to London two days later, as were Foulkes and Viollet, giving rare outings to Wilf McGuinness, Geoff Bent and Bobby Charlton, though none of the normal first-choice trio were missed as United treated the ninety minutes at the Valley as little more than a training session, the bottom-of-the-table side simply making up the numbers as the visitors strolled to a 5-1 victory. One of the 'stand-ins', Bobby Charlton, claimed a hat-trick, following on from his debut double against his namesakes.

That the home side had a poor record on their own ground, having conceded 93 goals in their 31 League games, mattered little as the result reflected the devastating power that United could unleash, their hunger for goals and their desire to succeed. Fifteen goals in the last three League outings was not achieved by good fortune, the feat made all the more remarkable considering the games were interspersed with a difficult FA Cup tie against Everton and the devastating 3-0 victory over Bilbao. The lyrics from Edric Connor's 'Manchester United Calypso' certainly rang true –

"If ever they're playing in your town, You must get to that football ground. Take a look and you will see, Football taught by Matt Busby. It's the greatest thrill that you've ever seen,

They are known as a soccer machine. They are the best, there is no doubt, So raise a cheer and give a shout. Manchester, Manchester United. A bunch of bouncing 'Busby Babes'; They deserve to be knighted."

All good things must come to an end and, sure enough, the Manchester United machine ground to a halt on February 23rd against Blackpool at Old Trafford. Revenge for the Seasiders was sweet. It didn't make up for losing the title to their Manchester rivals last season, but it did give them a glow of satisfaction, the first club since Everton way back in October to leave Old Trafford with points. If excuses were required, the atrocious playing conditions could not be used, as they were the same for both clubs, but the loss of Tommy Taylor ten minutes into the second half with a cracked bone in his left leg, with the game still goalless, was a major factor in the surprise defeat.

The absence of the Yorkshireman was a concern for the weeks ahead, particularly the delicate FA Cup quarter-final tie at Bournemouth. The Third Division South side, delighted with the outcome of the draw, made live on BBC TV for the first time, would certainly be no pushovers, as they had already defeated Wolves at Molineux (1-0) and Tottenham at home (3-1), ensuring that United's visit to the south coast would not conjure up a repeat of the visits to Hartlepools or Wrexham.

The long journey to Bournemouth on March 2nd was of little concern to the United support as according to the *Echo*,

"Since 7am today, Mancunians have been streaming into Bournemouth singing, shouting and generally making it known that the great day had arrived.

"Bournemouth West Station saw the start of the invasion, four special trains arriving in ninety minutes. Two trains were cancelled at the last minute, but this did not mean fewer people were coming, as coaches brought hundreds by road.

"At West Station, a dining car in a siding provided breakfasts for 152 at one sitting. Inspector Browning said it was an innovation, but one that could possibly be developed for Saturday mornings in the season.

"As each passenger left the station, he or she was handed a brochure on Bournemouth, with instructions about getting to and from the ground.

"Over the public address system, United fans heard: 'We wish you a pleasant day in Bournemouth. Up the Cherries!'

"Stepping from the train, a man played 'Lassie from Lancashire' on his cornet, then led the singing crowd to waiting Corporation buses which took them to the Pavilion for breakfast and a wash and brush up. Nearly 800 people arrived in the first two trains after an eight-hour journey."

Rosette sellers had arrived at the station around 4.00am, with others arriving later from London, all doing a roaring trade as the United supporters, already wearing red-and-white favours, snapped up the blue-and-white ones due to the change of colours for the day. £3 was being asked for a 2/- ticket. One member of the travelling support declined to have his photograph taken, saying: "The missus thinks I'm working nights."

Such was the demand for tickets, one enterprising individual, whose garden adjoined the Dean Court ground, constructed a makeshift stand of scaffolding and planks, enabling himself and a few friends to watch the game.

Those travelling United supporters seemed confident and carefree, but if the United management and players had any concerns about the trip to Dean Court and its potential pitfalls, these were magnified within ten minutes of the kick-off when Mark Jones was carried off with a knee injury, leaving the visitors to face the giant-killers with ten men for the remainder of the first half. The United centre-half did make a re-appearance after the interval at centre-forward, with a heavily strapped leg, but this was for nothing more than effect, and it was a move that failed to have any bearing on the game, as he had only been on the pitch a minute or so when he collapsed following a tackle by Hughes and had to leave the field once again. This time for good.

Following their results in the previous rounds, Bournemouth were far from overawed, taking the game to United from the first blast of the referee's whistle. Stiffle and Bedford both came close to opening the scoring, the latter hitting the crossbar, before the visitors inevitably found themselves a goal behind in the 35th minute. Following yet another attacking foray on the United goal, which resulted in a corner, Stiffle swung his kick into the penalty area where Ray Wood made little attempt to punch clear, merely palming the ball on to his crossbar. As it rebounded into play Bedford reacted quickly and headed the ball into the net. "The corner kick had already gone behind," claimed the United keeper. "I was amazed when the referee allowed the goal."

A goal behind, and without Jones, United were up against it, Bournemouth looking at times to have more than a one-man advantage; but remember, this was no ordinary team they were up against. Setbacks merely acted as a spur. Byrne, as always leading by example, pulled Edwards back from centre-forward to centre-half, presenting Bournemouth with an even greater obstacle than the departed Jones, while Colman and McGuinness, like two demented whippets, chased everything.

Having stood firm in the ten minutes remaining prior to the interval, despite a hint of panic, United used the half-time break to their advantage and came out for the second half prepared to battle. Having managed to keep Bournemouth at bay for the opening fifteen minutes of that second half, luck finally came their way.

With the forward line interchanging positions due to there being only four men up front, Berry, having moved inside, was picked out by a through pass from Foulkes. As the home defence stood looking for an offside decision, the diminutive winger raced forward and slipped the ball past Godwin in the Bournemouth goal.

If Bournemouth had dreams before, then four minutes later they turned into nightmares, realising their golden opportunity was gone as the ten men stepped up a gear and dramatically took the lead. Pressing forward, Berry, a constant thorn in the Cherries' side, beat four men on a run that took him into the Bournemouth penalty area, but his final shot was blocked by Godwin. The ball rebounded to Viollet, his effort cannoned off a defender to Whelan, who headed towards goal. On the goal line, Brown managed to stop the netbound effort, but was adjudged by the referee to have used his hand and a penalty was awarded.

Brown later professed his innocence to Frank McGhee of the *Daily Mirror*, stating that the ball hit him on the shoulder, with the televised highlights of the game simply revealing a blur of action, the appeals of the United players and Berry's subsequent successful spot-kick.

United had taken yet another step towards the Treble.

Busby, at times, seemed loath to rest players, to refresh his side, but with a six-point lead over Tottenham, albeit having played a game more, and with Real Madrid lurking menacingly on the horizon, the pack was reshuffled for the trip to Goodison Park where Everton sought revenge for their cup defeat a few weeks previously. Out went Foulkes, Colman, Edwards, Viollet and of course the injured Jones, and in came Bent, Goodwin, Blanchflower, Webster and Doherty. The changes made little difference to the well-oiled machine.

"Reserves? They're in Top Class" proclaimed the heading above the Derek Wallis report in the *Daily Mirror*:

> "If these Scintillating Six (McGuinness, who had also played at Bournemouth was included in this total) are manager Busby's idea of reserves, then no wonder Manchester United are cruising towards the most astonishing Triple Crown sport has ever known.
>
> "The first team can never afford to play badly. They know there is always a man behind them ready and willing and able to take over." In the *Daily Express*, Terence Elliot penned: "You haven't a chance Tottenham! Nor you Preston. That flash shooting ahead into the straight for the League championship is Manchester United.
>
> "If United were going to fall, it was in this test of their strength at Goodison Park, where they fielded six reserves.

The stand-ins just turned on a Busby display and did what their seniors couldn't do at Old Trafford."

Everton were beaten 2-1, thanks to two Colin Webster goals, but then two Midlands sides, Aston Villa and Wolves, attempted to throw a spanner in the works, holding the team every football supporter wanted to see and every opponent wanted to beat to 1-1 draws at Old Trafford and Molineux respectively. Another Midlands side, Birmingham City, lay in wait in the FA Cup semi-final, confident of derailing the plans for a trip to Wembley on Cup Final day.

With the footballing public ensnared by United's performances, their attacking flair and determined approach to games, many journalists sought to capture that special ingredient, to earmark what gave United that certain pulling power, making them a major attraction throughout the country. In *World Sports* magazine, assistant editor Phil Pilley decided to make the trip to Manchester for the match against Aston Villa, just to see what all the fuss was about. Under the headline "United They Stand" he wrote:

> "Rarely have I known a people so unconditionally in support of a local team. The Mancunians regards the United as a product of his city – like cotton, but more entertaining and more human.
>
> "And this is not a blind or totally ignorant adulation. The fever grips not only the gullible but the discerning. Take Tony Walker, a young man who works at the Town Hall. On Saturday afternoon you will rub shoulders with him at the United ground; next week you will see him in his regular place listening to a Halle Concert.
>
> "Another regular soccer goer is the Lord Mayor Harry Sharp who said: 'No praise is too high for them… and, I put it down to good leadership and discipline.'"

Upon making his way to the ground, Pilley continued:

> "The Old Trafford ground is industrial; it settles in a clearing flanked by factories, chimneys, smoke. As I jostled

with the crowd surging down Warwick Road, I fancied from their chat that they had come not to see who would win but to see how many goals their idols would score.

"Inside the ground the Beswick Prize Band were blowing it hot and strong; and a man who injects the personality cult into the art of spectating paraded gaily round the pitch clad in white bowler, red jacket and white trousers. Eventually he dissolved into the crowd, like the star nosed comic lining up with the chorus at the end of a revue."

Although the game in question finished 1-1, Pilley was impressed enough to ask:

"How have United come by all these splendid youngsters and managed to keep them happy? I heard various theories from the naïve and cynical. The most interesting was that the club holds a powerful attraction to Roman Catholics, and that any Catholic lad of high promise is soon recommended to Old Trafford. Busby denied this to me: 'It's one of those stories that get around,' he said. 'Only three of the team playing against Villa were Catholics.

"'Our scouting policy is to find young players and develop their football ourselves. One of the reasons behind their success is that, as youngsters, they have much in common and work together here in a happy-family atmosphere.'"

Of the players on view, Pilley, like many others, was impressed by a duo of complete opposites.

"As a result of these blended policies, Manchester now have a side whose technical strength lies in all-round efficiency – based largely, I fancy, on the support the 20-year-old wing-halves, Edwards and Colman, supply to an attack of tremendous fire-power.

"A great team, then; a team that proves soccer-good, attractive soccer – can still capture public imagination and cash; a team that, in a city which has moral problems, sets a stirring, healthy example to youth. The greatest in the world? Steady there! It's a hypothetical question; certainly not one for an insular Englishman like myself – nor kerbside salesmen in Manchester – to answer.

"But, judging merely from a distance on records and reputations, I would say this: day in, day out, they must be among the world's best. And who knows? If United can continue to keep their 'Babes' content, and if success does not breed complacency, what heights may they reach in the future?

"What Manchester thinks today... I wonder?"

League matters were thrust to one side on Saturday March 23rd, as United, their supporters and local members of the press headed across the Pennines to Hillsborough, Sheffield, for the FA Cup semi-final against last season's losing finalists Birmingham City. Henry Rose, the regular United correspondent for the *Daily Express*, who had fallen foul of all connected with the club following his comments regarding Tommy Taylor, did little to reclaim his standing amongst the faithful by declaring that Birmingham City would be the team that would head to Wembley for the Cup Final. Admittedly, Rose had tipped the St Andrew's side from the third round, whilst also naming United as one of his last eight, declaring that he was not going to cheat at this late stage and switch to the favourites. He would stick with the 11-4 outsiders.

Having done their pre-match training at Blackpool, United travelled from the Lancashire resort on the morning of the match, getting caught up in traffic after stopping in Manchester for lunch and arriving at Hillsborough only thirty-five minutes before kick-off. This perhaps hindered their approach in the opening minutes, but they were soon to settle and looked the better of the two teams even without the injured Tommy Taylor.

Cup semi-finals can be dour affairs, seldom reaching the heights commensurate with the occasion, and this was a classic example with the outcome decided within the opening quarter of an hour. In a cup-tie, perhaps more so than a normal League encounter, the opening goal can prove vital and it was to come United's way after only twelve minutes. Byrne picked out Pegg who evaded two defenders before passing to Charlton, whose crossfield ball fell to Berry. The United number seven got the better of Green and as the Birmingham defence backtracked, he hit a low, left-footed shot beyond the outstretched left hand of the diving Merrick.

A minute later it was 2-0. Edwards sent Pegg scurrying down the left, the winger rounding Hall before attempting to cross into the centre. His attempt was blocked twice but, regaining possession, he rolled the ball towards an unmarked Charlton who beat Merrick with a left-footed drive to celebrate his first FA Cup-tie in style.

Birmingham, to their credit, battled admirably to get back into the game, causing the United defence a number of problems, but could not manage to score the goal that would allow them to regain a foothold in the game. The two early goals had been enough to kill both the game as a real contest and the Midlands side's hopes of a second consecutive trip to Wembley.

"Every week is a terrible ordeal, but the lads take it all in their stride. They just keep winning these vital matches. We were the better team and I am sure we deserved to win," said a contented Matt Busby, with his assistant, Jimmy Murphy adding: "Everything went according to plan."

Floodlit football was no longer a novelty now that ever more clubs were scrimping and scraping to install systems of varying types. Thus they were enabled to play at any hour of the night and day, with no need to bring kick-off times forward to an unsuitable hour, forcing supporters to go AWOL from their workplace. United, however, whilst trailblazers in the production of young footballers, lagged behind many lesser sides when it came to installing floodlights at Old Trafford, despite a system having been in place at their Cliff training ground for a number of years. "Waiting to see how other clubs go about it," or "looking for the best system" were the normal replies when confronted about the subject.

Having done some homework, they went as far as to publish an illustration of Old Trafford, complete with floodlight pylons on the cover of the *United Review* for the fixture against Portsmouth back in September. The accompanying text read:

"According to electrical experts we should have a floodlighting system as good, if not better than any installation in the country! From the model photographed here you will see four pylons – each to be 160 feet high. At the top of each tower will be 54 floodlights – equal to millions of candle power – and the whole installation will be controlled by a single press-button. The work has been commissioned and completion is expected early in the year."

The estimated cost for the project was over £40,000, the work going on throughout the season, causing little disruption as three of the four tall pylons were outside the stadium walls. Thankfully, everything went according to plan with the big 'switch-on' scheduled for the visit of Bolton Wanderers on the night of Monday March 25th.

With the night sky around Old Trafford bright in the early evening air compared to the usual gloom, the footballing public were attracted like moths to the banks of the ship canal, along with the simply curious. "One to the illuminations, please," was the tongue-in-cheek request to the bus conductors, with the official attendance given as 60,862, but others had to admire the new structures from the outside, as the 'full house' notices quickly appeared, and the gates were locked around half an hour before kick-off with an estimated 15,000 still outside.

Seventy extra police were called in to cope with the vast sea of human bodies outside while, inside, the scene took on a surreal appearance when the United players took to the field in an all-red playing kit, the visitors in all white. A dress rehearsal for the forthcoming European Cup semi-final tie against Real Madrid? Hopefully it wasn't, as things did not go according to the script. Taking full advantage of their inactivity on Saturday, Bolton outplayed their jaded-looking hosts, scoring twice without reply. Strangely, it could well have been the Madrid giants who were christening the Old Trafford lights instead of unglamorous Bolton, but despite being in agreement to taking part in such a prestige fixture, the Spaniards had to decline the invitation due to their European Cup commitments against Nice.

One person who was there the night Old Trafford took on a completely different look was Ray Morgan, but the youngster from Collyhurst was to remember it for more than the 'new look' surroundings of which he was already quite familiar. Ray recalled:

"I met my dad at the United Cafe on the Warwick Road bridge and the roar when they were switched on was deafening. Bolton were something of a jinx to us, as their 2-0 win showed, but it wasn't the lights or the score than stands out in the memory, but the fact that my dad knocked out a guy who had peed down my leg through a rolled up newspaper... common in those days but not down young lads' legs... my hero... my dad the Red.

"One thing about going back then was how much time my old man took out to make sure I got to the games. For a Saturday game he would have been working in Metro Vickers in Trafford Park for the usual Saturday half day and then he would make his way to the ground and meet me at the United Cafe. After the game, we would get the bus into Piccadilly where he would treat me to roasted chestnuts. For a midweek game it would be the same again and taking into account the fact he left the house at six in the morning and we wouldn't get home until ten at night I owed my dad a lot... not least the fact that I'm a Red."

"I find it difficult to pinpoint my first United game, as it's so long ago. We lived in Collyhurst and football was all we lived for. I went to St Pat's school, and although he was about four years older than me, I was an altar boy with Nobby Stiles, who was soon to be playing in the United youth team.

"Basically your mates would ask you on the Saturday morning if you were going to the match. Not, are you going to see such and such, as we couldn't really care less who United were playing, just that there was a game on. Having agreed to go, we would simply jump on a bus heading in the right direction and keep jumping off between stops in an attempt to avoid paying the fare until we got near to Old Trafford. Once at the ground, it was down to the nearest turnstile where someone would always lift us over and we would then scramble down to the front for a good view. From time to time we would also manage to blag a pie. Getting home would simply be a reversal of the getting there process. A good afternoon out for free."

Although the press handout on the night of the big 'switch-on' declared that the lights would "produce the effect of continuous sunlight", the ninety-minutes that followed produced nothing but gloom for the United players and supporters alike. Twice in the opening stages, Gubbins came close as United struggled to put their game together and, after thirty minutes, the visitors eventually took the lead. A crossfield ball from Lofthouse found Gubbins, whose forward pass to Parry was blasted past Ray Wood. David Pegg came close to an equaliser, as did Johnny Berry and emergency centre-forward Duncan Edwards, but it was the visitors who continued to impress.

Within four minutes of the game resuming after the interval, it was 2-0 to Bolton, courtesy of a controversial goal. McGuinness was fouled and with the linesman flagging for the free kick, Bolton counterattacked. Full-back Hartle, still some distance from goal, decided to try his luck with a shot and was as surprised as anyone to see his effort fly past Wood, via the head of Foulkes. Booing echoed around the ground, but the referee was unmoved and the goal stood. United proceeded to storm the Bolton goal, but to no avail, as the Burnden Park side held out until the final whistle. The lead at the top was cut to three points, but there was still the cushion of a game in hand.

Victory by the odd goal in three was enough to get back to winning ways against Leeds United at Elland Road, a quick reply to their critics who had voiced the opinions that United were wilting under the stress of having to compete on three fronts. Performances could be expected to suffer as the season began to take its toll, but there was the underlying strength in depth coupled with in-built determination to succeed on all fronts.

However, they could have done without the crucial First Division encounter against Tottenham Hotspur coming the week before the European Cup semi-final first leg against Real Madrid in Spain. Because there was so much at stake, the game failed to reach the heights expected, with Tottenham anxious not to lose and United happy to have a point and steer clear of injuries. The game entered the record books with little to report beyond the 0-0 scoreline.

And so it was to Madrid and the imposing Bernabeu Stadium. This was United's true test, ninety minutes against the European champions, a team they had to match, and indeed defeat, if they wanted to claim that unprecedented Treble. A defeat within this towering structure would not signal the end of the dream but, if it did come to that, it had to be a scoreline that could be overturned in the Old Trafford second leg.

Pre-match formalities took so long that the game got under way five minutes late; but when it did, United were able to show that they were more than capable of causing an upset – this despite finding the home side well versed in the underhand tactics all too familiar on foreign shores, as well as in skilful football.

But it was the dark side of the game that caused United problems and a stronger referee might have turned the game in their favour. Di Stefano should have been sent off for a blatant kick at Blanchflower, later admitting that he did "see red".. Lesmes tripped Berry inside the Madrid penalty area only for Dutchman Leo Horn to lack the courage to award a spot-kick. Alonso committed a horrendous tackle on Taylor, while Whelan was punched in the stomach by Munoz as he attempted to pass the Madrid defender.

Such incidents were certainly off-putting, knocking United off their stride, but taking everything into consideration, the visitors did well to remain on level terms until the 63rd minute when Madrid finally opened the scoring when Rial dived headlong to head a Gento cross past the outstretched arm of Wood. Ten minutes later, Di Stefano made it 2-0, a shattering blow; but with eight minutes remaining the majority of the 125,000 crowd were silenced when Tommy Taylor climbed above the white-shirted defenders to head Whelan's cross past Alonso to give United a glimmer of hope.

Had Blanchflower, on one of several upfield forays, managed to level the score, the result would have gone down as one of the greatest in the club's history, but the miss was to prove crucial as Madrid quickly counter-attacked, with Kopa and Rial presenting Mateos with the opportunity to make it 3-1.

Whilst there was praise for United's overall performance despite the defeat, many were critical of the red-shirted forwards. "Blame Forwards" said Tom Jackson of the *Manchester Evening News*, under the heading of "It Will Take Supermen to Pull United Through", suggesting the team lacked "forward rhythm". His counterpart Alf Clarke in the *Evening Chronicle* had similar thoughts and penned: "Unless the forwards play better than they did yesterday Manchester United can say goodbye to the triple crown." Henry Rose, not every United follower's cup of tea, echoed a similar opinion in the *Daily Express*, going as far as to suggest that "Busby must have the courage to make a change in the forward line. He MUST find a place for BOBBY CHARLTON."

The general opinion was that Madrid were at least three goals better than United, with some suggesting that the Spaniards would have won by an even greater margin had they shown their best form. Roger Byrne, whilst praising Madrid, said: "They are the best club team I have ever played against," but was equally confident that his team could turn things around in the second leg.

> "Any team must be good to beat Madrid by three goals, but my confidence in United's ability to win through is increased by the way the team rallied in the last 20 minutes and began to dictate the run of the game.
>
> "We can be masters if we reproduce that form all through the match in Manchester.
>
> "United are not out of the cup yet and all the players are determined to win through at the second attempt."

Returning to home soil, United were perhaps fortunate that their domestic programme continued with a trip to bottom-half Luton Town, where a lacklustre performance,

> "rarely rose above the mediocre" with the "Not so majestic Manchester United still seeming to be recovering from their

Spanish trip. They really went through the strolling players' act. They strolled on, strolled about the field, and strolled off at the end of a tame 90 minutes, comfortable and so leisurely winners."

These comments were echoed in the other Sunday and Monday newspapers, all the correspondents who had watched United confidently reporting that the championship was once again heading towards Salford.

Easter. One of the major dates on the footballing calendar. Four days when the hopes and dreams of many can be either fulfilled or dealt a savage blow.

Six days after the lacklustre 2-0 victory against Luton it was off to Turf Moor, Burnley, not the happiest of hunting grounds for United, with only two victories in the last eight visits. Here they were looking for another two points that would take them a step closer to the retention of the First Division title. Tottenham, who had been clutching at United's shirt tail for most of the season, had been joined in their pursuit by Preston North End in recent weeks, a two-pronged attacking front eager to upset the champions' Treble joust.

On Good Friday, the First Division table read: 1st – Manchester United with 55 points from 37 games; 2nd – Preston North End with 51 points from 38 games, and 3rd – Tottenham Hotspur with 49 points from 37 games.

A more energetic performance at Burnley followed with what was considered United's best ninety minutes for some time. A sublime performance and hat-trick from Billy Whelan, his first league goals since February, were more than enough to record a rare victory at Turf Moor. Preston kept up their challenge with a solitary goal victory over Sheffield Wednesday, but Tottenham were wilting under pressure, managing only a 1-1 draw at London neighbours Charlton.

With Real Madrid Manchester-bound for their forthcoming semi-final second-leg tie, Busby had the championship almost guaranteed with four games remaining, and resisted the temptation to rest his star performers for the visit of Sunderland to Old

Trafford. He did make one or two minor adjustments to the team that had played at Burnley twenty-four hours previously, but he actually strengthened his eleven, by replacing Goodwin, Viollet and Scanlon with Colman, Charlton and Pegg. "Let's get the points that will ensure us the title and worry about Madrid later," seemed to be the manager's philosophy. Neither was he intending to rely on Blackpool defeating their near neighbours Preston, a result that would allow the championship trophy to remain at Old Trafford as long as United triumphed.

Blackpool failed to take both points off Preston, managing only one in a 0-0 draw, while a few miles down the A6 there was no nervous nail-biting or clock-watching as a Sunderland side, who had toiled against relegation for long periods of the campaign and were renowned for their cheque book approach to team building, were ironically defeated by the side who had become a role model in the production of their own players, beginning at grass roots level.

The visitors' side was awash with seasoned professionals, eight full internationalists, but they were no match for the effervescent red shirts who bubbled away like a witch's cauldron from the first whistle.

But despite their superiority, having outpaced and outplayed their opponents, United had only a sixth-minute Whelan goal to show for their efforts with fifteen minutes remaining. Surprisingly, they had eased off during the second half, despite Sunderland's keeper going off injured; but suddenly, as if awoken from a spell, they then surged into life. Whelan added a second, equalling the club's scoring record of 30 goals in a season previously held by Jack Rowley. Edwards made it 2-0 with a thirty-five yard special, with Tommy Taylor rounding off the scoring with the fourth in the dying seconds.

Former Manchester City goalkeeper Frank Swift, now reporting for the *News of the World*, wrote:

> "There are hardly any superlatives left to describe this great United team. Limited space makes it impossible to do full justice to all the fine work once again building up to a first-

class, all-round team display. For me they are champions…
by a mile."

Down below in the Old Trafford dressing room, it was teacups of champagne in the bath for the United heroes. The real celebrations could wait, with captain Roger Byrne taking time to say:

"Although the League title is the least glamorous of the
three, it is the most arduous. Our ambition now is to win
it three years on the run, like Huddersfield and Arsenal."

Real Madrid flew into Ringway Airport and headed straight to Old Trafford, arriving seventeen minutes after United's Easter Monday fixture against Burnley had kicked off. If their journey had been intended to cast their eyes over their opponents as well as to take in the Old Trafford atmosphere, they were to be disappointed in the first instance and to receive a rude awakening in the second.

With the League title secured, Matt Busby finally had no hesitation in leaving the majority of his first-choice players – Byrne, Colman, Blanchflower, Edwards, Berry, Whelan, Taylor, Charlton and Pegg – out of his team to face the Turf Moor side, bringing in Greaves, Goodwin, Cope, McGuinness, Webster, Doherty, Dawson, Viollet and Scanlon, with perhaps Viollet the only one who might have an outside chance of facing the Spaniards. But even fielding what was more or less a reserve team line-up, Burnley were still outclassed. Goals from Webster – what did he have to do to secure a regular first-team place? – and debutant Alex Dawson gave United a comfortable 2-0 win.

Word that the Madrid players were in the stand quickly spread around the stadium, and the noise level was subsequently cranked up in order to let them enjoy a little of what their forthcoming encounter would produce, at least in atmosphere. From the safety of their seats it might have been relatively tame or unimpressive compared with the noise echoing out of their own much larger arena, but as they left the ground at full time, their coach was caught up in traffic and they were subjected to a volley of abuse from sections of the United support who remembered the treatment that had been handed out to their favourites in the Bernabeu.

To say that the Madrid players were shocked by the fist-shaking, abusive Mancunians is an understatement. "We were disgusted," said Real president Senor Santiago Bernabeu. "It was not the sort of welcome we had expected. I was disgusted by it all. And so were the players. They never expected to be shouted at." The stories even made their way back to the Spanish newspapers, where quotes appeared saying: "The fans surrounded our coach and booed us and when someone shouted something, they mocked us." One paper, *Alcazar*, even carried a story of the Madrid players being stoned upon their arrival.

Interest in what was expected to be a feisty encounter was huge, but for those without a ticket or unable to get to Manchester, there was the option of being able to watch the action unfold on television. That was if you actually owned one! Granada TV had trumped their BBC rivals and secured the rights to televise the match in its entirety, not just the usual second-half-only screening. However, they faced a problem before a ball was even kicked.

Planning to use three cameras, finding ideal positions for them proved to be difficult. Each side of the ground had covered accommodation and placing cameras near the halfway line would block the view of a few spectators. Using either end of the ground behind the goal would mean that although above the heads of the crowd, they would be perhaps too far from some of the action. Putting a camera in the main stand would also be far from ideal, as this would mean the removal of some seats. Architects and structural engineers – stress and strain experts – were called in, and it was even suggested that part of the stand roof could be cut away to accommodate the necessary cameras. In the end, ideal positions were found behind the goals and along the side. Everyone was happy, that is, with the obvious exception of the BBC!

Outside Old Trafford on the night of the match, the *Manchester Evening News* gave out thousands of red and white caps, along with red and white megaphones, in the hope that the crowd would make it the most colourful and noisiest night in United's history. Leading up to the kick-off, the police found themselves in the unusual position of giving away hundreds of tickets, as supporters with spares found them difficult to pass on and, not wanting to hang about outside the ground, gave them to the police. Even the ticket touts had difficulty selling their wares, offering £1 tickets for 4/-. The payment of such cash could all have been for nothing, as unbeknown to those outside, there had been drama inside even before a ball had been kicked in anger. In the days running up to the game, United had kept the Old Trafford turf well watered, but upon inspection by the Madrid officials on the morning of the game, they had informed their United counterparts that if the puddles on the pitch were still there an hour before kick-off, then they would call the game off. As it was, the United groundstaff turned off the sprinklers and covered the soft, wet areas with sand, enabling the game to go ahead as planned.

The United players had spent the days leading up to the match at their regular pre-match haunt of Blackpool's Norbreck Castle hotel, confident in their own ability, but knowing full well that they had to function as a team in order to score the necessary goals to claw back that 3-1 deficit. They were also well aware that Real Madrid were no Bilbao.

This was proved within half an hour of the start, as the visitors increased their advantage with goals in the 24th and 30th minutes through Kopa and Rial. Both goals saw Real tear the United defence apart with their swift, attacking play. 5-1 down, the tie was now undoubtedly beyond even Manchester United's reach.

Half-time allowed for a brief period of thought, an opportunity to re-plan the strategy for the second forty-five minutes, but even that did not go entirely to plan, nor did the switching on of the floodlights brighten the dismal evening.

On the hour, a Byrne throw-in sent Pegg dashing down the wing and his cross was met by Taylor who managed to scramble the ball home at the second attempt. Could United achieve the impossible? A Taylor back-header and a powerful shot were both dealt with by Alonso as the minutes slowly ticked away and it was five minutes from time before a second goal materialised. Pegg again caused problems down the flank, crossing the ball towards Charlton who snatched an equaliser, but it was too little, too late.

There was, however, much more to the game than the four goals and the end of United's interest in the competition, as the following morning's newspapers were once again as quick to acknowledge Matt Busby's team's failings as they had been their successes of recent weeks. "I Was Ashamed" declared George Follows in the *Daily Herald*, writing:

"Manchester football fans helped to knock their own Red Devils out of the European Cup at Old Trafford last night and at the same time they threw away their own good names as sportsmen. They were guilty of a squalid show of one-eyed partisanship, a public display of bad manners that made me ashamed to be English.

"They booed the players of Real Madrid when they did a victory dance in the centre circle at the end.

"They cheered when Duncan Edwards fouled Mateos near the end of the game disfigured by 48 free kicks – 22 against United, 26 against Madrid.

"They bombarded two Spanish men and one girl with empty cartons as they carried a Madrid banner around the ground at half-time.

"They incited Edwards and Roger Byrne to actions that they will want to forget.

"Edwards lost his head. He attempted to drag injured Torres off the pitch so that the game could be restarted.

"Byrne ended the match on an unhappy note by a blundering foul on Mateos."

"United Die With Their Clogs on," declared the *Daily Express*, while Arthur Walmsley's article in the *Manchester Evening Chronicle* was preceded by "This Was a City's night of Shame". Even Matt Busby got caught up in it all, going onto the pitch at the final whistle to question the referee if he had actually played a full ninety minutes.

The disappointment of defeat and the fallout from the after-match criticism was a major blow to everyone associated with the club, but the ramifications of the ninety minutes against Madrid had to be dismissed immediately as, with two League fixtures still to fulfil, full attention had to be focused on the FA Cup Final against Aston Villa. The 180 minutes against Cardiff City and West Bromwich Albion would provide Busby with the opportunity to once again rest some of his stars without provoking the wrath of the Football League. Between the two fixtures, when the Central League stalwarts once again proved their capabilities beating Cardiff 3-2 at Ninian Park and drawing 1-1 at home against West Bromwich, he would field seventeen different players, giving a debut to goalkeeper Gordon Clayton in the latter of the two fixtures.

Rather surprisingly, the number of spectators attending those two final games, a mere 38,065, would have fitted comfortably into Old Trafford, with a disappointing 20,357 trudging down Warwick Road and its neighbouring streets to see Roger Byrne presented with the First Division championship trophy at the end of the match against West Bromwich Albion on April 29th. Many were so eager to obtain a good view of the trophy presentation that they invaded the pitch with five minutes still to play. An announcement from secretary Walter Crickmer to get back behind the touchlines was thankfully heeded, but when the final whistle did materialise, the police were powerless to prevent a full-scale pitch invasion.

With Wembley now firmly on the horizon, Matt Busby had a problem in the centre of his defence. Mark Jones had been out for a lengthy period with a knee injury, but had returned to the side against West Bromwich Albion for his first League outing since February, playing with a cut eye received in training. Jackie Blanchflower had damaged thigh and stomach muscles against Cardiff, while third choice number five, Ronnie Cope, had an injured toe. There were one or two other positions to take into consideration as well, the number eleven jersey another concern as Albert Scanlon had proved a capable deputy for David Pegg. Furthermore, Dennis Viollet had also taken over the number ten shirt from Bobby Charlton, giving Busby much to ponder over.

As per normal, it was off to the seaside for the United squad, taking up residency once again at Blackpool's Norbreck Castle on the north shore and posing for a team photograph in their all-white Wembley kit. It looked as though Mark Jones had got the nod over his stand-in Jackie Blanchflower, as he was included in the line-up, but on closer inspection only ten players featured in the posed shot, with Tommy Taylor, like Blanchflower, nowhere to be seen.

No matter who got the nod from Busby, United were favourites to lift the trophy. "The Biggest 'Certs' Since the War" proclaimed the heading above Arthur Walmsley's article in the *Manchester Evening Chronicle*'s Cup Final supplement, the reporter going on to write:

> "The plain fact is that Manchester United have been made favourites for the cup simply because they are, on all known form, by far the better footballing side – and that, among other things in United's favour, is what is really going to count tomorrow."

In another Cup Supplement, this time in the *Weekend Mail*, alongside a teamgroup and pen pictures of the United players was an interesting snippet entitled 'See How They Play':

> "Watch how Manchester build up their attacks. The centre-forward, with his back to the goal, will receive a pass and then push it square for his inside-forwards to race through for scoring efforts.
>
> "Keep your eyes on danger man Duncan Edwards, who possesses a hard shot and will often burst through for a crack at goal.
>
> "Follow Johnny Berry carefully. He has a body-swerve nearly the equal of Stanley Matthews. He likes to cut across the full-back and have a shot.
>
> "United base their attack on the through ball. Watch how they push it through for the forwards to race on to.
>
> "Follow carefully the mazy dribbles of Eddie Colman – until he delivers that telling pass."

Despite knowing the hard facts, few, if any, could prevent United from performing at the level they had set themselves.

Matt Busby also had the belief that his team was capable of pulling off the 'Double', becoming the first side to do so in sixty years.

"We have been showing top form throughout the last two seasons and we are unbeaten in our last nine League games, (it was actually eight) despite having had to switch and re-switch the team due to injuries. Contrary to the critics, I consider that the European Cup k.o. from Real Madrid will act as a spur to our lads on Saturday. And if more and more people are switching their Cup tip from United to Villa, that's just the thing to put our lads on their mettle."

After much debate behind the scenes, it was Jackie Blanchflower who got the nod over Mark Jones for a place in United's line-up, the Irishman delighted to get the call ahead of his friend, but unaware of the part he was about to play in one of the most controversial finals ever played.

When the game was in its infancy, with a mere six minutes gone, a cross into the United penalty area was headed towards goal by Villa outside-left McParland and easily gathered by Ray Wood. McParland, however, continued his forward run and instead of the legal shoulder-to-shoulder contact, he caught the United keeper on the cheek with the full force of his challenge. Wood immediately fell to the ground, whilst the Villa man, well aware as to the feelings of Wood's team-mates and his own ill-fated decision, decided against immediately getting to his feet.

Surrounded by concerned team-mates, Wood received treatment from trainer Tom Curry, but attempts to stand up saw him collapse back on to the turf and it was obvious that he would not be able to continue. His green jersey was pulled over his head and given to Jackie Blanchflower, Edwards moving to centre-half, with Liam Whelan also taking a few steps back to fill the void in the United engine room. It was a move that deprived the front line of the Irishman's attacking flair and shooting prowess. The ten incensed men of United resumed their fight even more determined to lift the trophy.

"Should I have sent McParland off?" questioned Frank Coultas the referee. "Personally I saw nothing vicious. It was clumsy but with no foul intent. If Wood had not gone down, I would not have given a foul."

Those clad in red and white both on the pitch and the terracing were of a much different opinion.

Wood, carried to the dressing room, was unconscious for some fifteen minutes and was bleeding from both the mouth and nose. Upon coming round, United physiotherapist Ted Dalton took him outside the stadium where the keeper's reactions were tested by throwing a ball towards him. His efforts at trying to catch the ball were like that of a novice, much to the amusement of two young boys playing nearby, but it was decided that it was worth throwing him back into the action and he returned to the fray in the 34th minute at outside-right. It was obvious to everyone that he was there only to make up numbers, as Villa paid him scant attention and when the ball game his way he was barely capable of lifting his leg, never mind kicking it in the right direction.

Even with ten men and an inexperienced keeper, United withstood all the Villa pressure, fortunate not to go behind on the hour when Myerscough shot wide with the goal at his mercy and again when Sewell hesitated and was robbed by Byrne. Seven minutes later, however, they finally wilted under pressure, the villain of the piece, McParland, heading home a Smith cross.

Few doubted United's ability to come back after going behind, they had seen it on numerous occasions in the past, but before such an opportunity could materialise, they were dealt a second cruel blow and once again McParland and the match official were flung into highly debated controversy. Dixon robbed Colman of the ball, turning to send a right-footed drive on to the United crossbar with Blanchflower beaten. As the ball rebounded into play, McParland, who had been standing in a clearly offside position on the byline to the right of Blanchflower, moved back into play, latched on to the ball and sent it past the helpless keeper. There was no doubt to even the most biased spectator that the Villa man was in an offside position when the ball was played, but the goal was still given.

United now had a monumental task on their hands, but continued to show determination in their play, never once considering throwing in the towel. For their efforts, they were rewarded with a goal in the eighty-third minute when Tommy

Taylor rose to head home an Edwards corner kick. Suddenly there was panic on the touchline.

During the half-time interval, Wood had once again collapsed and, having been diagnosed with a fractured cheekbone, was given a pain-killing injection. It was also advised that if United were to insist that he should continue to play, he should in no way retake his place between the posts. Nine minutes into that second period he was back to his meanderings on the right wing. But now, with United back in the game, although with time running against them, Matt Busby made the desperate decision to ignore medical advice and put Wood back in goal, and Blanchflower back to centre-half, allowing Duncan Edwards to press forward in search of an equaliser. It was a goal that was never to materialise. Villa stood firm to become arguably the most despised winners of the famous trophy. A victory, that no-one could deny, that was achieved purely due to strength in numbers.

There was much sympathy for the gallant losers, but once again they did not escape criticism from the press. In large bold letters, the front page of the *People* was of the opinion that "United Threw It Away" with Joe Hulme writing:

"My verdict on one of the most thrilling Cup Finals of all time is this: Manchester United threw the match away.

"They waited too long before putting the injured Ray Wood back into goal. Had they made the move fifteen minutes earlier, I am certain they would have got the equaliser.

"When the move was made, the babes were all over Villa. There just wasn't enough time left for them to get that second goal.

"I know that Roger Byrne, United's captain, does not agree with me. 'I didn't put Wood back in goal earlier because he wasn't fit enough. In fact, he should not have come back at all,' he said."

The debates lingered on, but the result would remain unchanged. United were FA Cup runners-up.

"Am I disappointed that we lost the Cup? Yes!" exclaimed Matt Busby. "Am I downhearted? Not likely! It was Villa's Cup…but Manchester United's Final. We lost – and that's football. But don't worry. While the boys play as they did in this Final we'll be chasing that League and Cup double and the European Cup again with every confidence next year. We Can Do It."

While basking in the glory of his team's success, McParland was quick to make a scathing attack on United captain Roger Byrne and his fellow white-shirted team-mates, claiming he was "roughed up" following his collision with Ray Wood.

"I was made the target for a personal attack that was obvious retaliation by players who considered I had purposely hit the goalkeeper. It was the worst handling I have ever experienced in football," complained the Villa winger. "I was struck on the jaw as I went up for a ball in the air," he further alleged, "while on another occasion when I leapt to head a ball an elbow was rammed into my back. Later I was hit in the back of the neck as I fell in a tackle with a United player sprawling across me."

The Villa man added that when he suspected a personal attack he moved into the penalty area as often as possible in the hope of winning a penalty.

It has to be assumed that those comments, and indeed the actions of the United players if in fact they were actually true, were little more than uttered and carried out on the spur of the moment, as shortly afterwards peace resumed, in rather surprising circumstances. Soon after the Cup Final, Roger Byrne was married and, with his wife Joy, headed to Jersey on honeymoon, both looking forward to a relaxing break away from the rigours of life at Old Trafford.

"After arriving at our hotel, Roger left me to finish off the unpacking and headed off to the bar for a pre-dinner drink," recalled Joy. "When I went to join him I noticed he was in conversation with a rather familiar looking face. When recognition did come, it was something of a shock, as I had last seen our fellow guest a few weeks previously at Wembley in the colours of Aston Villa and I can't say I took favourably to him then. It was Peter McParland. Roger, however, was speaking to him like a long lost friend. I suppose though that was typical of Roger who bore no grudges."

Messrs McParland and Byrne were not the only footballers on holiday on the island as two other members of United's Cup Final side – Jackie Blanchflower (who was also on honeymoon) and Duncan Edwards – were also there along with various other professionals from a variety of clubs. Before long they were involved in both a cricket and a football match against teams of locals.

Byrne was certainly no novice as a cricketer and could quite easily have followed his friend Brian Statham into the professional ranks, and in the first of the two sporting fixtures managed 20 runs before being caught out, whilst taking two wickets for eight runs. His competitive spirit showed through even in a friendly cricket match, as one of the balls he bowled lifted viciously and saw an opponent having to retire.

As for the football match, had he been aware of his captain and prize wing-half's involvement (Blanchflower had a 'slight disposition'!), Matt Busby would not have been too pleased. Played in 80 degree heat, the holidaymakers won 11-1. The *Jersey Evening Post* were most complementary to the United captain, despite him only managing one goal from the inside-right position:

> "Manchester United's immaculate left-back, Roger Byrne, demonstrated that his forward ability is on a par by also notching an excellent goal. International or friendly fixture, Roger always gave 100% and was a credit to his profession."

If there was any consolation to the United players, having captured only one of their three targets, it was financial. The club had managed to have European Cup bonus payments sanctioned by the Football League and, although minute in comparison with the Real Madrid players' claims, saw them earn £210 for their first-round success, £240 for the second, £360 for the third and £480 for the semi-final. This was over and above the normal £3-a-man win bonus. Had they actually triumphed in all three competitions then payouts of around £2,900 would have been the norm.

Chapter Seven

The Dream Becomes a Nightmare

Season 1957-58

I T is open to debate whether Manchester United had been genuinely on course for that unprecedented 'Treble', or if their chances were wildly hyped by media speculation and by the misguided pipe-dreams of the most enthusiastic supporters. Certainly, even on an 'off-day', they had the beating of any other team in the country; but Real Madrid were a far cry from your Huddersfield Towns, Cardiff Citys and Leeds Uniteds. The Spaniards were a team of immeasurable talent, unmatched even by United's high standards – albeit not by much. Then, in addition, they had their gamesmanship and underhand tactics to add to their arsenal. This was the team that United would have to match, from a playing perspective only, if they were to rise to that ultimate pinnacle on the European front. On home soil, they had nothing to prove to anyone.

Matt Busby had achieved what few could ever hope for in top-class football, and that was to create yet another trophy-winning side from the ashes of a first. Comparisons were often futile, even impossible to make due to the timescale involved, but it was less than a decade since the United manager's 1948 FA Cup winning side were being lauded as one of the 'best ever'. How did they compare to the present-day eleven who had captured the country's imagination with their free-flowing brand of football, augmented by their youthful enthusiasm?

One man qualified to judge was Alf Clarke of the *Manchester Evening Chronicle*.

> "How do the Manchester United of today compare with Johnny Carey's team? I believe they are better.
>
> "The present United side have actually scored more goals, but the old forwards were magical. They had all the talents devastatingly blended to overcome any situation. I believe them to have been United's best forward line, better than the Meredith, Hales, J. Turnbull, A. Turnbull and Wall attack of 1908, which from my schoolboy recollections of them would not have stood up to the speed of the game today.
>
> "I think that the present United half-back line is better than the 1948 trio, largely because of the dominance of Duncan Edwards.
>
> "At full-back my vote goes to Johnny Carey and Aston, but there is little between Jack Crompton and Ray Wood. Both capable of making the superb save and permitting the simplest shot to beat them.
>
> "For sheer brilliance, then, I take the 1948 side. For power, the present team. This is a team built to WIN, to ride roughshod over the long League programme. Their greater speed and stamina are, in my view, the reasons why the present team are better and more effective than Carey's men."

The rise from being 'nearly men' to the team to beat on the domestic front had taken time. To now attain the same status on foreign shores was not seen as work in progress, but an urgent, pressing need. Those talented youngsters had grown into manhood, into players of quality. Their ambitions matched those of their manager and, as a new season approached, those ambitions were now considerably higher than twelve months before.

Even pre-season had taken a step up. Previous campaigns had slowly gathered momentum with nothing more than training sessions and runs around suburban Salford. The long-haul trips to

America and jaunts to Scandinavia to face the part-time joiners, students and all-comers had all been end-of-season trips, wind-down breaks with all expenses paid. August 1957, however, took United to Germany, a more testing and competitive environment in which to blow away the summer cobwebs. The results were par for the course, clear-cut victories, with Berliner Stadtelf and Hanover offering little and conceding seven between them. United were once again ready to roll.

Much to Matt Busby's relief, the German trip had gone broadly to plan, without the intrusion from unwelcome visitors who had surfaced during the visit to Copenhagen at the end of May, forcing Busby to throw a security cordon around his players.

Whilst relaxing at the team hotel in the Danish city, Busby had been approached by Lajos Cseisler, a Hungarian, but an agent for Internazionale Milan, who did not bother with any smalltalk, asking the United manager: "Are you prepared to transfer Tommy Taylor to Italy?"

Busby's reply was equally brief, telling the agent that he was wasting his time, as he had no intentions of selling Taylor, or any of his other players for that matter, to a club at home or abroad. The United manager added: "No fee was mentioned because the interview never got that far. These things can be very unsettling to a team and I don't want my players to become the target of those foreign agents."

Busby didn't want to find himself in the same shoes as his Leeds United counterpart, as the Yorkshire club had lost their most prominent player, the Welsh international John Charles, to Juventus.

The £55,000 fee did little to compensate for the loss of such a talented individual. The player himself pocketed a £10,000 signing-on fee plus added extras such as bonuses and a house. A similar fee was on the table for Taylor and, to a £15-per-week professional in Manchester, it was a very tempting offer. It was not surprising that Busby did not discuss the matter face-to-face with his centre-forward.

Money was now becoming a serious issue within the game. Since the war, crowds had risen gradually, with United achieving better attendances than most. The opening-day figures for season 1957-58 showed an increase of some 100,000 on the previous year. Players were beginning to feel that they perhaps deserved more for their efforts, even with a new-season wage increase to £17 per week.

Duncan Edwards felt that £20 per week was a more acceptable figure:

"I suggest that increase not out of any exaggerated idea of our importance but because in these days that seems a reasonable living wage for a family man. Emphatically I would keep the increased bonus system. There is no greater incentive than extra money at the end of the week.

"Equally emphatically, I would throw out any suggestion of paying a star player more than his team-mates. In any case, how does one define a star player?

"At Manchester United, all the players are stars. We believe that each man fits his position as well as it is able to be filled, so what kind of trouble would it cause if Matt Busby suddenly started paying me extra because I scored a couple of goals?

"No, I am happy as things are, with a flat rate of wages."

There was, however, discontent at Old Trafford as regards to money. Recent times had seen an upturn in media interest surrounding the club, and with television becoming more and more popular it was of little surprise that such a medium wanted to feature United in more than actual match footage. Assuming they only had to turn up at a training session to film the players going through their daily routine, a television crew from the *Sportsview* programme was given a rude awakening when Roger Byrne politely told them that they could film as much as they wanted, as long as he and his team-mates were 'adequately paid' for their 'public relations' exercise. Neither side got what they wanted.

Some were critical of the United players' actions, but others, such as former captain Johnny Carey, supported the United captain's stance:

"I feel that there ought to be more than a token payment for sportsmen taking part in a television transmission which is, after all, providing entertainment for millions of people.

"It is not a new problem. I recall, being confronted with much the same sort of thing as captain of Manchester United's 1948 Cup Final team, although it was not then the BBC that were involved. I went into the question very thoroughly at the time because I felt, as I do now, that in many cases footballers are exploited in the matter of pictures.

"Yet I was convinced then that whatever monetary gains were to be derived by players demanding fees for posing while in training would not amount to any appreciable figure. Therefore on the question of press photographs I was opposed to sticking out for payment.

"We owed it to the club to allow photographers to come along and take pictures, for publicity was good for United. It was also good for us personally.

"I remember the case of Jack Crompton, who was out with me for twenty minutes making spectacular dives in order to make the pictures life-like. He had both knees badly grazed, but was happy to oblige. The photographer thanked him, but Jack never even got a proof of a photo. A week later, about half a dozen small boys came to Jack for his autograph, brandishing copies of those photographs, for which they told him, they had paid half-a-crown each. That sort of thing would sour any player."

But all thoughts of money were soon forgotten as season 1957-58 got under way, United picking up where they had left off by brushing their opponents aside and scoring goals for fun – twenty-two goals from the opening half-dozen fixtures.

Leicester City collapsed under a Liam Whelan hat-trick on the opening day at Filbert Street: "Here we go again! That United blend of continental craft and British precision still has the championship look about it" and "Moving with the superb poise and grace that belongs only to really great champions, Manchester United started the new season as they left off last – in winning vein," were only two of the numerous warnings to the other First Division sides.

If they had aspirations towards the title, then they would have to overcome the formidable champions.

Everton were then then beaten 3-0 at Old Trafford, while neighbours City meekly surrendered under a 4-1 hammering. Former City goalkeeper Frank Swift, watching from the Old Trafford press box penned:

> "I am seriously concerned about the form of Manchester United. Concerned about the all-round team brilliance which methodically wore down their Maine Road neighbours and finally tore them to shreds.
>
> "Why? Because there's hardly a superlative left to heap on their proud, young shoulders. Even that has been said before! Which means, I fear, that the critics may find themselves looking for faults this season in the finest side to grace our game for years."

Others were concerned that it would be too easy for United in their quest for further glory.

Everton, on their home turf, proved that United's march forward would not be entirely without a hitch, as they managed to earn a point from a 3-3 draw after being 3-1 down at half-time. During that ten-minute break, the 72,077 inside Goodison Park debated how many the champions might rack up, but a 42nd-minute injury to Jackie Blanchflower forced United into playing the second half with basically ten men, finding a determined Everton side just too much of a handful to contain and proving that Manchester United were, after all, only human.

United's next opponents, Leeds United, were not the club to test any tentative theory of United's susceptibility: they were to fare worse than any of the other early-season opponents by conceding five without reply. However, if the excuse of Blanchflower's injury was raised in defence of the collapse on Merseyside, then it should be mentioned here that Leeds played with ten men for the majority of the second half and were only 1-0 down at the time of Hair's injury.

"Blackpool has the illuminations, the Tower and Stanley Matthews. But what would that bright town give to add this tag to its famous galaxy of attractions… THE GREATEST SOCCER SHOW ON EARTH" wrote Terence Elliot in the *Daily Express* following United's 4-1 victory beside the seaside. "Exaggeration? Maybe, but you know what I mean," he continued. "Blackpool more often than not looked as though they were there to act as stooges to the great performers who pulled out the tricks you can only see from the masters and the stars."

Top of the First Division, United's success was mirrored off the pitch with the announcement of record profits of £39,784 for the previous year. The second highest recorded in the history of the club, falling behind the £50,810 in 1948-49. Gate receipts, less the visiting clubs' share and payment to the Football League, were record breaking, amounting to £178,769, an increase of £58,425 on the previous season.

Entertainment tax claimed £30,498 as against £23,805 when the profit was a mere £1,463. Some 140,000 spectators – another record – had watched the Central League side.

Since football had resumed in the wake of the Second World War in 1945-46, United had made a profit of £294,016, despite having to pay out £240,981 in entertainment tax. Club assets stood at £156,445, wages and bonuses claimed £43,694, benefits to individuals amounted to £5,800, while travelling and hotels jumped from £15,554 in 1955-56 to £27,416. £1,000 was written off for depreciation of the ground and a further £1,371 for depreciation of the club-owned houses. The £45,000 for the cost of United's own floodlight system had been paid, with those same accounts also revealing that Manchester City had been paid a sum of £3,147 for the hire of their Maine Road ground for the three European Cup ties played there prior to the installation of United's own system.

But it wasn't the figures that were being bandied about that brought gasps from those shareholders in attendance at the club's AGM, it was the announcement that,

"...the Board were now concentrating on a ground development scheme which will include extra accommodation and additional cover which would be of course governed by the funds available for capital expenditure."

With plans having been put in place to increase the capacity of Old Trafford to 100,000, Mr W. H. Petherbridge, one of the directors, revealed that

"plans were well in hand to build a double-decker grandstand, with the entire 'Popular Side' (United Road) being covered."

Work, it was said, was scheduled to begin the following year, but at the board meeting of November 26th the following was recorded:

"Mr Petherbridge stated that as requested by the Directors he had met the representatives of Edward Wood & Co and Goldsmiths regarding the provision of additional covered accommodation on the popular side of the ground and now submitted plans by Ed Wood & Co to survey the terracing at the Stretford End of the ground to the height of the covered corners which would increase the capacity of the ground by approximately 6,000 and cover the whole of the Stretford End terracing apart from a slight cutaway to provide for floodlighting requirements."

Such a proposal would have meant a smaller, although still significant outlay, with the 'Popular Side' plans put on the back burner for the time being at least.

All good things, however, must come to an end and the headlines in the newspapers of September 15th told of "A Buffeting for the Champions", "Busby's Forecast Boomerangs", "Birch gives the Champs the Stick" and simply "United Crash". For those unaware of that afternoon's fixtures, it would have been imagined that Busby's team had encountered a superteam – perhaps Madrid were back in town? But, no. It was none other than the local bogey team, Bolton Wanderers, once again proving a jinx.

"I've been sitting here trying to think what happened," said a stunned Jackie Blanchflower, while even the most hard-nosed United supporter was to admit, "we've no complaints today. The lads were well and truly licked," following the 4-0 defeat at Burnden Park. Ironically Matt Busby had tipped Bolton to be one of the surprise packages of the season, but he was not expecting United's 'bogey' team to trounce his boys by such a scoreline.

A fifth-minute goal from Stevens set the scene for the afternoon, but in effect this could have been the home side's fourth goal, as only Parry's poor finishing and a superb save from Wood had kept the scoreline blank. Bolton continued to be quicker and sharper than their visitors, who were never given the opportunities to slow the game down and employ their favoured system of ten- to fifteen-minute spells of possession, grabbing a couple of goals and putting the game beyond reach. Instead they were outfoxed and made to pay for it with their first defeat of the season – their first in the league since the previous March when they lost to… Bolton Wanderers.

> "It makes our win even greater when you remember that Dennis Stevens had to go off with a nasty ankle injury… and Johnny Ball was limping on a wing with ligament trouble. We never stopped fighting, despite these handicaps," said a delighted Nat Lofthouse, who rounded off the scoring with his team's fourth.

Jealousy is a strange trait and often those who show such a streak should be aware that they simply cannot match or obtain what others have. Instead of bemoaning the facts, they should simply get along with what they have and enjoy life. Bolton Wanderers could certainly never claim to have the players to stand shoulder to shoulder with Manchester United (Lofthouse perhaps excepted); but they simply rolled up their sleeves and got on with the job at hand, revelling in the praises of an unexpected (outwith the boundaries of the town at least) victory.

Blackpool, another Lancastrian near-neighbour, were similar to Bolton in that their successes, as a whole, would always be limited. They could, however, claim to have a superior playing staff, with the likes of Stanley Matthews and Ernie Taylor, but again they could be considered inferior to United's all-star cast. For their visit to Old Trafford on September 19th, they were without Matthews, who some claimed only shone when in front of the bright lights of London grounds; but this mattered little as the Seasiders overturned the form books to claim a memorable 2-1 victory.

Again, United were behind early on and 2-0 down by the interval, an excellent average for the Seasiders as they had only managed three attempts at goal. In the second half, United threw everything into attack, but were too rushed in the search for that breakthrough. Edwards did manage to pull a goal back, as Blackpool frustrated their guests with their time-wasting tactics, but with only three minutes remaining, it was too little too late. United were beaten and knocked off the top of the First Division by Nottingham Forest, who now claimed a two-point advantage.

The disappointment of two successive defeats was considered little more than a minor setback. Every great team had their off-days, and it was not going to be easy to knock United off their pedestal of being the country's top side and major footballing attraction. Such was their popularity, it was close to becoming problematic, especially for the home support. With the European Cup waiting to nudge its way into the fixture list along with the FA Cup, where United were once again favourites to lift the trophy, demand for tickets would always increase when major fixtures came around. United, however, thought they had overcome this problem with the introduction of the programme token scheme at the start of the previous season, where a 'token' was issued in every copy of the *United Review* and also on the reserve-team single sheets. These could be stuck on a sheet to prove an individual's attendance at those particular fixtures. When it came to an 'all-ticket' fixture, priority would be given to those with the greater number of tokens. Due to Central League games being played on Saturday afternoons when the first team were away from home, away programme covers would also be taken into consideration. Simple. What the United officials did not foresee was a 'black market' in both home tokens and away programmes.

Many supporters began to talk of a 'free-for-all' in the normal leisurely process of buying a match programme, with "brawling teenagers attempting to buy all they can get hold of." Matters were worse at away games, where travelling United supporters searched the vicinity of the stadiums for programmes as if they were buried treasure. At Goodison Park, many spent so much time racing around outside the ground that they were locked out as the gates were shut prior to kick-off. Many of those unfortunates had even failed to locate that elusive programme. At Bloomfield Road, Blackpool, boys bought copies of the programme in batches and sold them at inflated prices after the game. Bolton was little different, with more bulk buying. One United supporter offering to buy a programme from a thirteen-year-old boy who had purchased a bundle of them, was told that they weren't for sale as he already had buyers for them. Another supporter who had been unable to obtain a programme prior to kick-off waited for two hours after the game in order to get a piece of paper rubber-stamped by Bolton Wanderers officials in order to prove he had been at the game.

Such situations saw United being accused of not caring about their supporters. Further claims that the club had not printed enough copies of their own programme to satisfy demand were rebuffed when it was revealed that they had ordered a print run of 60,000 for the recent match against City. There was no easy solution to a problem that would continue as long as United remained successful.

Like a ship amid stormy seas, it was hoped that the recent turbulent times would subside quickly, and following those two successive defeats, normality was restored with a 4-2 win over Arsenal at Old Trafford. The London hoodoo remained in place, it being nineteen years since a club from the capital had left Old Trafford with both points. It was an ideal warm-up fixture for the first of what was hoped to be numerous European Cup ties this season, against Irish minnows Shamrock Rovers. If Anderlecht could be hammered 10-0, what hopes had a bunch of Irish part-timers?

Hope they certainly had, along with much determination, but unable to register any local leprechauns to play, they had little in the way of luck and were soundly beaten 6-0. However, the match was not as one-sided as the scoreline suggests, as Shamrock had clung on bravely throughout the opening thirty-five minutes; but once United had taken the lead, the outcome was never in any doubt.

Sandwiched in between that trip over the Irish Sea and the return leg in Manchester was a trip to the Midlands to face Wolves. Without the flu-stricken Byrne, Colman, Whelan and Viollet, United struggled, a matter not helped by Busby's strange decision to play Wilf McGuinness at left-back, leaving a player with attacking tendencies, more accustomed to playing in the half-back line, exposed to the skilful play of Deeley – who was to score two of the Wanderers' goals in their 3-1 win. The result left United in the unfamiliar League position of fourth. As for the Irishmen, with nothing to lose and their pride to play for in the second-leg tie, they put up a gallant show and despite going a goal behind in the fifth minute and conceding another seventeen minutes later, they earned the respect of the Manchester public with a spirited performance. Pulling a goal back ten minutes into the second half, they were unfortunate to concede a third five minutes later. To their credit, they continued to take the game to United and were rewarded with a second in the 68th minute. Unable to snatch an equaliser on the night, they left the field to well-earned applause, content in their endeavours against England's best.

England's best, however, were always a target for criticism, with the sports editor of the *Manchester Evening Chronicle* even prepared to have a pot-shot at United:

> "Manchester United are Britain's No.1 team, but they are in great danger of being the most hated side in Britain if they don't drop one idea taken – and 'improved' upon – from the Hungarians.
>
> "It is those nauseating, time-wasting tactics of short inter-passing between a tight group of three players. I know Manchester City did it when they won the cup in 1956 but

they, like the Hungarians, did make some progress, whereas United stand still.

"This is not only an insult to the opposing players but may one day lead to a United man being seriously hurt, for I can visualise an a opponent losing his temper and going straight for the man and not the ball.

"The United supporters do not like it either – I have a great many letters to prove it – but, what is more important, it is un-British."

Matt Busby was, as ever, quick to respond, agreeing that perhaps such tactics were frustrating to both opponents and supporters alike, but:

"it has its purpose in our plan of victory and cannot be condemned as deliberate time-wasting or a 'big-headed' policy of showing off at the expense of the other fellow.

"First, let me make it quite clear that there is no intention by the United players to make their opponents 'look small'. A man left floundering after tackling thin air may look 'silly' to the spectator. But there's been a chap doing that to opponents for more than 20 years, name of Stanley Matthews – and nobody's ever suggested that Stan does it deliberately. So why pick on United players?"

Time wasting, gamesmanship or whatever, it did have the makings of results, and following the 3-1 defeat at the hands of Wolves, United went back to what they did best – winning games. They followed up the 3-2 victory over Shamrock Rovers with the vengeful 4-1 defeat of Aston Villa at Old Trafford, and a 2-1 success over early claimants to their First Division crown, Nottingham Forest.

The November 5th fixture against Villa held the promise of fireworks on and off the pitch, but turned out to be little more than a damp squib, although last season's cup winners reverted to some crude tackling in an effort to knock United off their stride. Such tactics were ignored as was May's Cup Final defeat, and a Tommy

Taylor double, one from David Pegg and a Dugdale own goal helped secure a comfortable victory.

Against Forest, it wasn't so easy, nor was it expected to be; it proved to be a 'classic' match, spoiled only by the referee's whistle to signify full time.

This was not some blinkered assessment, but the overall view and opinion of those who shared the steps of the terraces and the hard, wooden seats in the cramped press box. "No One Wanted This To End", "An Occasion to Remember", "Five Stars! But Worth Six" were only three of the national press headlines, while Nottingham's Saturday-night *Football News* showed a sniff of excitement with "Babes Snatch 2-1 Victory in 'Thriller'". Surprisingly, its Manchester counterparts, the *Pink* and the *Green* did not go overboard, simply proclaiming "City and United Victory Double" and "Viollet Winner for United".

None of the headlines, however, could do justice to the ninety minutes. Words were not enough to convey the thrills and spills that confronted the 47,654 crowd.

> "Never a foul nor a childish tantrum in the whole of the absorbing ninety minutes"... "a record crowd were held entranced by a classical Soccer battle which no one wanted to end and no one who saw it will ever forget"... "Skill, the only arbiter at Nottingham! For one traveller at least this was the perfect occasion, a case where flawless manners of players, officials and spectators alike gave to a routine League match the flavour almost of an idyll. There was glorious sunshine for a start, so comforting for those who had queued from 8.00am, the impeccable turf, the cosy intimate atmosphere of the ground where spectators are not held back by concrete walls or wooden palings, but are allowed, nay welcomed, to advance and sit on the fringe of the turf itself" and "But what will be acknowledged without dispute is that this was a great exhibition of football, in which skill was the final, the only, arbiter, and where the splendour of the performance was enriched by the grace of sportsmanlike behaviour."

Such reports can only convey a sketch of the occasion without the complete masterpiece.

Whelan claimed United's first within four minutes of the start, collecting a throw from Ray Wood before dashing seventy yards along the touchline, crossing impeccably for the Irishman to volley home. It was cat-and-mouse for the remainder of the half, but within ninety seconds of the restart, Forest were level when Quigley centred and Imlach headed past Wood.

This was a signal for Forest to up the ante, and it was only the brilliance of Wood that kept United on level pegging until the hour mark when they scored what was to be the winner, Berry sending Viollet through to convert the type of goal he could put away blindfolded.

Saturday October 19th once again saw Busby forced into making changes to his first-choice line-up. This time, however, it was not due to influenza striking at the heart of his players, it was something most probably more annoying to the United manager – international call-ups. Removed from his options for the visit of Portsmouth to Old Trafford were Roger Byrne, Duncan Edwards and Tommy Taylor, arguably the backbone of the team. On this occasion, Wilf McGuinness took over Duncan's number six shirt, 18-year-old Alex Dawson wore nine, and in place of captain Roger Byrne came debutant Peter Jones, a 19-year-old Salford-born youngster. The changes inexorably affected the outcome of what should have been a routine fixture, the champions conceding three without reply.

United simply never got going, the Old Trafford crowd left bemused at the accolades that had been handed out only seven days previously following that supreme display against Forest. It was a sorry show indeed, with Whelan and Viollet – who to date had scored sixteen of their team's thirty-four League goals – looking completely out of sorts. Berry and Pegg created numerous opportunities, but none were seized upon. Players held on to the ball too long, some tried to walk the ball into the net, while the majority lost every vestige of form.

Although shaken by the manner in which his team had lost to the Fratton Park side, Matt Busby had much more to command his attention, a more worrying item on the agenda than the loss of two points which could easily be made up in the weeks ahead. The Italians were back on the hunt for his players.

This time it wasn't Internazionale Milan, but Lazio and Juventus who, despite a current ban on importing foreign players, had Tommy Taylor, Duncan Edwards and Eddie Colman in their sights.

The Lazio interest could have been taken with a pinch of salt, due to the fact that their mission to watch Taylor and Colman in action against Aston Villa had been made public through the *Manchester Evening News*. This revelation followed a telephone call to the newspaper by a gentleman with a "pronounced Scottish accent", who nevertheless claimed to be Italian and involved in the ice-cream business in Glasgow. Juventus, however, were to be taken seriously, as it was 'Mr Moneybags' of Italian soccer, Gigi Peronace, who was putting Taylor and Edwards under the microscope when he watched them in action for England against Wales at Ninian Park, Cardiff. Peronace had been responsible for spiriting John Charles off to Italy, and capturing the likes of Taylor and Edwards would have been well within his capabilities. With the embargo of signing foreign players due to be lifted in March, he had time on his hands as well as money in his pocket.

Matt Busby had been relieved that Taylor had not pressed for a move to Italy during the summer, but lived in constant fear that one or more of his players could have their heads turned by sums of money that would take them a considerable time to earn in England. "We can't be free of this constant fear until the soccer rulers give us the same advantage our overseas rivals enjoy; the right to pay our players on merit," the United manager was to say.

In his weekly column in the *Manchester Evening Chronicle*, Duncan Edwards was quick to ensure the United support that,

> "there has been no official approach to me, and, if there were, I should refer it immediately to United manager Matt Busby.
>
> "I would regard such a situation as club business, and, after they had made up their minds, I might be in a position to consider it.

"I say emphatically that I am happy at United and can foresee no possibility of my wanting to leave.

"In addition, before I could even think of moving overseas, I would have to overcome my own belief that this poaching of our top players is a disaster for English football."

At the end of the day, it all boiled down to money, nothing else, and as Matt Busby had said, the Football League could go a long way in helping the clubs, and indeed English football, to keep hold of their prized assets, by lifting the maximum and minimum wage restrictions. Ironically, the matter had recently been looked into and a minor adjustment would be made to the payment of players as from the start of the following season.

The new campaign would see an increase in the maximum wage to £20 per week, a rise of £3 on the current figure, and it would be paid all year round and irrespective of age, giving the top professionals £1,040 per annum. At present, the maximum wage only covered those over the age of twenty, and fell to £14 during the close-season. The minimum wage was currently between £4.10/- (aged seventeen, during winter and summer) and £8.10/- (aged over twenty). In addition to this, players who had not requested a transfer would be entitled to 2½% of any fee, while signing-on fees would double from £10 to £20.

It was not just the players who would benefit from such changes, although the figures quoted would certainly not deter the money-laden Italians nor change the minds of their targets. Match officials were also to benefit, with a referee enjoying an increase from five to seven guineas per match and a linesman from 2½ to 3½ guineas per match.

With United having been unchanged for the opening nine league fixtures of the season, rumours began to surface that certain members of the Central League side were becoming increasingly dissatisfied with life at the club, going as far as to suggest that the reason behind two defeats at the hands of Everton was nothing more than their dissatisfaction at having to play second-team football. *Manchester Evening Chronicle* scribe Alf Clarke was quick to pick up on the whispers, stating that they were nothing but 'lies'.

'Lies' they might possibly have been, but there was no denying that many of United's 'understudies' were becoming impatient at the lack of first-team opportunities – even if, when stood side-by-side to those in the first team, they undoubtedly lacked that little bit extra required to oust them from their regular places. With the conveyor belt of players coming through the ranks, it was always hoped that ready-made replacements in the event of injuries, ageing, or the more unusual transfer seeking, would be available without the club having to move into the transfer market. A strong reserve team was a necessity due to the number of games on the fixture list; but those Central League fixtures, whilst not ideal for some of the players taking regular part, were a major attraction for clubs on the lookout for new talent, and United's strength in depth meant they were often under close scrutiny.

Central League football was acceptable to up-and-coming youngsters, to players returning from injury and those happy to remain at the club and let their careers wind down, but for others it was a hindrance, a poor substitute for a higher level of football and less attractive to the pay packet, lacking first-team appearance money and win bonuses. Even Matt Busby could not hold on to players indefinitely if they wanted to move on.

Within the space of a few weeks, United lost two members of what could be considered the first-team squad with the departure of twenty-two-year-old John Doherty to Leicester City for a fee of £6,500 and Jeff Whitefoot to Grimsby Town for £8,000. "Doherty and Whitefoot are exceptions because we happen to be well catered for in their positions. It is not the start of a reserve exodus from Old Trafford," explained Matt Busby, quick to add that there had been no change in the club's policy of holding on to reserve-team players.

Having gained revenge on Aston Villa for their unlikely FA Cup victory of last season with the recent 4-1 victory at Old Trafford, United were to enjoy a second sweet taste of revenge with a 4-0 win in the annual FA Charity Shield fixture, again at Old Trafford.

Matt Busby was still well aware of the resentment many felt towards Peter McParland for the Villa man's contribution to the outcome of those ninety minutes at Wembley in May. So much so that the United manager named Ray Wood as captain on the night, so that he would come face to face with McParland as Villa captain in the centre of the pitch prior to kick-off, shaking hands for all to see. McParland said:

> "I was really touched by what happened. When Ray and I stood there in the centre, the cheers of the crowd really got me. I had not had such a reception in all my career, not even when we won the cup.
>
> "I still can't believe it. This Old Trafford crowd were wonderful. I expected a roasting for my part in the accident to Ray Wood at Wembley, but the fans actually cheered me. I'll never have any fears about playing in Manchester again.
>
> "Some people had been trying to give me the idea that I should go out there tonight in a false moustache and a pair of shooting irons.
>
> "I hope all Manchester will now understand that if the odd disgruntled fan bears a grudge, the players certainly do not."

Ray Wood was of a similar mind.

> "I have been annoyed by some of the things that have been said about the game. I was as pleased as anyone that it all passed off so well.
>
> "Wembley is just another game as far as I am concerned. That goes for Peter, too. The only trouble is that some of the fans seem to think that we footballers can never forget when we take a hard knock. It is all part of the game."

As for the match itself, Tommy Taylor exacted his own revenge on the Midlands side, smashing home a second-half hat-trick in a nine-minute spell, Johnny Berry rounding off the scoring from the penalty spot to give United a 4-0 victory. They gained custody of the trophy they had first won way back in 1908, but one that appears in the record books as little more than a friendly. It was also a fixture that was quickly erased from the memory, as seven days after the 3-0 home defeat by Portsmouth, those supporters who had not travelled to the Midlands for the match against West Bromwich Albion were quickly put off their tea, or perhaps choked on it, as they listened to the results programme on their radios. "... West Bromwich Albion four, Manchester United three." Household pets and children ran for cover.

Conceding four at the Hawthorns, or anywhere else for that matter, was almost a record in itself. Eight had been conceded before in the space of 180 minutes, as had nine, but the last consecutive heavy defeats had been back in February 1955 with the 'old' United. This was now the 'new' United and things like this were not supposed to happen.

The match against West Bromwich had been a genuine seven-goal thriller. United had taken the lead through Taylor, who later gave his side a 2-1 advantage; but Berry had missed a penalty when United were 3-2 down. Even with the score at 4-3, there were golden opportunities for an equaliser, but it was this poor finishing that had proven fatal.

Having suffered three defeats in their last five First Division fixtures, compared with having lost only six in the whole of the previous season, United now found themselves in an unfamiliar fifth place, six points behind leaders Wolves. A major downturn in form within a matter of a month when they could have been found sitting second, a mere two points behind the then leaders Nottingham Forest. "The Champions are Tottering", cried the headlines. Matt Busby exclaimed:

> "I must admit I am deeply concerned about the loss of vital championship points – but no more than that. I've no worries at all about my team's ability to hit the winning trail again and convince the doubters that they still retain the power and skill that have carried them to League honours in the last two seasons.
>
> "We had a number of 'rockets' launched at us by the critics last weekend and I would have found them disturbing had they not coincided with a United display last week against West Brom which was close to, if not right up to, the standard of our best last season.

"If proof were needed that there is nothing basically wrong with United, it was provided in that game."

True enough, it was back to winning ways the following weekend with a 1-0 victory over Burnley at Old Trafford thanks to a Tommy Taylor goal, and a point from a 1-1 draw at Preston in the following fixture was not to be sniffed at. Deepdale was then a fortress with the North End home support not having seen their side beaten in twenty-nine consecutive games. But even as United registered another four points with successive 2-1 victories over Sheffield Wednesday and Newcastle United, there was still continued criticism from far and wide relating to their indifferent form of late – along with a transfer request that rocked the club to the core.

The media continued to prophesy that United were on a downward spiral, and the recent transfers of Doherty and Whitefoot hinted that things were not all they should be. Colin Webster had asked for a transfer, which was not surprising considering his ability and eye for goal, as had Freddie Goodwin who was unhappy at playing understudy to Eddie Colman. Strangely, the Salford lad, a huge favourite with the supporters and often a key player in the United side, had also sought out his manager, hinting at moving elsewhere due to the fact that he had lost his place to Goodwin. His request was discussed at a board meeting towards the end of October, with the minutes stating: "A request for transfer by E. Colman was refused. A similar request by C. Webster would, it was decided, be considered when the time was opportune." Ian Greaves and Mark Jones were others who had become unsettled and had hinted towards moving to pastures new.

Colman had been omitted from the seven-goal thriller at the Hawthorns, many wrongly supposing that it was due to his involvement in the England 'B' international of that midweek; but the Busby policy was always to restore his first-choice players to the team no matter where they had played, or even how they had played if on international duty. The diminutive wing-half, however, had in previous weeks been playing below his usual standards, as well as turning up late for training – difficult to imagine, remembering how close to the ground he lived, hence the manager's decision to leave him out of the first team, allowing Goodwin to continue his impressive form. Captain Roger Byrne had even reportedly pulled his young team-mate to one side following a training session and had a serious talk with him due to his lifestyle off the field. An in-form Colman was an asset Manchester United could not do without.

The unrest within the ranks saw numerous fingers pointed at Busby. Many believed that he would weather the storm of indifferent results and transfer requests, but others felt that the United manager was not playing fair, keeping individuals in the first team who were not playing to the required standard, with their reserve-team understudies straining at the leash. One of many letters on the subject, sent to the *Manchester Evening News* read:

> "This spate of transfer requests from Manchester United players who 'haven't quite made it' (Doherty, Whitefoot, Greaves, and Goodwin) smacks of unrest behind the scenes. For years now manager Matt Busby has impressed upon his second team that they and their seniors are all one happy family, enjoying the same privileges. But now Busby's scheme to play off against one another 22 men of practically all first-team standards is misfiring. With so many of the reserves being given a senior run he's now having to exercise all his diplomacy to stave off a wholesale transfer request when these players fail to hold their places."

The problem within the Old Trafford camp was not so much 'trouble' being caused by certain players asking for transfers, but more to do with the 'ambition' of those same individuals, according to Alf Clarke in the *Evening Chronicle*.

> "Matt Busby released Jeff Whitefoot and Johnny Doherty only because he has ample coverage in their positions.
> "He said 'No' to Eddie Colman and Ian Greaves and he will say 'No' to Freddie Goodwin and Mark Jones – if Mark, like Freddie, seeks a move.
> "Whatever the outcome I'm sure it won't disturb the cordial atmosphere at Old Trafford.

"I have never known a happier lot of players in my long experience with the club. There are no favourites with Busby. He thinks as much about the young juniors as he does about the international stars – because the youngsters are the men of the future; the men who will keep United battling for honours.

"Whenever there are stories about trouble in the United camp, I remember a former United player who, upset because he had lost his place in the senior team, asked for a transfer – and got it.

"I met him a few months later, 'Any United player who wants to leave Old Trafford wants his brains examined,' he said."

Busby recognised the problems connected with having such a strong squad of players, all vying for a first-team slot, many frustrated with reserve-team football. He was quick to emphasise that those first-team stars with international caps and championship medals could well have lost out had they left Old Trafford for pastures new. He also knew that no other club in the country treated its staff better or more generously, with all the top players earning the same money, even if they were playing reserve-team football.

Sandwiched in between the 1-1 draw at Preston and the 2-1 win over Sheffield Wednesday should have been the European Cup tie against army side Dukla Prague, scheduled to be played at Old Trafford on November 13th. However, the death of the Czechoslovakian President Mr Zapotocky saw the fixture postponed the day before, much to the disappointment of the 58,000 supporters who had purchased tickets; Matt Busby, too, as he was now left looking at his team having to play eight games between November 30th and December 28th, an average of one every four days. "In the view of the circumstances, we have sent a telegram to Paris asking the committee if we can play the matches next month," said a United spokesman.

Dukla, who had just completed their domestic season runners-up to Spartak Sokolovo, returned to Manchester on November 20th, earlier than expected, to play their first round first-leg tie and had hinted at their inexperience at playing under floodlights. Given the nature of their overall performance, that could be considered as little more than gamesmanship designed to mislead their opponents.

In keeping with United's current haphazard form, a packed Old Trafford crowd was left chewing their fingernails for much of the opening hour, wondering if their team could produce something like the form that they had grown accustomed to, conjuring up at least a couple of goals as a safety net for the return leg. The Czechs, for all their flair and attacking football, lacked the finish that could have earned them a notable victory. At the opposite end of the pitch, their United counterparts were playing more as individuals than as a team, squandering what opportunities opened up for them, although Taylor's aerial power and Edwards's shooting from the edge of the penalty area caused their opponents some concern.

Although not decisive, a goal in the sixty-third minute changed the course of the game, coming from the only mistake the Dukla defence made over the course of the ninety minutes. Either goal-keeper Pavlis or his defender Pluskal could have cleared the ball, but as they hesitated, in nipped Colin Webster and United were in front. Suddenly, the trance was broken and within a further four minutes the lead had been doubled, Taylor rising to head home via a post.

Eight minutes later it was 3-0 when a pass from Whelan left Pegg in front of goal, totally unmarked, the winger making no mistake. His goal was considered the one that would ensure a safe passage into the next round. It was a game that was far from compelling, lacking glamour and panache, but it did produce superb performances from Byrne and Edwards. United, however, were still far from their normal selves, and from their best.

Albert Scanlon left his Central League team-mates behind, returning to first-team duty against Newcastle United on Tyneside in place of the injured Johnny Berry, and he grasped the opportunity with both hands in a game that once again saw United struggle. A goal behind after half an hour – in reality it could have been more – they huffed and puffed for the next fifty-five minutes, and it was only a shrewd decision by Busby to reshuffle his forward line that brought any reward.

With five minutes remaining, Taylor swung a ball into the centre and, before Simpson in the Newcastle goal could react, Edwards had slammed the ball home. Scanlon, having switched to the left, was suddenly back on the right, but was to be denied a goal when his thirty-yard drive rebounded off an upright. With a minute remaining, he was back on the left and once again saw another shot denied by the woodwork; but, as the ball bounced back into play, Taylor nodded it past Simpson for the winner.

In the Charity Shield fixture against City at Maine Road, ideal debut conditions had been contrived for David Gaskell. Playing in borrowed boots and denied the opportunity to feel nervous, he had thrived; but his League debut against Tottenham at Old Trafford was to prove a completely different occasion for the seventeen-year-old.

A mid-table Spurs side, particularly played at home, should have caused few problems for the debutant or for his team-mates, but in fact the young goalkeeper was let down by ninety minutes of shoddy defending. A goal in front through Pegg after seventeen minutes, United suddenly found themselves 4-1 down via a Smith hat-trick and a Blanchflower own goal. Even a fever-pitch crowd, superb play and goals from Pegg and Whelan could not prevent the third home defeat of the season.

Conceding four for the third time in just over three months was a concern, even more so when the latest defeat came only days before the all-important European Cup trip to Czechoslovakia to face Dukla. It was hoped that United would leave their recent poor performances at home as they flew to Prague; but it wasn't to be.

"Oh, United, Such A Dismal Show!" preceded Henry Rose's *Daily Express* report from the Czechoslovakian capital, where the reporter wrote of "the most listless, boring European Cup tie I have ever seen since I set out last season with Manchester United on their Continental adventures." The 1,600 mile trip itself was a drawn-out affair, taking United the best part of four days. The match itself was far from exciting, the 1-0 defeat being practically meaningless.

It could have been a creditable draw had Tommy Taylor not seen a header from a Pegg cross controversially disallowed. But according to Don Davies, such a result "would have been flattering", whilst adding: "Rarely can the attack of such a distinguished club have performed so fitfully in a match of such importance." His press box colleague, Henry Rose, also wrote that the bookings of Webster and Borovicka provided "one of the few moments of urgency, bite, and purpose, albeit misplaced, in this travesty of an important date in soccer's calendar."

"Little Wrong With United" and the verdict of the Dukla hangover were surprisingly added to the reports of the 3-3 draw against Birmingham City at St Andrew's. Some would have disagreed with the headline, as once again United took the lead before conceding two in a minute and going in at the interval 3-1 down. Credit had to be given for pulling back a point from the jaws of defeat, but all was still not well down by the banks of the Manchester Ship Canal.

The point was underlined the following week when Chelsea sent United crashing to yet another home defeat with a goal five minutes from time. It was a defeat that left the champions ten points adrift of leaders Wolves, a game in hand offering scant cause for optimism.

> "Are Manchester United on the decline?" asked Alf Clarke. "The club's playing record compared with last season – and many critics – say yes. But I disagree, and I'm going to tell you why.
>
> "The plain truth is that since the war the United supporters have been fed on soccer caviar. A smaller portion of the dainty dish and you'd think they were starving!
>
> "That's precisely what has happened. United have not been playing as well as we know they can or did last season."

There had been much criticism of Tommy Taylor's performances, and even more so his selection for the England international side. As Clarke continued:

> "Tommy Taylor has his limitations, but he can still be the most dangerous centre-forward in the country, if he is permitted to play his own type of game.

"Don't get me wrong. I'm not suggesting that United or England should change style of play to suit the individual, Taylor. But is there a better header of the ball – apart from Lofthouse – than Taylor? Then why will the United wingmen persist in holding on to the ball instead of centring it?

"I have been hammering this point for weeks.

"On the eve of the game against Dukla I urged the United forwards to move the ball quickly to the man running into position. I suggested it was time the ball came into the middle as Taylor lay in wait and United's front-line men went to town.

"I agree that United's attack has not been functioning as we know it can. I attribute that to wrong tactics on the wings, yet it is so easy to remedy.

"Still the knockers do not appear to be satisfied. The criticisms go on and on. Some even say that Duncan Edwards goes too far upfield, leaving defensive gaps. Yet United's main objective, as it should be with every club, is to score goals. Any complaints about that?

"I still think Manchester United will win their third championship in succession, because I believe the Wolves and West Bromwich Albion, their two most serious rivals, will crack up. Why? The lack of reserve strength."

Clarke continued in his assessment as to why United would be champions again by saying:

"Is there any team in the country who could bring in four or five reserve players in any one match and still prove themselves in the championship mould? Could Wolves or West Bromwich, or Preston or any other club, emulate such achievements? I doubt it. This is why I believe that United have nothing to worry about.

"The Central League side is top of the table at the moment. You don't get there, and stay there, without having resources to achieve it.

"I agree that United's attack has not been functioning as we know it can.

"I attribute that to wrong tactics on the wings, yet it is so easy to remedy. The United wingmen go on inviting the challenge, then lose the ball. That gets you nowhere, except that United's defence is then subjected to unnecessary pressure.

"The season has a long way to run and because United are not leading the League now does not mean to say that they have thrown away the chance of making it a triple run of League championship victories in succession. I think they will be champions next May."

Gaining support from one of the press corps was all very well, but the support was still concerned at the downturn in form. It was a worry to all associated with the club, leaving doubts in the back of their minds that they had perhaps seen the best of the current crop, whilst secretly hoping that it was no more than the kind of minor blip that happens to all teams at some time or other. In the *Manchester Evening News* a 'Special Correspondent' wrote:

"The excuse has, of course, been offered that every team which visits Old Trafford tries that little bit harder. Of course they do. The champions are always there to be knocked off their pedestal.

"But if they are champions in the true sense they can take advantage of their opponents' over-eagerness. This is what Matt Busby's men are not doing.

"There are two vital essentials necessary to success which unfortunately Manchester United do not possess at the present time. These are adaptability and experience.

"The first has never been one of United's strong suits, except in that grand era of Johnny Carey, Jack Rowley, Stan Pearson and the like. Not only were they brilliant individually, but they could bring their rivals down to the tempo they desired to set and then maintain it.

"Unfortunately the present team fail to do this.

"Although no criticism can be levelled at one man on the grounds of determination or ability, or against their teamwork – who will ever forget that stirring second half against Tottenham! – the Red Devils en bloc lack adaptability.

"When things are going badly in a match there is a tendency to become ragged. Furthermore, the new idea of marking, with players switching about all over the field in an effort to confuse the immediate opponent, has led to a general decline in power. It has also led to a considerable and noticeable change in attacking play."

Strong words indeed, but the writer had a point.

As for the players, defeats, especially if they were frequent, did little for their overall confidence, deterring them from trying the unexpected and forcing them to take a more cautious approach. They did, however, maintain the belief that it was something that would correct itself sooner rather than later, and Manchester United would be back on track again in search of the game's top honours, as Duncan Edwards proclaimed:

"What a glorious time the 'knockers' are having! Manchester United are fourth in the First Division – and to hear some people talk you would think we are heading for relegation.

"Somewhere you will always find people who consider it a crime to be successful, and right now they are forecasting gleefully that United 'have had it'. The Old Trafford bubble, it seems, has burst.

"So let's get this straight. United may not be playing as well as they have done, but we are still a power in the football world. Stan Cullis's wonderful Wolves may look as if they have the League championship sewn up, but don't bank too much on that.

"Wolves have to keep up their own pace for at least another month before they can say with any degree of certainty that they are prospective champions.

"In that time anything can happen. A slip or two and West Bromwich Albion could nip into the lead – and if that happens United will not be far behind.

"Alright, so eight points is a long way back. Perhaps United at the moment are no more than fancied outsiders, but stranger upsets have happened in football."

Duncan also spoke of the ambitions he shared with his team-mates, to do well in both the FA Cup and the European Cup, but was realistic enough to say that perhaps they would not triumph in either. He was quick to add:

"But this much I can tell you. When next you hear somebody whisper that United are depressed or dejected because they have not whipped everyone within sight in the League, just forget it.

"The dressing-room at Old Trafford is a bright and gay a place now as ever it has been.

"All the recent situation means is that we will have to fight a little harder – and there is nothing we enjoy more than a fight. That is why we are proud to be Manchester United."

Defeats were now a more regular occurrence than Matt Busby's ventures into the transfer market, the club cheque book stuck away at the back of a drawer gathering dust, used only for paying accounts and the like. In the past, the United manager had only bought when he felt a position needed strengthening from outside the ranks. A replacement had been required for the ageing Jimmy Delaney – out came the cheque book and in came Johnny Berry. Likewise, Tommy Taylor had been introduced as a replacement for Jack Rowley. So on December 19th, the cheque book was once again brought out into the sunlight, as Busby decided that perhaps a new signing could alter the course of recent results and restore some confidence into his side. The incoming player on this occasion, however, was not replacing a player edging towards the end of his career. For once Busby was going against the grain.

The goalkeeping position had always been something of a problem for the United manager since the immediate post-war days when Jack Crompton was the last line of defence. Finding a back-up, never mind a replacement, had been a lengthy process. At present, Ray Wood was holding down the first-team spot, with youngsters such as Gordon Clayton, Tony Hawksworth and David Gaskell, the latter pair both very inexperienced, waiting in the wings. But the recent deluge of goals against had nudged Busby into seeking another goalkeeper. A player who could be thrust into action without any concern about how he would cope under the spotlight.

Busby's eye had fallen upon the twenty-three-year-old Doncaster Rovers and Ireland international keeper Harry Gregg, who had been a recent target for Sheffield Wednesday. Three weeks previously the Yorkshire side had tabled an offer, but this was immediately dismissed by the Doncaster directors. After a fortnight of deliberation, in stepped United with a £22,000 bid, confident of success, but a two-hour directors' meeting at the Yorkshire club brought a similar response, with an additional statement from manager Peter Doherty saying: "There's only a little margin between what we are asking and United's offer."

"We've made our offer but it was not accepted. That's it as far as we are concerned," was Matt Busby's reaction to the knock-back; but twenty-four hours later, the Yorkshire air tantalised the United manager and his assistant Jimmy Murphy as, following an FA Youth Cup tie against Leeds United at Elland Road, talks with the Doncaster club were renewed when it was revealed that they would increase their original offer by a further £1,000.

A meeting of the Doncaster directors was hastily convened at the Belle Vue ground, which dragged on for two hours. At its conclusion a telephone call was made to Manchester. Ten minutes later Busby and Murphy were heading for Yorkshire and the home of Peter Doherty.

Upon arrival they were warmly welcomed by the Doncaster manager, their transfer target Harry Gregg and countless refreshments courtesy of Mrs Doherty. An hour later, fed and watered, they were also contented to have the goalkeeper's signature on the required forms, prompting a statement to be released by both clubs:

> "In view of the expressed desire of Gregg to move to Manchester United, we contacted United and re-opened negotiations. The player was transferred for a fee satisfactory to both clubs."

It was a transfer that caused some surprise, United's first venture into the transfer market in four and a half years, and one that prompted suggestions that perhaps the club was moving away from its production-line ways and edging towards purchasing ready-made replacements in order to maintain their place at the top.

> "I don't mind the critics who say that United are slipping a bit," countered Matt Busby, "that's a fair opinion. I may dispute it, but I know it's sincere and it's the price we have to pay for past successes.
>
> "United have ruled the roost for the past two years and it's my job to see that they go on doing it. That's the real reason I have signed Gregg. It's not because I seek to make Ray Wood a scapegoat for recent results going against us, but because you just can't hope to keep right on top in this hectic soccer world without doing everything possible to duplicate every position with first-class men. With reserve goalkeeper Gordon Clayton out of action until well into the New Year because of injury; Tony Hawksworth with the army in Germany and David Gaskell, at 18, too immature in my opinion to be called on in an emergency for the fierce programme of League, FA and European Cup matches ahead, I was quite naturally concerned about the goalkeeper position. That's why I've had my eye on Gregg."

Despite losing their main asset, Doncaster were obviously more than happy with a record fee for a goalkeeper, having profited by £21,000 on the player they had signed from Coleraine five years earlier. Busby was unperturbed at having paid such an amount. As for Gregg, "It's the happiest day of my life. The only reason I want to leave Doncaster is to better myself and provide more security for Mavis, my wife, and my little daughter, Linda." Life would never be the same again for Roger Byrne and his fellow defenders, as Harry Gregg was no ordinary goalkeeper. He prowled his penalty area like a caged tiger. This was his domain, a territory he ruled, and woe betide anyone, friend or foe, who got in his way as he challenged for the ball.

Gregg went straight into the United side for the match against Leicester City four days before Christmas. Meanwhile, Ray Wood had spoken out at news of United's interest in Gregg, telling Bob Pennington of the *Daily Express*:

> "If Gregg signs for United, I shall want a transfer. It would show a lack of confidence in me. I know we have dropped points lately, but I don't think I am responsible. I'm a married man with responsibilities. Reserve team football would be no good to me. I've nothing against Harry Gregg, but I must consider my own future."

But in the cool light of day following Gregg's eventual signing, Wood had second thoughts – only to knock on the manager's door and ask for a move in early January.

Stepping into the First Division spotlight held no fears for the big Irishman and he came through his debut with flying colours, receiving praise from a man who was no mean keeper himself. Frank Swift wrote in his *News of the World* match summary:

> "...that decision to pay out a record fee for goalkeeper Harry Gregg looks a certain winner in what is undoubtedly a bid to re-establish the Old Trafford team as the top attraction in Great Britain.
>
> "Gregg's command of the penalty area, collection of those dangerous crosses, sound judgment and anticipation, were the top features of this likeable Irishman's first outing for United. Once his defensive colleagues gain confidence in him, the team will benefit in general."

Gregg himself was more than happy with his performance, telling Swift:

> "My biggest thrill was our first goal… and the crowd's reception was just wonderful. The price tag? It never worried me. That was between Mr Busby and Doncaster Rovers."

As for the game itself, the 4-0 scoreline got United back to winning ways, but in the press box, Harry Peterson thought that United could do much better despite scoring four without reply. "Might have been a dozen, and should have been eight," was his opinion. But Peterson and his fellow hacks were all in agreement as regards the performance of another debutant, Kenny Morgans, who impressed on the right wing.

Welsh teenager Morgans had joined United as an apprentice as a fifteen-year-old, a target of numerous other clubs, as he recalled:

> "There were five or six other clubs down at the house before I signed for United. One club was in the living room, another in the back room and someone else in the kitchen, all at the same time.
>
> "When I first went to Old Trafford I had a job at one of the joinery companies in Stretford and I stayed there until I signed professional at seventeen.
>
> "The first team players were like gods. They had their own dressing room and nobody went in there who was not a first team player. Tommy Taylor and Jackie Blanchflower had a party piece where they would fight each other for real, while Tommy used to say that he worked down the mines, so he would get under a table and show us what he did. It was a scream.
>
> "Before a game Roger Byrne had lunch with Matt Busby, never with the players and the captain was not expected to go out on the town with other members of the team. That was why he was such a fantastic captain. If he said something to you on the field, you did it."

Christmas Day brought little rest for the United players and just under 40,000 supporters made a hasty retreat from the turkey, crackers and discarded wrapping paper to enjoy goals from Taylor, Charlton and Edwards that gave United a 3-0 victory over Luton Town, nudging them into second place and back into title contention – although they were still eight points behind leaders Wolves. The pot, however, did not continue to boil, but merely simmer, as three successive draws saw them drop back to fourth, albeit still eight points adrift.

The return fixture with Luton on Boxing Day ended 2-2, with a similar result at Maine Road against City leaving the title of the 'best team in Manchester' up for debate, a Bill Foulkes own goal denying his team both points. At Elland Road, it was thanks to Harry Gregg that third-bottom Leeds did not claim victory, but with relegation on their minds, the Elland Road side were more than happy with the 1-1 draw.

Sandwiched in between the Manchester 'derby' on December 28th and the trip across the Pennines to Leeds on January 11th was the FA Cup third round, with United given a daunting trip to Cumbria to face Third Division Workington. United's form had shown some extent of improvement, but they did not enjoy much in the way of luck in this particular competition.

United travelled north on the Friday, stopping overnight at the Trout Hotel in Cockermouth. Upon arrival at the Cumbrian outpost the following day, they handed their opponents an expense sheet for £73.10/- to cover the cost of the eighteen second class train tickets from Manchester to Workington (£42) and the overnight accommodation (£1.15/- per head). At one point, it was looking like a fruitless journey as the Borough Park pitch was covered in a hard frost. But the work of groundsman Billy Watson enabled the game to go ahead. On the advice of the referee, he sanded the goalmouths and parts of the pitch that the breaking sunshine could not reach.

Workington manager Joe Harvey knew plenty about both the FA Cup and Manchester United from his time as captain of Newcastle United, with whom he lifted the famous trophy twice in 1951 and 1952, and he had prepared his players perfectly for what was undoubtedly the most important fixture in the club's history. As kick-off approached, the ground was a sea of red and white, the colours of both clubs, but on the day, as no compromise could be reached as to who would change, both agreed to play in their alternative shirts, Workington in white, United in blue.

Harvey had inspired his players with his pre-match team talk, and they stormed into the lead after only five minutes, catching United cold. Purdon sent Robson through on goal and, as Gregg raced from his area, the Workington player's shot rebounded off the keeper's leg and into the path of Colbridge who had the easy opportunity to slip the ball into the vacant net. Not surprisingly, the forty minutes that followed continued along similar lines, the home side putting their exalted visitors under almost constant pressure. In the Workington goal, Newlands did not make his first real save until five minutes before half-time, when they deservedly left the field to warm applause for their solitary goal advantage. Those travelling United supporters who had smashed down a seven-foot steel barrier at Victoria Station, in a panic when they wrongly thought the 'special' pulling into one of the platforms was the last train for Workington, must have been wondering if their journey was going to prove a waste of time and money.

After the break, however, it was a different story, as United began to show their capabilities, stretching the home side as they slowly took control. An equalising goal, which had never looked too far away, came in the 54th minute when Taylor set up Viollet. Two minutes later, before Workington could regroup, Viollet scored a second from a Colman centre, completing his hat-trick in the 62nd minute from yet another cross into the area, this time from Scanlon.

There was to be no dramatic last-gasp fightback, as the home side had nothing left to give, their opponents having stunned them with those three quick goals. Two bad misses from Taylor near the end could have ensured victory by an even greater margin.

The 1-1 draw against Leeds United at Elland Road had been considered far from satisfactory, but with a European Cup quarter-final tie against Red Star Belgrade next on the agenda, minds might have been elsewhere. But there had been change in United's make-up in recent weeks. No longer did they rely on footballing skills to overcome opponents, they employed strength and speed, much to the dismay of their opposition. The introduction of Morgans, Scanlon and Charlton, in place of the more experienced Berry, Pegg and Whelan, had also brought about an upturn in fortune over the course of the past few weeks.

But it was a confident Red Star side that arrived in Manchester to take in United's game against Leeds. Although they pinpointed the threats from the inter-switching moves between Charlton and Viollet and the skilful play of Colman and Edwards, their trainer still expected his team to progress into the semi-finals. Busby was more open-minded as regards the outcome. "I certainly want an improvement on the 1-1 draw we got in our only previous meeting with Red Star when they visited Old Trafford in 1951," he was to say, adding: "We could do with at least two goals in hand for our second leg game behind the Iron Curtain on February 5th."

An overnight frost had hardened the Old Trafford pitch, much to the delight of the Red Star officials and players, while a dense fog on the night of the game made viewing difficult from the terracing. Many of those straining their eyes through the gloom were surprised to find that Busby had not gone for experience in his starting line-up by re-instating Berry, Pegg and Whelan, but had given Charlton, Scanlon and Morgans the chance to prove they were more than capable replacements.

For the opening twenty minutes or so, United took the game to their opponents with shrewd passing movements and quick, direct breaks; but as in numerous recent fixtures they were to fall flat in front of goal. Then, as the fog began to lift, Red Star slipped into gear. Sekularac sent Tasic through, but he failed to control the ball properly; Mitic attempted a shot from long range, again to no avail; but then came a moment that the United support had envisaged and been all too familiar with over the past few weeks. As Red Star once again pushed forward, Gregg began to stray from his line, ambling slowly towards the penalty spot. The advancing Tasic looked up and seized the opportunity, chipping the ball elegantly over the Irishman's head and into the net. The keeper was left flapping at thin air as the ball flew over his head from thirty yards to be greeted by a wall of silence. Was Gregg's first mistake as a United player going to prove costly?

What was said in the United dressing room during the ten-minute interval was never repeated, but it was certainly effective. Five times in six minutes Beara, a former ballet dancer and arguably the best goalkeeper in European football at this time, denied United. Charlton did manage to beat the on-form keeper, but his effort smacked against the post.

United looked for inspiration and it was to come nineteen minutes into that second period from the single player most capable of turning a game around – Duncan Edwards. Seizing the ball inside his own half, he set off for goal, charging at the Red Star defence as if he had changed sports and had an oval ball tucked under his arm, brushing three opponents aside with ease. A pass to Scanlon saw the winger take his time to thread the ball inside towards Charlton, who fired past a helpless Beara. The same player should have made it 2-0 moments later but squandered an ideal opportunity created by Byrne.

The Yugoslavs, like most foreign sides, knew all the tricks in the book and were not averse to applying them when needed. Shirt pulling, body checks, elbowing and other sly digs were all employed, with the referee, although full of intent, content to give out little more than warnings that were never followed up when the perpetrators committed further offences.

Refusing to be dragged into such underhand tactics, the United players, although no angels themselves at times, remained focused on the game. As the minutes ticked away, a positive result began to look unlikely to materialise. Then, with nine minutes remaining, Viollet whipped the ball in from the right and Colman slid in to side-foot the ball beyond the reach of Beara to give United a slender advantage to take to Belgrade for the second leg.

For the time being, the European Cup could be forgotten, and priority given to the quest for that third consecutive League title. Eight points was a considerable margin to make up on current leaders Wolves, but the red enclaves of Manchester believed that such a feat was possible. Many, however, were shuddering at the thought of Bolton Wanderers' impending visit to Old Trafford, hot on the heels of the Yugoslavs and at a time when United were perhaps at their most vulnerable. Talk of the 'Bolton bogey' was rife in the pubs and workplaces and, despite their mid-table placing, few believed the Burnden Park side incapable of adding another victory to their impressive record, having only lost once in the previous ten meetings. None could have contemplated the actual outcome of the ninety minutes on January 18th.

If ever there were a game to silence the 'United knockers', then this was it, also lending the red-shirted under-achievers a boost in confidence at the most critical time of the season.

To their cost, some were still struggling up the steps on to the terraces when Charlton opened the scoring after only three minutes, having collected the ball from Byrne on the left, run forty yards beating three white-shirted defenders, and fired the ball past Hopkinson. It was a lead, however, that was held for only seventeen minutes, Stevens equalising with a twenty-five yard drive, releasing the groans of 'here we go again' from the home support.

But the expected Bolton onslaught failed to materialise as, within four minutes, they found themselves 3-1 down, the strong wind and muddy pitch doing little – like the Bolton defence – to subdue United. A Charlton shot rebounded off Hopkinson into the net for the second, then Viollet forced home a third from a Morgans centre.

Hopkinson in the Bolton goal was beaten for a fourth time prior to the interval when he miskicked a clearance, the ball falling to the feet of winger Scanlon, who calmly lifted it over the horrified keeper and into the net. It was the goal that left everyone in no doubt as to the outcome, despite Lofthouse scoring a second for the visitors two minutes into the second half, bundling Gregg and the ball into the back of the net, despite the protests of the United players. Others, including Gregg and Busby, thought the Bolton forward had punched the ball into the net. In hindsight, it was a goal that he would regret scoring, as it only prompted United into taking revenge.

Tommy Taylor thought he had made it 5-2 after Morgans had done all the spadework, but the referee chalked it off, hauling play back as he had already blown to award United a free kick for handball against Higgins. It was not to be the United centre-forward's afternoon, as he was also denied half a dozen times by Hopkinson.

Bobby Charlton claimed his hat-trick in the 57th minute, latching on to the ball after it had been headed around the Bolton goalmouth as if in some juggling act; then, ten minutes later, Morgans once again supplied Viollet, who accepted a simple scoring opportunity to make it 6-2. The United supporters were becoming intoxicated by the flamboyance of their favourites, while those who had travelled the short distance from Bolton were suffering the hangover from hell, many deciding to make an early exit for home.

But the scoreline was still not complete. Scanlon raced into the Bolton penalty area only to be upended by Higgins, and as Duncan Edwards placed the ball on the spot Hopkinson muttered a silent prayer. But it was to little avail, as the wing-half took one step back before hammering the ball home, almost ripping the net from the stanchions.

It was a result that kept United in touch with the leading pack. They were now a point behind second- and third-placed Preston North End and West Bromwich Albion, and six behind leaders Wolves thanks to Lancashire neighbours Blackpool recording a 3-2 victory over the leaders – who were due to travel to Manchester in three weeks' time. According to Don Davies in the *Guardian*, the victory over Bolton was the game that saw Bobby Charlton,

> "cross the borderline between promise and fulfilment and become a serious contender for the rank of master footballer.
> "Few will forget that moment, when Charlton gathered a loose ball somewhere in mid-field and slipped at once into a lovely loping stride which carried him past Hennin and Higgins in two capacious swerves until his final shot left goalkeeper Hopkinson petrified and helpless."

Over the past few weeks the Ashington-born youngster had indeed improved as a footballer, going from a mere replacement to a regular first-teamer, adding goals to his creditable work rate. He looked to continue his fine vein of form in the FA Cup fourth round tie against Ipswich Town at Old Trafford, although in the days leading up to the match it looked as though his plans would be thwarted.

On the Thursday prior to the game, the *Ipswich Evening Star* carried a quarter-page advert outlining details of the special trains that would be running between Colchester and Manchester for the cup-tie two days later, the earliest leaving at 6.10am on that Saturday morning. Many had already booked their trip north so paid the advert little interest, their attention more drawn by the article warning, "9 Inches Of Snow At Old Trafford – Pitch Now Being Cleared". It was a long way to go for nothing, but the article did add "Cup-tie Postponement Unlikely". Reading behind the headlines, there had been heavy snowfalls in Manchester that Thursday morning, leaving the Old Trafford pitch with a thick covering, but clearance plans had been quickly put in place to avoid flooding during a thaw. "Unless we experience very severe conditions, the match will definitely go ahead," United secretary Walter Crickmer told his Ipswich counterpart.

While the Ipswich Town supporters were contemplating what could be a long, fruitless journey north, their opposite numbers in Manchester were complaining about United's decision not to make the cup-tie an 'all-ticket' affair. Their argument was that while the regulars collected their 'programme tokens', they had to enter a 'free-for-all' in an effort to obtain a ticket, as there was no other cup-tie being played within forty miles of Manchester that afternoon. The club countered that Old Trafford was capable of holding over 60,000 and that Ipswich would only have an estimated following of 2,000, so there would be "more than sufficient room for all United fans to see the match." The biggest crowd at Old Trafford this season had been 63,103 for the 'local derby' against City, a match that had not been all-ticket. With the seasonal average standing at around 45,000, the supporters' argument seemed pointless. Even more so when an official attendance of 53,550 was revealed.

So Ipswich Town made their first ever visit to Old Trafford, the cup-tie definitely on, and their manager Scott Duncan hoping to knock his former club out of the competition. A tough prospect indeed, but one that was not beyond the realms of possibility despite the current upturn in form of last season's beaten finalists.

It was backs-to-the-wall tactics straight from the kick-off for the Ipswich Town defence, but they were relieved to see United miss three sitters in the opening eleven minutes, although for long periods their goalmouth was a mass of bodies, goalkeeper Bailey and his defenders doing as much to prevent United from scoring as the home forwards' appalling finishing. Scanlon shot across goal from eight yards out and Charlton blasted over when set up by Taylor in front of goal – and they were just two of the numerous misses.

After surviving a torrid opening spell, Ipswich showed they were a team to reckon with, playing some attractive football, with a Rees–Elsworthy move only stopped in its tracks by Jones. Minutes later, it was Gregg saving the day with a fingertip save from Rees. But it wasn't long before they were back on the defensive and, five minutes before the interval, their rearguard was finally breached. Collecting a cross from Morgans after Acres seemed to lose his footing, Charlton drove the ball past Bailey from the edge of the penalty area.

The second half was a mirror image of the first, United attacking in droves, Ipswich defending in numbers, but as the minutes ticked away it seemed likely that only Charlton's goal would separate the two sides. Many within the home support considered the East Anglian side worthy of a draw and a replay at Portman Road. However, there would be no last-minute heroics from the visitors, as with five minutes remaining, a long ball from Foulkes found Charlton who immediately shot for goal. Bailey dived, but as he launched himself across goal, the ball hit Elsworthy, cannoned off in the opposite direction and went into the net. United were in round five.

It was back to League business at Highbury against Arsenal before priority again could be given to the European Cup quarter-final second leg tie in Belgrade. These were two games on which Manchester United's season didn't exactly hinge, but victories in both would keep dreams of the Treble alive.

On the morning of the Arsenal fixture, United director, 82-year-old Mr George Whittaker, was found dead in his London hotel bed, making black armbands an unwanted addition to the all-white playing kit which was soon to be stained with mud and sweat from the afternoon's endeavours – ninety minutes of first-class football which left many hoarse from shouting and speechless from what they witnessed.

> "I've seen a few exciting games in my time, but by golly, this one gets into the final," began Joe Hulme in his match report for the *People*, continuing: "What can you do but praise a side that, by sheer good football, thumps away to a three-goal lead, as Manchester United did?
>
> "And what can you do but cheer a side who hit back to equalise with three goals in four minutes – as Arsenal did. After that you have to admire United because they didn't go to pieces. They didn't panic. They just banged in two more goals. So back come Arsenal to make it 4-5 with the 63,578 crowd shouting as they haven't had a chance of shouting for a long, long time."

Hulme wasn't alone in his praise, as the *News of the World*'s Frank Butler enthused: "I have never seen Manchester United greater, and I haven't seen such superb fighting spirit in an Arsenal team for many seasons." But it wasn't all praise from the men in the press box, as Jack Peart of the *Sunday Pictorial* considered United "Too Cocky", going as far as to write:

> "If I were Matt Busby I'd have a few harsh words to say to certain United players who give every impression of becoming far too cocky and casual.
>
> "Biggest offender is left-half Duncan Edwards. I cannot think his display in this thrilling game would impress England team manager Walter Winterbottom, who was watching.
>
> "I hope too that United will digest the lesson that real champions never ease up, even with a three-goal lead as they had at the interval."

This was echoed by W. Capel Kirkby of the *Empire News and Sunday Chronicle*:

"Manchester United had some of the cockiness taken out of them in some of the most amazing second half football I have ever seen from an Arsenal side, or any other side in years.

"United should profit from this lesson. Good as they are, they cannot afford to take any opposition lightly."

The opening minutes of the Highbury encounter had given little indication as to what lay ahead, as both sides shunned early opportunities, Morgans firing over and Gregg being called upon to make three excellent saves. He escaped injury by a hair's breadth when making the third, as Groves managed to hurl himself over Gregg's shoulder and into the back of the net as he charged in on the ball, as the United keeper attempted to grasp at the second attempt.

Morgans was proving to be a thorn in the side of the Arsenal defence, forcing Evans into using underhand tactics in order to stop him, but with ten minutes gone the United winger left the full-back floundering, cutting in from the right and squaring the ball into the path of Edwards, who fired home from twenty-five yards. Kelsey in the Arsenal goal managed to get his fingers to the ball, but was unable to stop it.

Charlton had the ball kicked off his toes after Kelsey blocked a shot from Taylor, then Edwards came close on a couple of occasions, but each time the ball was scrambled away to safety. At the other end, Gregg had to race out of his area to kick clear as Herd, looking suspiciously offside, raced after the ball in what was a rare Arsenal attack.

Despite enjoying the majority of the play, it wasn't until the thirty-fourth minute that United scored a second. Having saved a Groves header, Gregg cleared the ball upfield towards Scanlon who, gaining possession in his own half, raced past Stan Charlton before picking out Bobby Charlton with an inch-perfect cross. Kelsey was left helpless as the ball flashed past him and into the net.

Four minutes from the interval, Arsenal thought they were back in the game, but a linesman's flag cancelled out the goal. From the resulting free kick, United counter-attacked, and as Charlton's shot beat Kelsey, Evans appeared to push the ball round the post with his hand; but after consulting his linesman, all United got from the referee was a corner. Arsenal had little time to feel relieved, as with the match official looking at his watch, Morgans squared the ball inside to Taylor. Although the United centre-forward's initial shot seemed to hit Kelsey, the ball broke loose and the Yorkshireman was on it like a flash, to force it over the line. His first goal in seven games.

In the gloom of the late London afternoon, even the Arsenal supporters applauded United from the field. Yet within fifteen minutes of the restart their applause was reserved for their own heroes as they turned the game on its head with three goals in as many minutes.

Thirteen minutes into the second half, Arsenal pulled a goal back when Herd converted a Groves cross. On the hour, it was 3-2, Groves once again: having just failed himself to score, he flicked the ball through to Bloomfield who steered it past Gregg. A minute later, Arsenal were on level terms, completing an astonishing transformation with Bloomfield racing through the United defence, his shot beating Gregg and going in off the post.

Cruising at 3-0, United now found themselves with a real fight on their hands and the possibility of losing the game altogether. Meanwhile, fighting of a different kind broke out in the main stand, as police and stewards had to be called in to deal with a great commotion as rival supporters began throwing punches. All eyes, however, were soon back towards the pitch, where Byrne picked up a knock with yet another desperate clearance as Arsenal continued to press forward.

The home side's joy at having clawed themselves back into the game was to last only four minutes, as the seemingly neglected Scanlon harried down the left, beating full-back Charlton, before sending over an inviting cross towards Viollet. His header left Kelsey flapping fruitlessly at the ball as it flew past him.

A flurry of long balls into the United area caused some concern, as did the resilient Groves, with Gregg throwing himself at the Arsenal man's feet to make a brilliant save. But from the keeper's clearance, Morgans yet again rounded a defender before switching the ball inside to Taylor, who in turn beat Kelsey with a shot from an acute angle into the far corner of the net.

5-3 with sixteen minutes remaining, and with the game still liable to swing either way, Arsenal pulled it back to 5-4 in the 77th minute through Tapscott, setting up a rousing finale. Having witnessed six goals in eighteen minutes, no-one on the packed terracing and in the stands dared move in fear of missing something else in this compelling match.

Viollet almost notched a sixth for United, getting the better of Kelsey, but as the ball rolled tantalisingly towards goal, Fotheringham ran in and managed to clear at the expense of a corner.

There were to be no further goals and as the final whistle blew, the crowd, as exhausted as the red-and-white-shirted individuals on the pitch, stood as one, applauding both sets of players as they left the field together.

The suggestions in one or two of the newspapers that United had displayed a form of arrogance were refuted by David Herd, scorer of Arsenal's first goal:

> "I certainly would not have described them as cocky. They simply radiated confidence in their obvious ability."

The *Daily Telegraph* correspondent, however, had got caught up in the adrenalin-sapping ninety minutes, writing:

> "The 'Babes' played like infants in paradise. The ball, it seemed, had been placed in the arena for their own amusement. With the utmost abandon and cherubic cheerfulness the Manchester United marvels kicked, headed and dribbled among themselves. When, on a rare occasion an Arsenal player knocked them sliding in the mud and momentarily took their ball away, it was all part of the fun."

It had certainly been one of those "I was there" ninety minutes.

Forty-five thousand spectators flocked to Easter Road, Edinburgh, the highest post-war crowd for a game in the Scottish capital, on the evening of February 3rd to see Matt Busby's 'other' team, but the United manager was nowhere to be seen. This was not a United reserve-team fixture, nor indeed any combination of red shirts, but the dark blue of Scotland, Busby having taken over as manager of his national side a couple of weeks previously. But he would have to rely on others for feedback from the Scotland v Scottish League World Cup trial match, as he was in Belgrade for the second leg of the European Cup quarter-final tie.

Meanwhile, assistant manager Jimmy Murphy also had international commitments to add to those at United, as he was team manager for the Welsh national side. Although he had wanted to make the trip to Yugoslavia, Busby told him he had a more important job to do with Wales: their World Cup play-off second leg tie against Israel in Cardiff was a match he could not miss.

Belgrade was a far cry from Princes Street, Edinburgh, and the towering castle on its craggy rock, but United's reception as they disembarked from their aircraft in Yugoslavia was arguably even more enthusiastic than that they would have received had they been in the Scottish capital to play Heart of Midlothian or Hibernian. Countless photographers and reporters, along with hundreds of supporters, swamped the United players even before they had reached passport control or customs, all eager to snatch a photo, a word or an autograph. Strangely, those seeking the latter were no mere teenagers, but grown men, eager to get their match ticket for the following day's game or a scrap of paper signed by one or more of the stunned United players. The legend was not confined to Britain.

The flight to Belgrade was not without its problems, as heavy fog in Manchester brought a delay of almost an hour. Then following the six-hour journey, equally poor visibility in Belgrade almost prevented landing. The United plane was the only one to land that day.

Whilst energy-sapping, the ninety minutes at Highbury against Arsenal had also left Busby with a couple of injury concerns, Roger Byrne the main doubt with a badly bruised thigh; but constant treatment, mixed with good old Gorton determination, ensured that the United skipper was fit to play, and that Geoff Bent's journey had been a wasted one.

Tickets for the 1.45pm 'British time' kick-off had been eagerly snapped up, with a roaring black market seeing those with a £1 face value going for £5. Even a United training session was eagerly attended with some two hundred turning up to watch the United players go through their paces on a pitch partly covered in snow with ankle-deep puddles every few yards. One youngster got a better view than most, as Duncan Edwards lifted him on to his back and carried him on half a lap of the mudded pitch.

Belgrade had been under a blanket of snow, but United trainer Tom Curry had come prepared, not wanting to be caught out again, as in Dortmund last season. Now he carried four sets of boots for each player. Thankfully it was beginning to thaw, but with a blanket of snow left on Partizan's stadium – where the game was to be played due to its larger capacity of 60,000 – the playing surface underneath would be in as near perfect condition as possible come kick-off time.

Although considered as amateurs, the Red Star players were on £50 per man to win. United, on the other hand, were on £30; but at least one of the Yugoslavs, their star-man Sekularac, did not think he or his team-mates would be pocketing the cash. He surprisingly declared,

> "Manchester too strong. Manchester will win, Your team
> will be too much too strong for us. From our experience in
> Manchester we think they will be as fit and strong at the end
> as the start, so I don't think we have much chance."

Gusztav Sebes, manager of the Hungarian national team, who had seen both sides in action, was not so certain of the outcome: "If the weather stays the same as it is, it's United for me. If the ground is bone hard it will suit the Yugoslavs and they could score enough to win."

Henry Rose, a man whose *Daily Express* musings were read with disdain in Manchester and its environs, joined Sebes on the fence, writing on the day of the match:

> "My own view is we shall not see the end of this quarter-final
> tomorrow afternoon. I foresee a win by Red Star by the odd

goal (there will be no extra time) and a replay, probably in Milan.

"Key to the situation is the weather. This afternoon the players prodded with mixed feelings the blanket of snow on the Yugoslav Army pitch on which the game will be played. They have played on many a worse ground. And if there is no overnight frost the passport to the semi-final is on the way.

"United have the crowd to beat as well. For there will not be even a thin red line of supporters to cheer them on. Frost is not expected, but if it does arrive it will make the pitch bone-hard. The fight is on."

In his article, Rose had missed out another important factor that the visitors would have to overcome if they were to reach the semi-final for the second consecutive season: the referee, Karl Kainer (Kajner in some sources) from Austria.

When the time came, the man from the *Express* certainly did not omit him from his match report. "The most One-Sided Referee I've Ever Seen" exclaimed the headlines above Rose's quarter-page summary of the ninety minutes, going on to add, "They (United) had to fight not only 11 desperate footballers and a fiercely partisan 52,000 crowd, but some decisions of Austrian referee Karl Kainer that were double Dutch to me."

In the *Daily Mail*, Eric Thompson's report was preceded by – "Referee has Manchester United scared", while in the *Daily Herald* it was,

"Oh, Oh, What A Referee", their man at the match George Follows reporting: "The Blue Danube flows grey and cold through this city tonight, and, for all the players of Manchester United care, referee Karl Kainer, of Vienna, can go and jump in it – whistle and all.

"The Red Devils played the best football they have ever played in serious competition abroad and battled through again to the semi-finals of the European Cup.

"But they accused referee Kainer of robbing them of a resounding victory before an ultra-partisan crowd at the Partisan Stadium here today."

So, what exactly was the Austrian's contribution to this dramatic quarter-final tie that so upset United?

Within ninety seconds of the start, the loud, vibrating chants of "Plavi, Plavi" (roughly translated as 'Up the Blues') from the Red Star supporters were silenced, when United increased their advantage with a goal from Viollet. An attempted clearance by Spajic was charged down by Taylor and rebounded to Viollet who evaded two tackles before hitting a low shot past Beara.

Even in the early exchanges, United found the going difficult due to their sometimes overly robust opponents. Morgans was kicked on the thigh, Edwards on the ankle, but thankfully the United players kept their cool and maintained their momentum, managing to get the ball into the net once again in the fourteenth minute. Charlton's goal, however, was disallowed for an apparent offside but the general opinion was that he had simply moved too quickly for the linesman, who spotted him near goal and raised his flag despite having no real idea what had happened in the preceding seconds.

As if on cue, the crowd upped their vocal encouragement but, as earlier, were soon silenced again as the net behind Beara bulged not once but twice from Bobby Charlton efforts. First, a left-footed drive in the twenty-eighth minute: having robbed Kostic of the ball, he ran three yards before unleashing a twenty-five yard drive which left the Belgrade keeper helpless. Having already burst the ball with one effort, Edwards bulldozed his way through three minutes later, only to see his effort rebound off a wall of defenders – and Charlton shoot home from ten yards with his left foot. Now United were firmly in command with a 5-1 advantage. It was all over bar the shouting. Or so everyone thought.

Two minutes into the second half, Kostic pulled a goal back after Colman was prevented from getting a tackle in by another player. Eight minutes later the tempo increased dramatically when Tasic collapsed inside the penalty area, Foulkes stumbled on top of him and the referee pointed to the spot. Tasic himself converted the kick to turn the heat up to boiling point. Such was the excitement on the packed terracing that the surging crowd, pushing forward, damaged the wire netting on the concrete wall surrounding the playing surface, resulting in hundreds being injured.

Sekularac suddenly felt his pre-match forecast of a United victory was perhaps not his best press interview and began to do his best to alter the eventual outcome, threading his way through tackles that in the norm were only half-hearted due to the susceptibility of the referee. It was now a completely different game from the first forty-five minutes as United began to show their apprehension, playing a cautious game in fear of losing any further goals or incurring the wrath of the errant referee.

The match continued to be played out mainly around the United goal, with Gregg sliding out of his area amid the mud and slush with the ball in his hands. Kosic lobbed the resulting free kick over the United wall, hitting the side of Viollet's head and into the net via Gregg's hands. Thankfully, there was only a minute remaining. Even the referee couldn't conjure up the aggregate equaliser for the home side.

Such was the tempo of the game that the Red Star supporters had worked themselves into a frenzy during the pulsating ninety minutes, and the disappointment at losing out to United following such a spirited fightback was, for some, just too much to bear. At the end of the game, a troop of Yugoslavian soldiers had to be called upon to form a human barrier between the United players and the home support, who pelted their guests with snowballs as they left the field.

The full-time whistle had come as a relief to Matt Busby and his players who, after complaining that the match official was "so bad the lads had to stop playing their normal game", enthused: "Their second half revival was just desperation. But their fitness shocked us, and we were certainly glad to hear the final whistle. This was our best performance in the European Cup."

Captain Roger Byrne told the press that:

> "It had been a difficult game to play in, as the referee's performance had forced us to stop tackling due to good

tackles being penalised with free kicks. We were not so worried when we were winning, but after that penalty we became afraid lest a tackle would mean a free kick in the danger zone.

"Football is a funny game isn't it? I thought we were going to walk it after taking a three-goal lead, but it just shows you that you cannot give these continental sides an inch. Once they get a goal they play like demons. Never mind, we are through to the semi-finals."

Back in Manchester, supporters had been anxious for news of the match throughout the afternoon, many swamping the local newspapers offices with telephone calls in order to get any snippet of a score update. The *Daily Express* reported that they had received more than 5,000 calls in less than four hours and at one point, were receiving up to thirty calls a minute; but it was the local newspapers, the *Chronicle* and the *News* that were eagerly awaited for the on-the-spot thoughts of the respected Alf Clarke and Tom Jackson.

In the *Chronicle*, Clarke wrote:

"Manchester United were nearly frightened out of the European Cup – by the referee.

"I have played and watched football for more than 40 years,[8] but I have never seen a referee make so many amazing decisions as Austrian official Karl Kajner.

"I don't wish to detract from Red Star's brilliant second-half football, but with the referee accompanying every United tackle with his whistle, the United players became too scared to even challenge an opponent.

"It would be almost impossible for any team to give United a four goals start and then nearly catch them up, but with the help of the referee they did just that.

"With United three goals in the lead at the halfway stage plus one from the first game it looked merely a matter of

---

8 Clarke had actually played one game for United, on September 13th 1926, in a benefit match against South Shields. He set up Smith for United's goal in the 1-1 draw.

by how many they would win. But then Red Star shocked them. They swept to the United end like a well trained army.

"Some of their football was marvellous – skill and speed. They used the long ball better than in the first half and it was simply staggering to see United reeling.

"What caused this amazing decline? Apart from the referee, it was because Red Star had plenty of stamina.

"Duncan Edwards kept a pretty close watch on Sekularac in the first half, but it was the home player who did the dictating afterwards and I have seldom seen the England left-half play such a minor role."

Red Star were gracious in defeat with goalkeeper Beara saying:

"I have no grumble. Manchester are worth their place in the semi-finals. And this boy Charlton! Very good indeed."

This was seconded by team-mate Mitic, who added:

"United were better than our players. They deserve their win, even after the way we fought in the second half."

Don Davies in the *Guardian,* wrote:

"It was a battle of wits and guts and rugged tackling.

"The Austrian referee's performance on the whistle assumed the proportions of a flute obbligato due to the frequency with which fouls were committed by both sides."

"United can feel proud again, and Wolverhampton Wanderers beware. For United intend to make it a double-feature programme this week... a draw against Red Star, a win over Wolves on Saturday," said Frank Taylor in the *News Chronicle-Daily Despatch.*

As could be expected, the Yugoslavian *Politika* viewed the ninety minutes slightly differently:

"United were unsportsmanlike and often unscrupulous. In the second half the British players felled opponents in an impermissible manner. Many times we asked ourselves where was the renowned British fair play? That is only a legend. There was not a single professional trick they did not use to bring themselves out of difficult positions and were often unscrupulous when they tackled and pushed and tripped."

The referee simply waved away any criticism with a smile, saying: "This was the most attractive match I have ever seen and judged in my life."

Back in the warm confines of the dressing room, the United players were understandably in a joyous mood, buoyed by their success. Before they had even showered and dressed, a bottle of whisky (the same one that had eased the pain of Morgans's thigh at half-time) was doing the rounds. It was a painful sight for its owner, United secretary Walter Crickmer, although the joy of having reached the European Cup semi-finals for the second consecutive season must have eased his despair as the golden liquid slowly disappeared from his bottle!

Despite the tense and physical ninety minutes, the management and players of both sides relaxed and enjoyed the after-match banquet in the Majestic Hotel. As the official get-together drew to an end, Matt Busby was approached by Roger Byrne, his captain asking if he would allow the players to leave the function and go elsewhere for a few drinks. "Half an hour, then", replied the boss amid half-hearted cries of displeasure – and, with a smile on his face, agreed to a further half hour, in no mind to enforce his curfew.

Most of the players headed for the British Embassy Staff Club where the singing and dancing continued well past the manager's one o'clock cut-off. Even after a BEA rep drove Byrne and Mark Jones back to their hotel, it was decided that the night was still young. The two United players simply marched in the front door, out the back and into the same car. Accompanied by a member of the Embassy staff, they went to the home of a Canadian couple where they were to enjoy further liquid refreshment. It was 3.00am before the pair returned to their hotel, managing a few hours' sleep before it was time for breakfast – if, indeed, they could face it – and the return journey to Manchester.

There were certainly a few bleary eyes and sore heads amongst the United players as they made their way to Belgrade's Zemun Airport on the morning of Thursday February 6th, cups of strong coffee and the cold morning air helping to ease the memories of their late nights. A look at their club itinerary for the trip reminded them that following their 8.00am departure – which was eventually to leave an hour late due to Johnny Berry having packed his departure visa in his suitcase which had to be retrieved before he could board – they were to fly to Munich's Riem Airport for a forty-minute scheduled refuelling stop.

A few late souvenirs were purchased and the local sports pages scanned briefly before being called to the door of the departure lounge by a Yugoslavian official who handed out the passports to the forty-four passengers who then filed on to the awaiting *Lord Burghley* BEA Elizabethan-class Airspeed Ambassador – call sign 609 Zulu Uniform – selecting their seats at random.

No sooner were the players settled in their seats than the playing cards were out with games in full flow, some trying to use the last of their Yugoslavian change for the kitty, but to no avail. Jackie Blanchflower, Dennis Viollet, Liam Whelan, Ray Wood and Roger Byrne were quickly engrossed in their hands.

The flight to Munich passed quickly and the clear blue skies of Belgrade had soon become transformed into a dull grey, the noon landing accomplished amid a snowstorm, the runway already covered in a few inches of snow and slush as the aircraft touched down. Although the walk from the plane to the airport lounge was short, everyone felt the ice-cold wind that was blowing around the airport, and they quickly made their way inside to the warmth and relative comfort, giving latecomer Roger Byrne an earful for leaving the door open slightly longer than was necessary.

Warmed by the coffee and refreshments, the final call for boarding came at 2.00pm, half an hour later. The card school had not bothered to deal another hand as lunch was due to be served shortly after take-off, and everyone was settled and ready for the flight home. The tyre tracks made by the plane when it had landed some forty-seven minutes earlier were now almost invisible due to the continuously falling snow. Following dialogue between the cockpit and the control tower, the thin layer of ice on the wings was adjudged to be already thawing, so no de-icing was required. Clearance was given for take-off, and it was all systems go as Captain Thain announced,

> "We are now about to start the last leg of our journey. We will fly at 17,500 feet. The flight will take approximately four hours. Lunch will be served as soon as we are airborne."

Slowly the plane began to move forward, the sound of the engines increasing by the second as it gathered momentum; but around 450 yards down the runway the brakes were applied and it came to an abrupt halt as captain James Thain and his co-pilot Kenneth Rayment detected a surging on the port engine with the boost pressure becoming too high. If this reached a certain critical pressure, there was the possibility that it could cut out altogether.

Having returned to its previous position on the runway, clearance was given for a second attempt at take-off, but once again the plane came to a shuddering halt halfway down the runway. Upon taxiing back once again towards the terminal, the sound of the captain's voice echoed through the cabin: "There is a slight engine fault. We are returning to the airport buildings and it is hoped that it will not be a long delay." The passengers were ushered off and told to go back inside as the technicians and other ground staff tried to detect the problem. It was 2.35pm. Albert Scanlon recalled:

> "When we got back on board for the first time, we all sat in the same places. Then when we got off the plane again, Mark Jones went to the airport shop and bought a St Christopher medal. Five or ten minutes later we went out again and this time people started changing seats. Bobby and Dennis came up front. Eddie and Tommy and David went to the back. Bill Foulkes came over to the side and I sat where David Pegg had been."

No one knew exactly what was happening. Some, including Duncan Edwards, were of the opinion that they were here for the night, the United half-back deciding to send a telegram to his landlady – Mrs Dornan of 15 Gorse Avenue, Stretford, which read simply – "All flights cancelled. Flying tomorrow – Duncan."

There was little time to get comfortable as, ten minutes later, an announcement informed the now-impatient travellers that they could re-board. Busby wanted to get back to England to prepare for Saturday's game against Wolves, whilst not wanting to incur the wrath of the Football League if any delay in Germany led to this vital fixture being postponed. The authorities would have liked nothing better than to slap United's wrists for such an infringement, as they had carried some resentment ever since United's initial involvement in the competition. The journalists wanted to get back as they had the more pressing engagement of the 'Press Ball' that evening. A quick headcount revealed they were now one passenger short, who turned out to be Alf Clarke, who had taken the opportunity to telephone the *Evening Chronicle* office to give them an update of the current situation.

Clarke's earlier message back to Manchester had been nothing more than a brief injury update:

> "Manchester United are almost certain to be without Ken Morgans (thigh injury), but both England left-half Duncan Edwards and £23,000 goalkeeper Harry Gregg are expected to be fit for the vital championship clash with Wolves at Old Trafford on Saturday.
>
> "Both Edwards and Morgans carried on under difficulties against Red Star in the European Cup game in Belgrade yesterday after being injured in the first half, and Gregg was injured later in the game.
>
> "The players will have a check over at Old Trafford tomorrow morning."

His hurried update, which appeared on the front page of the 'Last Extra' edition (the Stop Press of this edition carried the result of the 3.15 race from Wincanton) was brief and to the point –

"United are held up in Germany – The triumphant Manchester United footballers, on the way back from Belgrade to Manchester, are held up in Munich by engine trouble, and they may not be able to get away until tomorrow.

"United, who drew 3-3 with Belgrade Red Star and so qualified for the European Cup semi-finals, broke their journey at Munich where they had lunch.

"They were due in Ringway this evening, but their plane developed engine trouble and it is doubtful if they will get away today as it is snowing very heavily."

It was now 2.59 and with everyone settled, albeit uncomfortably, clearance was once again given for take-off.

Three minutes later a voice from the control tower boomed into the cockpit:

"Clearance void if not airborne by zero four. Time now zero two. Wind is three zero zero." James Thain replied: "Roger. Understand. We are ready for take-off."

"Check full power," instructed co-pilot Rayment. "Full power set confirmed," replied Captain Thain. "Temperature and pressure okay, warning lights out." The attempt at taking off began for a third time.

"Running through my mind was the slogan 'third time lucky'," said *Daily Mail* photographer Peter Howard. "Steward Tom Cable, who had previously been busy between the bar and the galley, was now belted into a seat. Harry Gregg settled himself into his seat a little more firmly. Roger Byrne had pushed himself well back in his seat. I took the leaflet from the seat pocket in front of me and started to read through the crash emergency drill. I got as far as a diagram showing the use of a chute escape in the event of a crash.

"I put down the leaflet with the consoling thought that this wouldn't be necessary. We had stopped twice and surely could stop a third time if things were going wrong. Now, we were speeding down the runway again."

The plane once again rolled down the all-too-familiar slush-covered tarmac. Sixty knots, seventy, eighty… one hundred and seventeen. Two-thirds of the runway had been covered, V1 – the point of 'no return' – was passed, but the plane was now running over the undisturbed snow and slush on the runway, and the speed slowly began to decrease. Soon it was back down to 105. Rayment pulled frantically on his control column in an attempt to get the plane off the ground. There was no reaction.

It was now that Thain and Rayment realised that they were not going to make it.

Inside the cabin there was an eerie silence, everyone deep in their own thoughts. Bill Foulkes recalled his, as the plane continued to pick up speed with the buildings flashing past the small windows:

> "I remember sitting in the plane facing Albert Scanlon. David Pegg had gone up to the back of the plane where he thought it was safer and Eddie Colman had also been told to sit up there out of the way, as he was always carrying on and being a nuisance. On the opposite side, there was a six-seater table where Roger sat along with Jackie, Ray, Dennis and Billy Whelan. Billy, a devout Roman Catholic, muttered something I didn't at the time understand and Roger also said something, which again I couldn't really make out as the noise inside the plane grew louder."

Others gripped tighter to their arm rests as the end of the runway flashed past.

Suddenly, the sound of the engines were drowned by an ear-splitting crash as the aeroplane shook violently, spinning off the runway, crashing through the perimeter fence and into a nearby house. Everything was plunged into darkness before the crunch of the breaking fuselage echoed through the cabin.

It was 15.04. Silence enveloped the scene. The final whistle had blown for many on board.

Sources Used

Scottish Daily Record
Scottish Sunday Mail
The Guardian
Manchester Evening Chronicle
Manchester Evening News
Daily Herald
Daily Mirror
Daily Dispatch
News Chronicle
Sunday People
Daily Express
Daily Mail
The Sun
News of the World
The Observer
Sunday Post
The Times
Sunday Times